Also by David Howe

Social Workers and Their Practice in Welfare Bureaucracies
An Introduction to Social Work Theory
The Consumers' View of Family Therapy
Half a Million Women: Mothers Who Lose Their Children by Adoption
   (with P. Sawbridge and D. Hinings)
On Being a Client: Understanding the Process of Counselling and
   Psychotherapy
Attachment Theory for Social Work Practice★
Attachment and Loss in Child and Family Social Work
Adopters on Adoption: Reflections on Parenthood and Children
Patterns of Adoption: Nature, Nurture and Psychosocial Development
Attachment Theory, Child Maltreatment and Family Support★ (with M.
   Brandon, D. Hinings and G. Schofield)
Adoption, Search and Reunion (with J. Feast)
The Adoption Reunion Handbook (with L. Trinder and J. Feast)
Contact in Adoption and Permanent Care (with E. Neil)
Child Abuse and Neglect: Attachment, Development and Intervention★
The Emotionally Intelligent Social Worker★
A Brief Introduction to Social Work Theory★
Attachment across the Lifecourse: A Brief Introduction★

★Also published by Palgrave Macmillan

Empathy

What it is and why it matters

By

David Howe

palgrave
macmillan

First published 2013 by

PALGRAVE MACMILLAN

Palgrave Macmillan in the UK is an imprint of Macmillan Publishers Limited, registered in England, company number 785998, of Houndmills, Basingstoke,

Hampshire RG21 6XS.

Palgrave Macmillan in the US is a division of St Martin's Press LLC, 175 Fifth Avenue, New York, NY 10010.

Palgrave Macmillan is the global academic imprint of the above companies and has companies and representatives throughout the world.

Palgrave® and Macmillan® are registered trademarks in the United States, the United Kingdom, Europe and other countries

ISBN: 978–1–137–27642–1

This book is printed on paper suitable for recycling and made from fully managed and sustained forest sources. Logging, pulping and manufacturing processes are expected to conform to the environmental regulations of the country of origin.

A catalogue record for this book is available from the British Library.

A catalog record for this book is available from the Library of Congress.

10 9 8 7 6 5 4 3 2 1

22 21 20 19 18 17 16 15 14 13

Printed in China

Contents

Acknowledgements

Gentle counsel and subtle direction from Palgrave's publisher and editor, Catherine Gray, have, as always, kept me from straying too far. Thank you, Catherine. Thanks, too, must go to the anonymous reviewers who offered me generous and considered advice on how to improve the book. I have tried to follow most of it, but time, space and a stubborn streak of wilfulness meant that a few, probably key, suggestions have not found their way into the final draft. Sorry. The copyediting team of Sally Osborn and Linda Auld have also done me proud. The book has benefited hugely from their literary attentions. My friend Roger Hennessey knows more than a thing or two about empathy. I am grateful to him for the several conversations we have enjoyed discussing the subject of this book. And it is at this point that I realized, 'Oh! That's not many people to thank.' Surely the acknowledgements page for a book on empathy should – as so many are – be gushing with thanks to all manner of family, friends and colleagues who have all shown me boundless empathy. But I have to confess that writing the book became something of an indulgence, a solo pursuit, a secret pleasure. Nevertheless, now I have emerged, smiling but shamed into trying to practise what I have preached in the following pages. Be warned.

David Howe
Norwich

1
Introducing Empathy

Empathy, high and low

'I thought about killing myself.'

'Really? Suicide?'

'Yes. Everything and everyone I loved seemed to have gone. Especially after my mum died at the end of last year.'

'Right. Wow. Well, well. I mean, when you're thinking about it, did you think about, like, how you'd do it? Had it got that far?'

'Well no, but, you know, I sometimes feel there's no point in going on. It all seems so bleak. I can still, you know, sometimes, feel very alone.'

'Still, a pretty extreme thing to do. Ending it all. Big stuff.'

'But it didn't feel quite like that. Life, you know... I mean sometimes I wonder what there is to keep me going.'

This conversation might have taken place between two friends, two strangers who met on their way to visit a holy shrine, or a client and counsellor, although admittedly not one cut out for a long or successful career. Here is another similar conversation:

'My mother died last year. I miss her.'

'It can hurt. It's surprising how it can affect you.'

'Yes. I can still feel my stomach tightening. And I get these feelings of such emptiness. They come in waves out of the blue.'

'You look very sad.'

'Yeah. I do feel sad. It hurts. And the pain, the sadness won't go away.'

'Tell me a bit about your mother.'

'She was good. We got on well. Nothing dramatic, you

1

know [said with a quick smile]. But after Dad died when I was still quite young, she was always there. And that was nice. And now she's not there. And I still can't quite take it in.'

'That sounds really hard.'

These exchanges both involve someone who is feeling very low and in a state of some despair. Where the conversations differ is in the quality of the other person's responses. The first respondent is clearly failing to tune into the other's feelings of bleakness and desperation. He or she continues to run on his or her own agenda. We might say that this individual lacks empathy. As a result, the connection and conversational flow stutter as cues and needs are missed.

In contrast, the second respondent is picking up some of the other's pain. He or she is trying to tune into the person's feelings: imagining, sensing what it must be like to be someone who is hurting and in grief. This effort helps the other stay with their feelings, perhaps with the prospect of exploring them in the safety of a caring relationship. We might say that the respondent is showing some empathy.

This is a book about empathy. It is one of those skills that, when present, humanises people and their relationships. When empathy is missing, however, the world feels harsh, indifferent, less caring, even brutal. Like most human traits, individuals vary in their capacity to empathise. Even one individual can be empathic sometimes but a little less attuned at others. Levels of empathy might shift depending on mood, the people involved and the situations in which we find ourselves.

We recognise empathy when it is present, but it can be hard to sustain. Not surprisingly, this seemingly virtuous but often elusive capacity has interested people from a wide range of disciplines and practices. Over the last hundred years or so, interest in empathy has steadily grown. In fact, the twenty-first century appears to be witnessing something of an explosion of enquiry and scholarship into the capacity to empathise, as a quick scan of this book's bibliography will confirm. We might also note that of all the groups that have taken an interest in empathy, the helping professions have probably shown the most enthusiasm and greatest commitment.

Mind reading

There is something heroic about our need to know and under-stand. Indeed, the need to know how the world works seems to be part of our very nature. Even babies, writes Bruner (1990), arrive with a readiness to search for meaning; meaning, note, not only knowledge. It is the search for meaning, rather than simple explanation, that makes life particularly interesting. Thinking based on cause and effect is all well and good, but when it comes to handling human relationships we seek mean-ing, we look for purpose, we fret over intention. We rarely take matters at face value. We observe, then interpret. We are a mind-reading species.

We take this ability to recognise and reflect on what other people might be thinking and feeling so much for granted that we sometimes forget what an extraordinary skill it is. We could say that this intense interest in what other people do is one of the defining characteristics of our species. We do it constantly, as we talk, gossip, plot and ponder. It explains our obsession with TV soaps, the fixation of newspapers with the lives of the rich and famous, and the fact that romantic fiction and crime thrillers are the bestselling genres of literature. We are fascinated by other people's behaviour.

Most of our everyday talk, whether we are taxi drivers or teachers, heart surgeons or hairdressers, is about who is doing what with whom, why they're doing it and what will happen next (Dunbar 1996). It isn't sufficient simply to observe behav-iour; we want to know what is going on in people's heads that might explain it. 'Don't trust him. He may be all smiles, but he's really ambitious and will slag you off behind your back.' 'Do you know why she's in such a good mood today? She's won a holi-day in a newspaper competition! How amazing is that?' It turns out that success in the social world depends on our ability to recognise and understand, interpret and anticipate the mental states and behaviour of others.

Indeed, so pervasive is this urge to make sense of behaviour and understand experience from the inside out that it has conjured up an astonishing range of human enquiry. Philosophers wonder how we might know other minds, and whether knowing other minds makes us moral. Artists explore the world of form, substance and sensation, trying to feel things from the inside in order to communicate the experience in words, music, paint and stone. Social scientists and psychologists marvel at how we 'do' social life. How we relate, cooperate and create seems to depend on the ability to observe, interpret and understand the minds of others. And when our hearts are broken or our heads are in a muddle, we want to be understood. We seek love, we need comfort, we search for safety. At such times we turn to close friends and caring family, nurturing teachers and skilled counsellors.

And whenever there is talk of minds and morals, love and relationships, care and concern, there is also talk of empathy – that is, the capacity to read and maybe connect with other people's minds and their interior experience.

Outline and aims

There is therefore a story to be told about empathy and its rise. In Chapters 2 to 5 we shall consider first what empathy is, why we have it and how it develops. These opening pages look at empathy as it crops up in art, aesthetics, evolutionary psychology, developmental psychology and the work of neuro-developmental scientists, who study the brain and how it processes social information.

In Chapters 6, 7 and 8, we recognize that the capacity to empathize varies between individuals, and we wonder why this might be so. In particular, scientists have taken a great deal of interest in people whose empathy levels appear to be low, including individuals diagnosed with autism, psychopathy or borderline personality disorder. This interest in 'disorders of empathy' is partly driven by a concern for those who suffer an empathy deficit and the impact this has on their social life, and partly by a recognition of the role that empathy plays in defining our shared humanity. Of course, it should follow that if low empathy predicts problems with social relationships, then high empathy should sponsor a more successful social life. The importance of empathy in the skilful conduct of relationships has long been appreciated by psychotherapists, counsellors and others in the helping professions. It is to these groups and their work, via client feedback studies, that we therefore turn to in Chapters 9 and 10. And given that empathy is recognized as a key component of effective treatment, Chapter 11 considers what might make it therapeutically so efficacious.

Recognizing the many virtues of empathy, Chapters 12–16 review what philosophers and politicians, literary theorists and educationalists have to say about the part that empathy plays in behaviours that are regarded as moral, altruistic, decent and human, and how these might be promoted in both children and adults. Whatever the disciplinary background of the expert, there is a shared belief that empathy helps define and enrich our humanity, and by the same token its absence diminishes us.

It can be something of a surprise to learn that empathy has such an exotic and interesting provenance, and that so many disciplines have taken long, serious looks at its nature and potential. My hope is that if you are able to appreciate empathy's deep roots and marvellously varied and colourful character, you will be as excited, intrigued and committed to the concept as I have been in researching this book. The more one appreciates and celebrates empathy's long-standing appeal to writers and philosophers, artists and educationalists, psychologists and sociologists, counsellors and social workers, brain scientists and health professionals, the richer becomes one's understanding of this most human of qualities. I also hope that professionals – indeed all thoughtful citizens – who explore empathy at its widest and best will find their understanding a fraction improved, their practice a mite better and their nature a little more forgiving.

2
Origins and Definitions

Art and aesthetics

Empathy has its origins in the philosophy of aesthetics. As we discuss these beginnings, it will become obvious why the concept of empathy also attracted the attention of psychologists, humanists and psychotherapists. Appreciating empathy's rather colourful start reminds us that getting on the emotional inside of an experience can be extraordinarily energizing. This is true whether that experience is aesthetic, relational or therapeutic.

Late nineteenth-century German philosophers used the word *Einfühlung*, later translated as empathy, when discussing aesthetics. One of the earliest appearances of the word was in 1846. Philosopher Robert Vischer used *Einfühling* to discuss the pleasure we experience when we contemplate a work of art (e.g. Vischer 1873/1994). The word represented an attempt to describe our ability to get 'inside' a work of beauty by, for example, projecting ourselves and our feelings 'into' a painting, a sculpture, a piece of music, even the beauty of nature itself.

'For the romantic,' comments Stueber (2006: 7), 'nature is properly understood only if it is seen as an outward symbol of some inner spiritual reality.' As the work of art or the beauty of nature resonates with us, the feelings generated are projected into, and then felt to be a quality of, that work of art, that glorious nature.

If we can 'feel our way into' a work of art in an act of empathy, our understanding increases and our appreciation deepens. With particularly powerful works of art, we feel ourselves reacting both viscerally and emotionally (Freedberg and Gallese 2007). As our bodies resonate with the flow of the paint, the pain of a face, the strength of a buttress, the flight of a spire, our feelings vibrate in tune with the emotions of the work we are contemplating. We have an aesthetic experience. We are moved in our contemplation of a sensuous object.

The aesthetic doctrine of the early Bauhaus school 'taught artists that externalizing their inner experiences of things was integral to rendering the outer physical appearances of things' (Wix 2009: 153). Inspired by this philosophy, the artist Paul Klee encouraged his students to:

> sense the total nature of things [by] entering the conception of the natural object, be this object plant, animal, or human being ... The object grows beyond its appearance through our knowledge of its inner nature.
>
> (from Paul Klee's 1923 essay 'The Play of Forces in the Bauhaus', quoted in Wix 2009: 153)

The idea that we might understand the world by contemplating art and nature harks back even further to the Romanticism of the late eighteenth and early nineteenth centuries. The Romantics reacted against what they saw as the impersonal logic of the new Enlightenment sciences. They agreed that it was possible to explain nature, but they considered that science and its objectivity had nothing to say about what it feels like to be in the world, what it is like to experience life, to be in the midst of colour, shape and sound. The human experience can only be understood and appreciated if we recognize that we are found in and formed by nature. We cannot stand apart from it. We are embodied creatures: more than reason, more than thought. The Romantic view was that in human affairs, experience outbids explanation. Reflecting on the *subjective* self is what gives life its meaning. Poet William Wordsworth wrote in 'The Tables Turned' (1798):

> Our meddling intellect
> Mis-shapes the beauteous form of things
> We murder to dissect.

The eighteenth century also saw the emergence of literary works of a reflective, autobiographical nature. Michel de Montaigne's late sixteenth-century writings were a remarkable precursor of this genre, but a century or two later, Giambattista

Vico, Jean-Jacques Rousseau, Johann Wolfgang von Goethe and many others were exploring the human condition through their own reflective essays. Writers began to analyse the self with increasing honesty. It is in their reflections that we begin to see the growth of the modern, empathic mind.

The artistic temperament valued meaning above measurement in its contemplation of nature. By appreciating the form and feel of an object from within, we are emotionally affected. Poetry, said Samuel Taylor Coleridge (1798/1983: 5), has 'the power of exciting the sympathy of the reader by a faithful adherence to the truth of nature'. In this sense, aesthetic empathy describes a projective fusing with the object of contemplation (Keen 2007: 28). An aesthetic experience involves both thought and feeling, the mind as well as the senses. The intellectual appreciation of the artistic work coupled with its emotional ability to move us gives rise to a complex mix of feeling, thought, insight and beauty.

> To experience a work of art ... means to awaken the essential in it, to bring the living quality, which is inherent in its form to independent life. The work of art is reborn within me ... a living representation is always something experienced, and something experienced is always experienced with life.
>
>   (artist Johannes Itten, cited in Wingler 1969: 49)

In these ways, we come to understand the object of study intimately. Our empathic engagement with a work of art allows us to feel the feelings captured in the painting, the sculpture or the symphony. For example, in his paintings Vincent van Gogh feels and captures something of the restless turbulence of nature. And so when we look at a van Gogh picture of, say, a field of windswept wheat beneath a roiling sky, we too begin to feel and understand something of nature's dynamic, seething quality as communicated by the art.

Defining empathy

The aesthetic stance set the scene for a major shift in the way the world, including the world of people, might be understood, not from the outside looking in, but from the inside looking out. This insight appealed to social scientists, who began to recognize empathy's potential to help them understand human experience from the subject's point of view.

It was the psychologist Edward Titchener who, in 1909, was the first to use the term *empathy* as the English translation of the German word *Einfühlung*. Its etymology is from the Greek word *empatheia*, meaning to enter feelings from the outside, or to be with a person's feelings, passions or suffering. If we are to *understand* people and their situations rather than explain them, we need to begin to interpret and find meaning.

The human capacity to recognize other minds and think about what might be going on in them has been called many things, but all commentators agree that the skill is vital if we are to make sense of behaviour and relate to others effectively. Dictionary definitions and paying attention to the origin of words help keep our understandings rooted. From the Greek for 'feeling', *pathos* acts as a suffix for a number of related words (Hennessey 2011: 82): *a*pathy (without feeling), *sym*pathy (with feeling, together feeling) and *anti*pathy (feeling against). And so in similar fashion, we have *em*pathy, meaning 'into feeling' or 'feeling into'. The idea of getting 'into' a feeling is particularly important, particularly when we see and *feel* the world from the other's point of view, attempt to understand it, and seek to convey that understanding as we relate with those around us.

As we shall see, as well as saying something about sharing emotions, empathy also suggests an active effort, a cognitive challenge. In talking about *empathic accuracy*, Hogan (1969: 308) sees empathy as 'the intellectual or imaginative apprehension of another's condition or state of mind'. His concept attempts to capture our ability to recognize other people's personality, emotional condition, beliefs and desires in order to make sense of, predict and anticipate their behaviour. Thus, empathy might also be defined as the 'ability to identify what someone else is thinking or feeling and to respond to their thoughts and feelings with an appropriate emotion' (Baron-Cohen 2011: 11). It involves complex psychological inferences 'in which observation, memory, knowledge, and reasoning are combined to yield insights into the thoughts and feelings of others' (Stompe *et al.* 2010: 44).

To some extent, empathy overlaps with similar 'mind-reading' abilities in which we attribute mental states to other people, as the following example illustrates:

> Elaine is silent. She looks both sad and distraught. She has just put the phone down after talking at some length with her boyfriend, John. Elaine's close friend, Alice, knows that things haven't been good between the two lovers and that John has been on the brink of ending the relationship. Although Elaine has said nothing, Alice knows that John has finished the affair. Elaine's pain is palpable. 'Oh, Elaine, Elaine,' says Alice in a voice that captures her friend's distress and hurt. She reaches out and holds then squeezes Elaine's hand. Elaine looks up briefly, bursts into tears and rests her head on Alice's shoulder.

Alice may not have said much, bus she is seeing and feeling Elaine's hurt, and Elaine understands this.

Personal distress and emotional contagion

There is a position more primitive than either empathy or sympathy, which psychologists sometimes refer to as *personal distress* (Batson *et al.* 1987). True, your situation or condition affects me, but the effect is entirely personal. Once excited, my emotional distress takes no interest in or account of you whose situation triggered my feelings. My feelings are entirely self-absorbed. Once they are aroused, my only aim is to relieve the distress I feel, not the distress you are suffering. Let us say that you recount your parents' divorce when you were a child. Your story raises memories of my own parents' divorce and I lose myself in those deeply unhappy, miserable times. I cry. The memories and the distress suffered are now solely mine, no longer connected to you, your situation or your story.

Emotional contagion is a similar phenomenon. Simply being in the presence of people who are sharing and expressing some strong emotion is likely to see us being swept along in the same emotional current. A powerful piece of music can make us weep or alternatively feel like bursting with joy (Davies 2011). In an emotionally aroused crowd, the looks on people's faces, the sounds of their voices, the movements of their bodies take on a common, almost synchronized appearance. If everyone around us is laughing hysterically or in a state of panic, we might find ourselves laughing or feeling panicky too, even if we don't know what caused the original laughter or fear. However, in these cases, although we are tuning into and picking up the emotional condition of those around us, the emotion of joy or panic becomes ours. It is our own emotional arousal that consumes us and to which we react and attend, not that of the others.

We see something of these fast, unreflective and cognitively unprocessed emotional reactions – sometimes referred to as *primitive empathy* – in many species when individuals react, say, to the cry of fear in others (another bird shrieks) or a sudden flight response (another zebra turns and runs). Most of these highly attuned and contagious responses involve fear. Fear triggers fast escape behaviour whenever there is any hint of danger. This very broad notion of empathy describes the rapid sharing of an emotional experience by all members of the group, leading to behaviours that look coordinated.

But we can also recognize some higher orders of empathy in animals (de Waal 2009, 2010). Dog owners know how sensitive their pets can be to their owner's actions, mood and intentions. Preston and de Waal (2002) recognize empathy-like responses in monkeys, apes and even rats. These species tend to be group living and sociable. To explain the phenomenon, these authors believe that 'continuous contact and coordinated activities are characteristic of a bond that develops as a physiologically adaptive response to stress, accurate communication of affect with others, and the capacity for empathic responding' (Preston and de Waal 2002: 301).

Empathy and sympathy

Both empathy proper and sympathy are more complex and sophisticated than shared emotional distress. As we have seen, empathy happens when we resonate with another person's

feelings. In contrast, sympathy is 'an emotional response stem-
ming from another's emotional state or condition that is not
identical to the other's emotion, but consists of feelings of
sorrow or concern for another's welfare' (Eisenberg and Miller
1987: 92).

More straightforward distinctions suggest that whereas
empathy puts me in your emotional shoes, sympathy simply
tells you that I've walked there too. Sympathy is me oriented;
empathy is you oriented. For example, in response to the quiet
and obvious sadness of a 91-year-old woman about to leave her
house for the last time before she enters residential care, a
young care worker says, 'I know how you feel, Amy, I do. I felt
really sad when I had to leave my nice little flat overlooking the
park. I get quite tearful thinking about it even now. You'll be all
right when you get there; I'm sure.' The worker recognizes
Amy's feelings of empty despair and sympathetically tries to
offer reassurance. The gesture is well meaning, but doesn't
quite manage to stay connected with Amy and her thoughts
and feelings.

The risk is that sympathy can sometimes cause anxiety and
lessen mindfulness. With similar thoughts in mind, practitioners
from a counselling and psychotherapeutic background sometimes warn against the dangers of sympathy. For them, sympathy can get perilously close to identification, even projection,
with the risk that the counsellor becomes too emotionally
involved. Sympathy can mean that objectivity is lost. 'I understand how you feel' is different to saying 'You feel hurt and
upset'. If I am in the same emotional state as you, then we're
both in danger of feeling lost and not in control. If I also feel
anger at the injustice you have suffered, this traps us both in a
state of excited distress in which we fuel each other's rage and
helplessness: 'You should complain, maybe get in touch with the
newspapers; make a fuss about this wrong. I would. It's outrageous. It's absolutely not fair.'

According to this analysis, sympathy, identification, projection and countertransference can distort our perceptions and
communications (Gelso and Hayes 2002). In contrast, empathy
is a sense of knowing the other's mind without their state of
mind being the same as ours.

Stepping back and acknowledging these various definitions, I think that we are on safer ground when we limit ourselves the etymological origins of the two words. To be sympathetic is to have feelings (*pathos*) that are the same as (*sym*) those of the other. To be empathic is to know, sense or enter into (*em*) the feelings (*pathos*) of the other. We shall try to hold on to these distinctions as we journey through the rest of this book.

Affective and cognitive empathy

In spite of pleas to keep it simple, whenever people stop and think about empathy, they are naturally inclined to deconstruct, elaborate and refine the concept. At its most visceral, empathy is felt in the body. We physically feel the other's joy, fear or sadness and so know something of their world. Perhaps more than any other component of empathy, the fact that we share the same biology and the same senses means that we know at the physical level what it is to experience pain or jealousy. On first encounter, we appear to someone else through our bodies, via our senses. More than any appeal to our rational selves, there is something direct and powerful about recognizing another's feelings as physically felt. 'At its most basic,' says Mensch (2011: 21), 'empathy is bodily'.

Physical sensations can be felt as subjective feelings, and subjective feelings can be thought about, both our own and those of someone else. Empathy, therefore, can be the result of thought as well as feeling, cognition as well as affect. It consists of affective and cognitive responses, feeling what another person is feeling and understanding why that person feels as he or she does.

Along similar lines, Feshbach (1987) sees empathy as comprising three *processes*: the cognitive ability to perceive, recognize and discriminate emotional states in the other person; the more mature cognitive skill of seeing things from the other person's point of view; and an emotional response to or experience of the other's emotional state.

These interesting and I think helpful definitions therefore recognize both *cognitive* and *affective* processes at work in empathy. *Affective* or *emotional empathy* gets us close to what we generally understand as an empathic response: I feel your pain, I notice and sense your despair, but I am clear that it is you who is in pain and despair not me, even though I am being emotionally affected by your distress.

Cognitive empathy is based on seeing, imagining and thinking about the situation from the other person's point of view. It involves a more cognitively based, reflective process of understanding the other's perspective. Some knowledge of the other's history, personality, circumstances and situation is necessary before we can set our minds to work imagining what it might be like to be that person. It involves actively thinking about the other's mind coupled with the capacity to feel the other's feelings. Appreciating how you might feel as you see a distant torch light flashing in the nighttime forest depends on what I know about your circumstances. You will feel relief and joy if I know that you are lost and your leg is broken. You will feel fear and trepidation if I know that you are trying to escape a deadly gang out to capture you. In contrast to emotional empathy, the cognitive components of empathy in which we think about the other's emotional point of view take many years to develop, and only then in the context of close childhood relationships (see Chapter 4).

When our empathy is at its most expansive, both affective and cognitive empathy are involved. I am able to understand *and* feel your world while, at the same time, keeping a clear sense of my own and your mental experience. We therefore have to remember that empathy involves imagining another's psychological world while maintaining a clear self–other differentiation (Coplan 2011: 5).

And finally, empathy not only entails knowing what a person is feeling and feeling what a person is feeling, but also *communicating*, perhaps with compassion, the recognition and understanding of the other's emotional experience. Thus, as commentators add communication to the mix, we might define empathy as an affective reaction to the emotions of another; the cognitive act of adopting another's perspective; a cognitively based understanding of other people; and the communication of such an understanding (Davis 1994: 11).

The socially skilled mind reader

Most definitions of empathy put it at the heart of social life. Good empathizers are those who tune in to emotional atmospheres. They are good at reading faces. They hear excitement or fear in a voice. They make good eye contact. They pick up on how people feel about others. If someone is being quiet and ignored, they seek to bring them into the conversation. 'A good empathizer responds intuitively to a change in another person's mood with concern, appreciation, understanding, comforting, or whatever the appropriate emotion might be' (Baron-Cohen 2004: 24).

Empathizers say neither too much nor too little, and what they do say and communicate contains an awareness of other people's feelings, perceptions and attitudes. There is much checking of what others think and feel. Other people are invited to express their views. Conversations are balanced and reciprocal. Moment-by-moment adjustments ensure that turns are taken and everyone is involved and given a voice.

These empathic skills are based on a strong awareness of the links between mind and behaviour, belief and action, feeling and response. We rarely observe someone else without wanting to know something of the mind that lies behind what they say and do. Other people's behaviour does not make sense unless we know what thoughts, feelings, desires, beliefs and hopes drove it into being.

The perceptual skill that recognizes that we have to know the mind of another to make sense of their behaviour has been called 'mindsight'. It 'is the mechanism', writes Siegel (2009: xiii) 'underlying social and emotional intelligence and permits us to know the minds of others and ourselves.' Comprehension is achieved by projecting oneself into the head of the other, or more generally into the object of contemplation. And if we achieve a strong sense of the other's feelings, they, in turn, 'feel felt'. There is resonance. There is attunement. There is empathy.

So valuable is the idea of empathy that in his bestselling book, Covey (1990) rates it as one of the key attributes of 'highly effective people', those who first seek to understand, then be understood. Empathy oils the wheels of social life. When we share, love, cooperate and give, empathy is at work. When empathy is absent, there is no intimacy and relationships break down. Violence, abuse, discrimination and selfishness become all too common when empathy goes missing.

Empathy in context and in person

We shall consider individual differences in empathy in more detail in Chapter 6, but here we might simply recognize that the quality and depth of empathy achieved depends on the individual's own characteristics (sex, personality, temperament, attachment style, mood); the relationship he or she has with the other person (family, friend, colleague, stranger); and the specific situation (casual encounter, therapy, hospital visit, request for help, danger and so on).

Different combinations of person, other and situation will therefore produce different degrees of empathy, from low to high. Each component will affect the quality and intensity of empathy felt and shown. For example, a dispositionally sensitive and secure sister listening to a brother talk about his recent diagnosis of cancer is likely to show a high degree of empathy. On returning from a hospital visit to see her brother, she finds herself sitting on a train next to an overweight, middle-aged man. In this case her feelings of empathy are not especially high as she listens to him complain that his knee joints hurt and that he is finding getting on and off trains increasingly difficult.

There is also a tendency for would-be empathic observers to explain people in terms of their personality and temperament, whereas we are more inclined to explain our own behaviour in terms of the situation in which we find ourselves.

For example, I might see your determination to achieve a good degree in law as yet another manifestation of your conscientious, competitive and ambitious nature. You, on the other hand, feel under pressure to achieve knowing that your parents are paying your fees and that they have hinted that a poor performance would sorely disappoint, even annoy them. However, if you do achieve a good degree, you are more likely to see the success as a result of your natural intelligence and willingness to work hard – self-attributed dispositional factors.

On the other hand, if you fail or perform poorly, you are more likely to blame the situation: an unreasonably difficult exam, poor teaching, friends who lead you astray.

In general, then, a clear knowledge and understanding of your own and the other person's disposition *and* situation, nature *and* circumstance are likely to lead to better and more accurate empathy.

As well as defining empathy, social scientists have also been keen to measure it (Truax and Carkhuff 1967; Baron-Cohen *et al.* 2001; Davis 2004; Schmid Mast and Ickes 2007). For example, Baron-Cohen and Wheelwright (2004) have developed an instrument that measures an individual's Empathy Quotient (EQ). It comprises 40 questions that test both empathic recognition and response. Respondents are asked to rate the extent to which they agree or disagree with a series of statements. Examples include 'I can easily tell if someone else wants to enter a conversation', 'I find it hard to know what to do in social situations', ' It doesn't bother me too much if I am late meeting a friend' and 'When I was a child, I enjoyed cutting up worms to see what would happen'.

Studies using these measures have shown that in any given population there is a spread of scores from low to high empathy, with most people lying somewhere in the middle. In general, the lower the empathy score, the more puzzling and difficult the individual is likely to find social life. Some very low-scoring individuals even find everyday chitchat baffling, even stressful. So much of ordinary conversation requires people to see and sense what other people are thinking and feeling in order that their responses are appropriate, tuned in and sensitive. If you can't do these things, even matter-of-fact conversations become a strain.

An idea whose time has come

The beginning of the twenty-first century has seen a big explosion of interest in the concept and practice of empathy. Pinker (2011) describes empathy as the latest fashion in human nature and increasingly bold claims are being made for its extraordinary properties. Empathy, it seems, defines our humanity. In fact, argues Rifkin (2009: 3) rather grandly, 'The Age of Reason is being eclipsed by the Age of Empathy'. And for Ickes:

> Empathic inference is everyday mind reading ... It may be the second greatest achievement of which the mind is capable, consciousness itself being the first.
>
> (Ickes 1997: 2)

Great claims are also made for empathy's ability to make us good, moral, connected and civilized. 'Empathy', writes Hoffman (2000: 3), 'is the spark of human concern for others, the glue that makes social life possible.' Any problem, believes Baron-Cohen (2011: 127), whether personal or interpersonal, can be solved when it is immersed in empathy's healing balm.

The fact that so many disciplines are waxing lyrical about empathy and recognizing its importance in the conduct of human affairs is in itself revealing. The common thread that links all these disciplinary interests is the idea that empathic minds foster cooperation, collaboration and civility; that good-quality relationships bring about the capacity to be empathic; and therefore that being empathic is a defining quality of what it is to be human.

As we survey empathy's appearance in so many fields of human enquiry, the case will be made that the way in which we develop the capacity to be empathic explains why empathic relationships continue to have the power to connect and bond, harmonize and heal. Empathy allows for human kindness. If early relationships are where we acquire the capacity to empathize, relationships are where we go to understand and be understood, explore and expand, be contained and cared for.

Conclusion

In this chapter we have defined empathy, given a quick overview of its character and composition, and recognized some of the grand claims made on its behalf. The more passive definitions of empathy reveal our shared psychology, our susceptibility to be affected by the feelings of others. The more active definitions capture our humanity, our efforts to understand others, our compassion, our desire to act and help as we think about and begin to see the world from the other's point of view.

In the rest of this book, we shall explore further what empathy is and why we might possess it. We shall think about how it develops and what it helps us to do. We shall worry about its absence and explore its return. We shall appreciate its value and celebrate its virtues. But before we look at empathy's social value, including its therapeutic properties, we need to explore how our species got to be empathic in the first place. What evolutionary advantages did empathy confer? This begins to tell us not only how empathy arose, but also why it continues to oil the wheels of social life and personal change.

3

The Evolution of the Empathic Mind

Connect and select

What makes human beings stand apart from other species? What accounts for our success? Many key characteristics have been suggested that mark us out from the rest of the animal kingdom: the use of tools, the growth of language, sociable behaviour, the cooking of food. But then, of course, on further reflection, many of these defining features are clearly not peculiar to human beings. Chimpanzees use tools, albeit in a limited fashion. Many mammals, including whales and dolphins, communicate in ways that suggest some kind of language is being used. Similarly, our ability to cooperate and reciprocate is not unique to our species, although we do seem to have taken these skills to a whole new level.

Nevertheless, most scientists agree that our species' mind-reading ability does suggest something extraordinary and special. And so they have wondered what evolutionary advantages mind reading and empathy might have given human beings.

If the bottom line of evolution is survival, any behaviour that promotes survival, particularly if it gets you into adulthood and reproductive activity, will inevitably be selected for. If survival was simply a matter of everyone for themselves, nature 'red in tooth and claw', then group living would not be possible.

In practice, survival and success are usually enhanced by cooperative behaviour. Living in groups and being sociable generally increase your chances of staying alive. There is safety in numbers. For animals inclined to live in close association, wrote Darwin (1871: 80), 'those individuals which took the greatest pleasure in society would best escape various dangers, whilst those that cared least for their comrades and lived solitary would perish in great numbers.' Being with people with whom we are familiar allows us to relax and feel safe. We know them and they know us. Social interaction is much more predictable and altogether less stressful. We can therefore drop our guard and switch off the stresses and strains of maintaining social vigilance. It is altogether less demanding when we are among family and friends.

The nervous systems of group-living mammals, including human beings, are particularly sensitive to the behaviour of others. When others react with fear, we immediately pick up on it and feel their fear viscerally, in the gut, in the body. This makes evolutionary sense, as threat and danger have to be sensed by all group members as quickly as possible for us to prepare for fight or flight (Sapolsky 1998).

The concept of empathy accounts for the phylogenetic advantages of these systems in promoting cooperative behaviors that enable *groups* of individuals to share in the responsibility for detecting danger and to facilitate social communication and social interaction within a *safe* environment. It is this ability to share knowledge regarding environmental danger that provides the basis for the subsequent development of social groups, societies, and their product.

(Carter *et al*. 2011: 173, emphasis in original)

Further evolutionary developments meant that there were advantages not only in being able to read other people's facial expressions and body language, but also in individuals' ability to become more expressive. The human face is extraordinarily mobile and can express dozens and dozens of different feeling states that other people can read and interpret with great speed and accuracy. It is worth pointing out that this ability quickly to tune into other people's expressions, body language and vocal intonations initially takes place outside conscious awareness. We feel and sense the other person's emotional condition before we actually stop to think about it, reflect on it and analyse it. The feelings are felt in our own facial expressions as we mimic the other's look. They are felt in our bodies. They are heard in our voices. This is embodied empathy. It is emotional empathy, immediate, direct and fast acting. It does not involve conscious thought or reflection.

This is in contrast to cognitive empathy, where we do make a conscious effort to think ourselves into someone else's shoes. Successful group living therefore requires members to be empathic, both at the more primitive emotional level to keep members connected and safe and at the more sophisticated cognitive level so that members can regulate, moderate, coordinate, refine and develop their individual and collective behaviour.

Thus although there is safety in numbers, numbers also increase the collective potential. Division of labour and maximizing of talent offer possibilities far beyond the capabilities of any one individual. Sharp-eyed hunters, clever trackers, cunning trappers, patient gatherers, abstract planners, gifted storytellers – acting together, such individuals make for a formidable survival machine. But in order to take advantage of and knit together these many talents, there must be mutual recognition. There needs to be give and take. The welfare of the group depends on 'not me or thee but we' (Dawes *et al.* 1988: 83). Once again we are picking up empathy's pervasive presence. If mind reading and perspective taking facilitate cooperation and group living, and a sociable life increases the chances of success and survival, the skills of empathy will be selected for.

> The degree of cooperative, prosocial behaviour displayed within human groups and societies is rare within the animal kingdom ... No other species has ever developed such large and complex societies that involve such an array of nongenetically related individuals ... Human prosociality is most likely the result of multiple selection pressures and multiple evolved mechanisms, all of which have pushed human evolution in an increasingly cooperative and prosocial direction relative to most other species ... Far from being competitive and antagonistic, our most reproductively successful ancestors may have been among the most cooperative and resourceful individuals within their group.
>
> (Simpson and Beckes 2010: 50–51)

Social participation has therefore been suggested as the primary 'survival strategy' of early humans (Brewer and Caporael 1990). The 'willingness to enter and maintain mutually co-operative, long-term alliances with others ... may have been essential to survival, successful reproduction, and adequate parenting' (Simpson and Beckes 2010: 37). And as well as safety, sex and succour, a skilled social life can lead to trade, resource distribution and the resolution of conflicts.

The cognitive challenges of social living

Humphrey (1986) has also taken an evolutionary interest in our social behaviour, although he has been more concerned with our competitive nature. His thinking and analysis also got him to a point where he was impressed by our ability to see things from other people's point of view, but his first thoughts were prompted by observing the behaviour of gorillas in their home environment of the African jungle.

It was while studying these apes as a research biologist that Humphrey began to wonder why they had such large brains. All they seemed to do for much of the day was lounge around in social groups eating fruit. Life seemed relatively easy and undemanding. The only issue that seemed to exercise them was dealing with other gorillas as they foraged, groomed, occasionally mated and looked after their young.

If the main challenges in a gorilla's day-to-day life were the behaviours and intentions of other gorillas, maybe this went part of the way to explain their sophisticated, albeit laid-back social lives and their largish brains. To cope with the social demands of the group, gorillas had to make sense of and predict the behaviour of their fellow apes. Gorillas

> know each other intimately, they know their place. None the less there *are* endless small disputes about social dominance, about who grooms who, about who should first have access to a favourite food, or sleep in the best site.
>
> (Humphrey 1986: 37, emphasis in original)

All of this social thinking requires a great deal of multiple perspective taking, awareness and calculation, and therefore brain power (Dunbar and Aiello 1993). But equally, it confers significant advantages. For social animals, the ability to antici-pate what others might do – share, attack, mate, deceive – is extremely valuable if social life is to be conducted with skill.

Reflecting on his own troubled social life, Humphrey realized that human beings also spend an awful lot of time thinking and worrying about what other people are feeling, thinking, wanting, planning and plotting. Social intelligence, believes Humphrey (1986), is the key to the success of apes and chimpanzees, but human beings too. This ability to recognize, understand and interpret the minds of others has played a key part in boosting our intelligence. Humphrey concluded that there was a distinct evolutionary advantage in being able to attribute mental states to other people, read other minds and understand and relate well with those around us. To do this, of course, we have to see things from their point of view. We are all natural psychologists. Evolution rewards the empathic.

Furthermore, we need to recognize the role that deception and its detection play in social life. It is possible for deceivers, scroungers and cheats to prosper if everyone else is playing fair. Deception also involves penetrating the minds of others, seeing how the world looks from their point of view, and seeking to manipulate those minds and their perspective on matters. Alvarez (2001), poet and gambler, says that good poker players are good mind readers. Not only do they play the cards and the minds of the other players, but they have to be adept at obscur-ing their own thoughts so that others are clueless about what they are thinking, plotting and feeling. Deception, and in partic-ular its detection, requires considerable brain power.

In everyday life, though, the cheat who is found out risks punishment, attack and social isolation. Shunning social wrong-doers is a universal activity. Only if cheats show contrition and seek reconciliation are they likely to be accepted back into the group. Cheats might also feel guilt, which can only be assuaged by acting with renewed and vigorous reciprocity in future trans-actions. Therefore, from an evolutionary perspective, the contin-ued prevalence of reciprocal, pro-social and altruistic behaviour depends on cheats standing a good chance of being found out and suffering the heavy social penalties of not playing fair. If cheating both paid and ran a low risk of detection, cooperation and trust would rapidly break down.

> If individuals only ever encounter each other once, then the best thing to do is cheat. However, if there is a high probability that you are likely to meet the same individuals time and time again, then cooperative strategies prove to be the better option.
>
> (Barrett *et al.* 2002: 30)

If reciprocal altruism is to work, we need to remember who has helped whom, who is related to whom, who owes whom a favour, who pulled their weight for the good of all. Such complex social reckoning requires advanced social cognition. The receipt of a favour is likely to encourage feelings of gratitude, and hence further reciprocal behaviour. In fact, Trivers (1985) suggests that many of our emotional responses to social life are tied up with the favours and exchanges that take place as we relate with each other. Our emotions help cement relationships and maintain the benefits of complex cooperative living. Feelings of pleasure, gratitude, guilt, sympathy, annoyance, rebuke and retaliation can all arise as we trade social, psychological, sexual, material and nutritional goods and favours.

In further developing his argument, Humphrey recognizes that part of our ability to read other minds depends first on our ability to know and reflect on our own thoughts and feelings. Once again, this leads him into ideas about the nature and origin of empathy. 'It is as if', he says, 'I, like every other human being, possess a kind of "inner eye", which looks in on my own brain and tells me why and how I'm acting in the way that I am' (Humphrey 1986: 68). Having some ideas about how to explain our own behaviour then allows us to hazard some pretty insightful guesses about what might be governing other people's behaviour, including their likely reaction to our behaviour. The ability to 'think forward' and imagine future consequences of our own and other people's behaviour generates a range of psychosocial skills. 'We could, in effect, imagine what it's like to be them, because we know what it's like to be ourselves' (Humphrey 1986: 71). To the extent that I know me, then I might be able to understand you. This is social intelligence.

Social life of this kind involves considerable reflexivity. The sophistication of our social behaviour is not only driven by our ability to see the world from the other's point of view, but also by the recognition that as we do this, the other is doing exactly the same: I see you, seeing me, seeing you.

Putting the family first

For most of their evolution, human beings have been hunter-gatherers, living in small, cooperative tribes and genetically related family groups. Thus, 'those in need were often one's children or close kin, and survival of one's genes was tightly tied to the welfare even of those who were not close kin' (Batson 2010: 26).

Reciprocal altruism and preferential treatment are most likely between family members. We tend to be most generous with close kin. Moreover, the more dense, supportive and involved relationships are between people, the better their health and the longer they live (Barrett *et al.* 2002: 65). Family and close friends make us feel safe. Belonging reduces stress, and low stress boosts the immune system. Kin networks are good for your survival and they are good for your health.

From an evolutionary point of view, the concept of 'inclusive fitness' is a reminder that it is the survival of genes rather than of individuals that is important (Hamilton 1964; Wilson 1975; Dawkins 1976). Our genes are not unique to us. The more closely we are related, the more genes we have in common. Parents share about 50 per cent of their genes with their children (although none, of course, with their partners). Full siblings also have half their genes in common. Cousins share approximately 25 per cent of their genes with each other.

Thus, from a genetic perspective, the survival of the greatest number of genetically related individuals is better than the survival of any one individual. You could make the genetic calculation that an uncle dying to save the lives of five of his blood-related nieces and nephews is better than the uncle living at the expense of these same close relatives. Those nieces and nephews represent 125 per cent of his genetic stock. On similar accounting, an evolutionarily savvy father might risk his life to save his three children.

It is therefore not 'individual fitness' but 'inclusive fitness' of close kin that drives the genetic calculus. It is out of this theory that the idea of empathy and altruism arises.

> If the essence of natural selection is the survival of genes rather than the individual, and if many of the same genes are shared by close relatives, then actions by individuals which benefit these relatives will generally increase the genes' chances of survival. This logic has led to the concept of *kin selection*, one of the major sociobiological explanations for altruism (Hamilton 1964).
>
> (Davis 1994: 25, emphasis in original)

It is helpful, cooperative and altruistic behaviour between related individuals that promotes the survival of shared genes. The ability to solve inter-group problems and navigate the social world with social skill depends on possessing a talent for perspective taking. And in order for behaviour to be helpful, cooperative and altruistic, individuals must recognize, interpret and understand what is in other people's minds, including what they want, intend, fear, hope, believe, think and feel. These capacities define empathy.

The ability to empathize and mentalize is therefore key to understanding our talent for social living. *Mentalization* is the capacity to understand how one's own and other people's mental states affect behaviour. It is a form of social cognition. It involves the capacity to 'think about feeling and to feel about thinking' (psychologist Mary Target in a personal communication to Slade, cited in Slade 2005: 271) and to 'hold mind in mind' (Allen 2006). It also involves an appreciation of how my behaviour affects your thoughts and feelings, and how your behaviour affects my thoughts and feelings. Equally, I recognize that as I am 'mentalizing' our interaction and modifying my behaviour accordingly, you are probably doing exactly the same. Human beings are 'intentional beings'; that is, we are authors of our own actions. We understand each other to the extent that we see intentional, purposeful mental states behind our own and other people's actions and behaviours. The individual who mentalizes has *reflective function*: the ability not only to think about their own and the other's mind but also about how each is affecting and being read by the other, cognitively, emotionally and behaviourally.

Empathy and care

If the wisdom of the tribe is to be passed on to the next generation, intimate and prolonged interaction with and socialization of the young are vital.

The ability to care about others, particularly close family members, is likely to have arisen out of mothers caring for their helpless, very dependent infants. Strong caring behaviours not only ensure the survival of babies, but if extended between genetically related kith and kin they also increase the chances of related gene lines surviving. The roots of empathic, caring behaviour therefore drive deep into our evolutionary beginnings.

In hunter-gatherer societies, the raising of dependent, vulnerable children depends on the close, attentive care of parents and other family members stretching over many years. Parents' empathic feelings for young children increase the sensitivity and likely appropriateness of their responses above and beyond any instinctive, non-reflective reactions. Empathy also helps parents anticipate their children's needs.

Nurturing mothers need the support of close family (particularly grandmothers) and friends if they are to protect, nourish and raise their young. Sharing the demands of child rearing requires cooperation, and cooperation depends on good social understanding. In her book *Mothers and Others*, Hrdy (2009) calls this strategy 'cooperative breeding' or cooperative parenting. It increases the chances of babies, and mothers, surviving. By the same token, it is also in the baby's interest to be attractive and socially attuned. Cooperative, shared caring of babies helps young children develop sharp observational and mind-reading skills to help them detect who is likely to be safe and a source of comfort, and who is not.

Hrdy argues that these strategies would favour the selection of genes that enabled people to be sensitive and tuned into other people's feelings and mind states. Thus, cooperation, empathy, altruism, compassion and survival get linked. Caring behaviours increase success. 'Were it not for the peculiar combination of empathy and mindreading,' believes Hrdy (2009: 28), 'we would not have evolved to be humans at all.' She then goes on to make the interesting evolutionary case that prolonged breastfeeding also meant prolonged intimacy between mothers and their babies, which, in turn, helped promote the species' social intelligence and empathy (Hrdy 2009: 141; also see Seabright 2012). So important are these phenomena that Dunbar (1996: 150) believes that female bonding; the expression, recognition and understanding of emotions; and the language that supports them have been among the most powerful forces in human evolution.

Therefore, if caregiving is to be tuned into children's needs, it has to be empathic, and children of empathic carers are more likely to survive because their parents are recognizing need, anticipating danger and seeing risk. So not only do babies experience and display distress if they suffer pain or separation, the parent who sees and hears the distress also feels anxiety and distress. Tuning into and being affected by your babies' states ensures children's protection, safety and survival. In this sense, empathy increases the likelihood of the parents' genes surviving in their children. 'According to attachment theorists,' say Shaver *et al.* (2010: 78–9), 'the goal of the caregiving system is to reduce other people's suffering, protect them from harm, and foster their growth and development … Addressing another person's problems requires temporary suspension of one's own goals and plans.' Successful caregiving is therefore empathic caregiving.

Conclusion

Out of our evolutionary past, two types of empathy have emerged. First, there is the more *emotionally based* kind of empathy in which we feel the other person's feelings (of fear, excitement, interest) and which promotes cooperation, altruism, group cohesion and safety.

More *cognitively based* kinds of empathy developed as individuals had to read, recognize and negotiate the behaviour and intentions of others, particularly in matters of food, sex and status. Here, empathy is seen as 'the cognitive awareness of another person's internal states, that is, his thoughts, feelings, perceptions and intentions' (Hoffman 2000: 29).

All group-living species develop heightened sensitivities and awareness of the actions, responses and behaviours of others. A few higher-order mammals take these group-living skills even further and develop some understanding of their conspecific's plans and intentions. However, only in humans has this mutual perspective taking reached such a complex and sophisticated level. Advanced empathy seems to mark out and define our species' current success. We see something of this evolutionary story repeated in the empathic development of children from infancy to adulthood. It is time, then, to look at the development of empathy and social understanding in children.

4
How Children Develop Empathy

Natural differences in empathy

How do we learn to be empathic? The short answer is that before we can empathize, we must have been on the receiving end of another's empathy. The most important and influential of these early-years empathic relationships is that between young children, their parents and close family.

None of this is to deny the part that genetic, biological and innate temperamental factors play in the development of our empathic capacities, however. Empathy develops more or less as an individual's innate biological differences interact with their unique social experiences. Some people are just naturally better empathizers than others (see Chapter 6). They are born with the gift of empathy and relating well. They have temperaments and personality dispositions that grant them an emotionally attuned nature and high social acuity.

Most temperamental traits, including our emotionality, are genetic in origin, hormonally influenced and physiologically based rather than solely environmental (Kagan 1994; Plomin 1994). Empathic responses and pro-social behaviours therefore do seem to have a strong genetic component. These innate differences can be spotted even in young children, some of whom consistently exhibit pro-social behaviours that continue to be present throughout their lives (Eisenberg *et al.* 2002).

All parents know that newborns vary in terms of their ease of arousal, sensitivity and reactivity. They differ, too, in their tendency to approach or withdraw when they encounter new experiences. Babies modulate their arousal in many different ways. Eye gaze can be maintained or averted, facial expressions

31

can alter, bodies can get excited or not, breathing rates can go
up or down, hearts can beat faster or slower. Nevertheless, individual babies differ in their ability to do these things. Some
simply find it more difficult to regulate their arousal and reactivity than others. This means that some children are easier to
parent than others.

> Empathic competence may depend on how well physiologi-
> cal and emotional processes between mother and infant are
> coordinated, or 'attuned'. The interaction of temperament
> and maternal characteristics are generally considered key
> factors in the development of empathy.
>
> (Woodruff 2007: xv)

If temperamentally easy children are easier to parent, and less
stressed parents are more likely to be attuned and responsive,
such children enjoy a double bonus. Their naturally empathic
character will be nurtured by parents whose stress levels will be
lower, meaning that their ability to attune and respond will be
high. Parents, of course, form the major part of young children's
social environment. Genes, biology and temperament are
important, but the way in which they get shaped and expressed
depends critically on the quality of the social world in which
they find themselves. To make sense of any behaviour or trait, we
need to understand that genes are not destiny, and that genes
and environment interact in ways that are both complex and
dynamic.

The social origins of empathy

The evidence is strong that the quality of early caregiving relationships has a major impact on children's development of
empathy. If we are to be competent social players, we must learn
to make sense of our own and other people's actions and behaviours, thoughts and feelings, needs and desires. Much of everyday life, observes Schaffer (1996: 170), is taken up with thinking
about others. We need to develop social understanding. This
involves self-awareness and reflection. Failures in social understanding and empathy get people into social difficulty.

If children are to make sense of relationships and the social world, they need to interact with other people. The psychological development of babies, observed Winnicott (1984), takes place in the context of relationships. This suggests a 'relational view' of infant social development in which children gradually differentiate the self from others and the rest of the world (Carpendale and Lewis 2006). Babies slowly shift from an essentially egocentric view to one that recognizes and takes into account other people's thoughts, feelings, desires, plans and beliefs. As infants interact with and gain feedback from others, their self-awareness and sense of separateness develop.

All of this is nicely captured when we see babies first beginning to point to objects in their environment. That marks the onset of a truly social life. The baby sees something of interest and points to it with the intention of drawing the parent's attention to that object so that he or she will also look at it. Implicit in these actions is the baby's early sense that other people are separate mental entities whose mental states can be recognized, understood and influenced – the baby can get the parent to look at what the baby is looking at. Gesturing and shared gazing indicate the infant's growing knowledge of other people and how they work.

The ability to coordinate interaction with another person is an example of achieving *joint attention*. The shared gaze might then trigger a conversation: 'Yes, it's a birdie. Did you see it fly into the tree, did you?' And the baby might well babble in reply. This early form of interaction is often described as 'triadic' (Hobson 2002) – the baby, the object, and the other (for example the parent). Not only is this triadic interaction the basis of a relationship, it provides the foundation for language and, with that, even more sophisticated forms of social understanding and complex interaction.

The development of social understanding therefore arises out of social interaction. As children engage with other people, they learn to take the other's perspective into account. Recognizing that other people have different views, feelings, beliefs and intentions forces children to coordinate their world with that of others. And as they do this, their own sense of self becomes more distinct and better understood.

Although babies are born emotionally attuned and sociable, it is in their interaction with others that they gradually learn to make sense of themselves and other people and how to form and maintain relationships. The quality of relationships plays a major role in how well they can understand the social world and how competently they can handle it. In such relationships, children gradually learn to 'de-centre' their world view (Piaget 1932). They become aware of how to recognize and simulate (mentally role-play) the other's perspective perceptually, cognitively and emotionally (Eisenberg 1986).

Children who suffer neglect miss out on intimate, reciprocal relationships. They are denied empathy. Children starved of social interaction run a high risk of not being able to make sense of themselves or their social lives. As we shall see in Chapter 8, to miss out on close, attuned, empathic care is to run the serious risk of failing to develop the ability to empathize, to show compassion and to handle relationships well.

The sociable baby

From birth, babies show great interest in other people. Fairbairn (1952) saw babies, right from the day they are born, as socially oriented, person-seeking individuals. They appear to have an inbuilt need to connect, relate and find companionship. Objects might be of passing interest, but people and what they do are endlessly fascinating for new minds. In the early weeks of life, babies are especially responsive to human voices, faces and eyes. The baby's gaze, in turn, stimulates the mother's look, and at the point of shared eye contact a potent, highly arousing line of communication opens up.

Babies constantly present a wide range of needs along with the emotions that go with them. Any delay in being fed when hungry is frustrating and quickly leads to crying and distress. A loud, unexpected noise is frightening. The sudden appearance of a looming face is startling. A full stomach, a smiling mum and a shared 'conversation' are fun. However, babies find it difficult to regulate their state of arousal on their own. If they are to regulate their emotions, they need help from one or other of their primary caregivers. What they need at times of distress is a relationship with someone who can comfort, contain and regulate them, someone who can help them make sense of what is happening.

The sensitivity provided by responsive parents gradually helps children to manage and make sense of their minds and bodies. Empathic parents are able to tune in to their baby's experience and perspective. Seeing things from their child's point of view helps carers manage needs with more skill and accuracy. They accept and recognize that babies have no choice but to communicate behaviourally, whether by crying or by otherwise expressing physical distress. Psychologically minded parents know not to take crying and being upset personally (Holmes 2006: 45).

When attuned parents deal with their distressed babies, they help them regulate their arousal using a variety of soothing and containing responses. This indicates to the baby that although the distress may feel all consuming, it is in fact manageable. During these soothing and regulating encounters, parents engage most of the senses as they try to help babies recover a sense of equilibrium and well-being. Touch, talk, singing, eye contact, cuddles and kisses are used to communicate, connect and calm. When a mother (or father) wants to comfort and regulate her baby, her voice becomes higher pitched, slow, relaxed, singsong, rhythmical, quiet, gentle and soothing. Pauses are relatively long and there are fewer syllables per phrase. The mother's face expresses love and understanding. The infant's body is gently rocked and stroked.

All of this verbal, visual and tactile regulation typically accompanies practical tasks such as preparing a feed, having a bath or changing a nappy. In effect, carers help shape their infants' early coping strategies. Repeated exposure to these regulating experiences assists children with beginning to make sense of their arousal and what triggers and helps manage it.

Parents who can soothe and regulate, contain and manage arousal are helping their children develop the capacity to empathize and the ability to 'mentalize'. They are helping their children to make sense of their own and other people's emotions and mental states. When parents share their babies' interests – what they are looking at, listening to, puzzled by, laughing at – they communicate recognition and mutual understanding.

Caregivers who are sensitive and responsive help children develop secure attachments (Bowlby 1969). Baron-Cohen (2011: 48) says that empathic parents, in helping their children develop secure attachments, give them an 'internal pot of gold'. This resource, or resilience, grants them the social and emotional skills to deal with life's challenges and setbacks, as well as facilitating children's own empathy. 'Empathy', adds Rifkin (2009: 20), 'is the psychological means by which we become part of other people's lives and share meaningful experiences.'

The *co-regulation of affect* between parent and child is therefore critical if maturing infants are to develop emotional intelligence and social competence. When parents are emotionally attuned to their babies, they are in a state of 'being in the rhythm of the other', emotionally, physiologically and psychologically (Stern 1985). When parents relate with babies as psychological partners, when they recognize that collaboration is more likely to sort out problems and meet needs, babies begin to appreciate that feelings need not necessarily overwhelm you. Feelings can be understood, handled and contained, in others as well as the self. In these various ways, then, both emotional regulation and self-organization emerge out of our relationship with others.

The language of feeling

Emotionally attuned parents are good at reflecting back what they perceive their child's emotional state to be. This is known as 'affect mirroring' (Fonagy *et al.* 2002; also see Winnicott 1967 on maternal mirroring). Affect mirroring describes how carers credit their infant with an emotional state that they believe is *congruent* with the child's behaviour (angry cry, look of disgust, surprised reaction, frightened yell). These experiences are key if children are to develop the capacity to empathize.

If a mother thinks that her baby is looking cross because he isn't allowed to play with the TV remote, she is likely to mimic his anger by exaggerating her own facial and vocal expression of 'mirrored' anger, albeit sympathetically. 'Oh dear, who is a cross little boy? What a cross face! You can't play with the remote, no you can't! Here, have the wooden blocks to play with instead, you grumpy old thing.' From the baby's point of view, this is a kind of 'psychofeedback' in which 'my carer shows me my feelings' (Gerhardt 2004: 25). The carer's exaggerated facial expressions and expressive tone of voice give back to the child an idea of what the child is feeling. Mirroring and the emotional synchrony that goes with it take the infant's distressed psychological state and organize it for him.

Children in this kind of relationship feel emotionally recognized and understood. They begin to develop an understanding of their own psychological makeup and how other people work emotionally. We learned to recognize and regulate our own feelings because we had carers who recognized and regulated our arousal when we were young. Regulation improves further when children learn to think about and identify the cause of their own and other people's emotions: 'I'm sad because Susie won't play with me. But I think she's cross because her mummy said she can't go swimming this afternoon.'

Emotional understanding and interpersonal awareness continue to develop as carers and babies interact and play for pleasure, enjoy companionship and seek stimulation. Storytelling and verbal explanations of psychologically complex situations also help children see the links between thought and feeling, emotional cause and effect. Therefore being understood by another person promotes self-understanding. 'Feeling felt' conveys a sense of emotional connectedness between parent and child. This is a pleasurable, reassuring, confirming and psychologically constructive experience in which children feel safe. It is in the safety of these early relationships that children begin to recognize, understand and reflect on other people's mental states and how these affect behaviour.

During their second and third years of life, children, encouraged by parents, refer more and more to their own and other people's feelings. Emotions are given names. Explanations are provided about what causes feelings and how they affect us and other people. Much of this talk about emotions incorporates cultural beliefs and expectations. Embedding emotional talk in a cultural context means that children learn which emotions are appropriate in particular situations: whether guilt or shame, reserve or delight is the right emotional response.

Talk and discussion about negative feeling states are particularly effective in helping children recognize and understand the nature of their own and other people's emotions. Children's ability to talk about their own and other people's thoughts and feelings adds hugely to their capacity to interact with skill and competence. Schaffer (1996: 181) gives the following example of a conversation between a 3 year old and his mother in which the little boy is learning to talk about inner states:

Child: Why is Billy [*a baby brother*] crying?
Mother: Because he is tired but just can't get to sleep.
Child: Does that hurt?
Mother: Yes, I suppose it does.
Child: But going to sleep doesn't hurt me.
Mother: You cried when you were a baby and were tired.
Child: Does Billy have a pain?
Mother: Well, being tired is I suppose a sort of pain.
Child: There (*patting the baby*), you go to sleep and the pain will stop.

Playing *with* others provides children with a further key developmental opportunity. Play not only requires empathy but also helps empathy develop. Play involves pretending, role taking and the use of imagination. It requires communication and cooperation. It works well when children learn to share, take turns and appreciate the other person's point of view. Play promotes social bonding and friendship. Play and the exploration of imaginary worlds depend on children's growing empathic capacities.

From toddlerhood, parents increasingly encourage children to take the other's point of view. If there is a quarrel between two young children, parents typically highlight the victim's distress and the child's actions that caused it. This can contribute to the development of empathy, guilt and a moral compass. In short, the child develops a 'prosocial moral script' in which he or she routinely begins to consider others (Hoffman 2000: 11). Children's moral intelligence and conscience are not based on learning rules but rather on observing what their parents do and say in their everyday lives (Coles 1997; Baron *et al*. 2006: 396). Encouraging children to be kind seems to be particularly good for their empathic development and moral sensibility.

Helping children to see things from the other's perspective is most common when they are playing together with toys. Typical 2 year olds will hang on to a toy if another child tries to take it off them. They might even attempt to snatch back a toy that they feel belongs to them. Conflict in the use of toys is endemic at this stage. However, when a parent is present, children are encouraged to share their toys. Schmidt and Sommerville (2011) have shown that children as young as 15 months will relinquish a favourite toy if prompted. The researchers suggest that even in babies there is a connection between altruism and fairness. The more sensitive the infant and the more emotionally attuned the parents, the more likely it is that very young children will not only have a sense of what is fair, but also be more likely to share and show some basic empathy.

'Parents often spend much effort', notes Schaffer (1996: 274), 'in attempting to ensure that their children become generous, helpful, and caring individuals, for in our society at least these are socially approved behaviors that bring credit to child and parent alike.' Hoffman echoes similar thoughts:

> only in discipline encounters do parents put pressure on children to control their behaviour and consider the needs of others. If parents do this right, they can give children the experience of controlling their behaviour through their own active processing of information about the consequences of their actions for others, which contributes to their developing an empathy-based internal motive to consider others.
>
> (Hoffman 2000: 10)

The reasons given for children sharing typically involve seeing things from the other child's point of view: 'He's only a baby and he wants to play with your car. He doesn't understand that it's yours. Let him have a play and then you can have it back.' 'Ella has come round to play with you so it would be really nice and kind if you let her play with your dolls. She'll be very sad if she doesn't have any dolls to play with, won't she?' 'Here, you have this blue train and let Andi have the red one. That'll make him happy, won't it? That's a good boy. That's very kind of you. Look you've made Andi smile!' Interestingly, most parents side with the visiting child in these conflict situations. Issues of fairness frame the negotiations. Encouraging empathy helps resolve conflicts. The result is harmony. In contrast, parents who simply punish and shame children into behaving well add nothing to their empathic development.

All such talk about how behaviour affects feelings and feelings affect behaviour, both in the self and in other people, helps children develop intelligences that are both emotionally and socially sophisticated (Dunn *et al.* 1991). For example, a young child might ask why her friend Billy is crying. Her mother replies, 'He was playing in the garden and his balloon burst when it swished against the rose bush. Poor Billy. He liked his red balloon, didn't he? Do you remember how sad you felt when your skipping rope broke?' Parents who invite their children to reflect and wonder why another person might be feeling and behaving the way they do are more likely to raise emotionally literate and empathic children. 'Children who are more capable of explaining emotions in conversations with parents are also more sympathetic in response to peers' emotions' (Denham 1998: 39).

The accumulation of these everyday lessons in social life delivered by emotionally attuned, morally smart and other-inclined parents produces children who are both fair and socially skilled (Zahn-Waxler *et al.* 1979; Hoffman 2000). Families in which children are encouraged to be other oriented rather than self oriented in their understanding of relationships and social behaviours raise children who score high on empathy.

Mind-mindedness

Meins (1997) argues that caregivers who are interested in what their children are thinking and feeling, and seek to share this understanding with their children, are showing what she calls 'mind-mindedness'. Mind-minded parents are good at translating psychological experiences into involved two-way conversations with their children. This helps children link feelings and words. An emotionally attuned parent might ask a young child: 'Are you frightened by that noisy jet?' or 'Are you worried because mummy isn't well?' Cozolino (2006: 232) reminds us that such questions guide children's attention to their thoughts and feelings and how these affect mind and body. Children are helped to understand that they have an inner experience that is unique to them and different to those of other people.

Such mind-minded interactions facilitate emotional understanding and bring about mind-mindedness in children. Parents who focus on their children's subjective experiences help them understand their own and other people's thoughts, feelings and behavioural states. These early signs of emotional intelligence also predict good relationships with peers. 'Overall,' report Fabes *et al.* (2008: 304), 'early talk about feelings and the causes of behaviors have consistently predicted children's concurrent and later social and emotional understanding.'

It seems, then, that children are born psychologists. They constantly enquire about the reason for things, particularly why other people are behaving the way they do. Much of children's talk is about feelings – their own and other people's: 'Why is daddy laughing? Why is Tanya cross?' These questions about other people's feelings invite a psychological answer. In order to understand other people's behaviour we need to know what is going on inside their heads. Behaviour is not random, it is not arbitrary. We need to be curious about people's motives, desires, feelings and plans to make sense of the social world.

This early psychological 'training' by parents and others helps children develop the ability to interpret other people and their behaviour in terms of mental states (thoughts, intentions, desires and beliefs). It helps children learn 'to empathise with others' states of mind, and to predict how others will feel, think, and act' (Baron-Cohen *et al.* 2000: 355). Empathic, attuned parents interact with their children as psychological partners. They credit them with minds that are valued and worth knowing. As a result, their children grow up to be more empathic, secure and socially skilled.

Theory of Mind

There is another tack that psychologists have taken in their explorations of social understanding, empathy and the awareness of other minds, and how such skills develop. This involves what they call 'Theory of Mind' (ToM). ToM is the idea that we gradually realize that other people have minds just like our own. Their heads, like ours, are also full of thoughts, feelings, beliefs, desires, hopes and intentions. We also appreciate that they are thinking about us as a complex mental entity, just as we are thinking about them in the same way. ToM plays a key role in helping people attribute mental states to themselves and others. This helps explain and predict behaviour. As children acquire ToM, they get better at interpreting behaviour in others, regulating their own feelings and managing social interaction.

By the age of 3 or 4, most children develop a ToM in which they recognize that what people think, feel and believe is a good predictor of their behaviour, even if what the other person believes is actually false.

In everyday life, beliefs rather than reality determine what people do. Hence the acid test of mentalizing is understanding a false belief. False beliefs play an important role in social communication, especially in the detection and use of deception, persuasion and trading.

(Frith and Frith 2001: 151)

For example, if Maxi leaves his bar of chocolate on the kitchen table and then goes out to play, the first place he will look for the chocolate on his return is the table (Wimmer and Perner 1983). However, in his absence his mother has tidied the room and put the chocolate in a cupboard. When Maxi returns, he has a mistaken (false) belief that the chocolate is on the table; that is where he left it, that is where he will expect to find it, and so that is where he will look first.

In order to predict Maxi's behaviour, we need to see the world from his point of view. We need to know that even though he has a mistaken belief, nevertheless this belief will predict what he will do. When asked where Maxi will look for his chocolate first the moment he returns from the garden, most 6 year olds get the answer right – on the table. Children younger than 3 or 4 tend to get the answer wrong. They hold a literal view of the world. The chocolate is in the cupboard, so that is where Maxi will look. They lack a well-developed Theory of Mind. ToM skills are quite hard, particularly for young heads:

> to succeed at a false-belief task, you have to hold in your mind two conflicting pictures of the world – the world as it really is ... and the world as it is in someone's mind ... This double bookkeeping is difficult for two- and three-year-olds.
>
> (Bloom 2004: 21)

This capacity for 'social understanding' based on the ability to see how things look and feel from someone else's perspective is the basis of empathy, relationship skills and moral behaviour. It supports children's imagination and their ability to enter the minds of others, to pretend and play. It also allows children to lie. Attempting to plant a false belief in someone's head by telling a lie is a way of trying to change their behaviour. If you say it wasn't you who broke the cup and you are believed, then you don't get into trouble. Social understanding, empathy and the ability to lie aren't a million miles apart.

> Children's capacities for empathy, for understanding how to comfort or to frustrate, for sharing imaginative worlds, for deceiving and teasing, and for negotiation and compromise in conflict are all linked to their growing understanding of the connections between what people want or believe and their behaviour.
>
> (Dunn and Cutting 1999: 201)

All in all, having a good Theory of Mind helps people deal with the subtleties and complexities of social life. Having a theory of other minds also allows us to experience most of the social emotions, including shame and embarrassment (Ramachandran 2003: 125). The close links between the development of Theory of Mind, emotional intelligence and empathy help prepare children for the rigours and subtleties of social life. Those who are best prepared emerge as the most skilled social players.

In practice, awareness of self and awareness of others requires highly demanding thought processes with many orders of reflection and reflexivity. 'I think' is a first-order condition; 'I think you think' is a second order of information processing; 'I think that you think that I think' represents a third order, and so on. Cartwright (2000: 182) says that most adults can keep track of about five or six orders of such reflexive information processing or 'intensionality'. This remarkable skill weaves itself into the power and potency of empathy.

Dunbar (1996: 101) believes that 'Theory of Mind is, beyond question, our most important asset. It is a remarkable skill ... ToM has given us the crucial ability to step back from ourselves and look at the rest of the world with an element of disinterest.' It allows us to explore the mental world of other people. Indeed, write Fabes *et al.* (2008: 300), the 'development of an understanding of the inner experiences of others represents an enormous accomplishment in the mental life of young children, and undoubtedly an important expansion of their social competence.' This being the case, it is very likely that ToM, mentalization and the capacity for *cognitive* empathy are closely linked (Shamay-Tsoory 2011).

Conclusion

Parental mind-mindedness, mentalization and mind reading predict the quality of the empathy and pro-social behaviours that develop in young children. Parents who relate to their children as complex, self-reflective mental entities help children achieve minds that are complex and reflective in their turn. Being talked to in psychological terms helps children become good psychologists, able to make sense of the world socially and interpersonally (Fonagy and Target 1997; Meins *et al.* 2002). In order for children to develop empathy, they must experience being on the receiving end of it. Although there are exceptions, mainly the result of genetically based neuro-developmental disorders, in most cases empathic parents beget empathic children.

If the outer mind highlights the power of the individual, the inner mind highlights the power of relationships and the invisible bond between people. If the outer mind hungers for status, money, and applause, the inner mind hungers for harmony and connection ... Your unconscious wants to entangle you in the thick web of relations that are the essence of human flourishing.

(Brooks 2011: xi, xviii)

Good Theory of Mind and empathy go together. They both predict a child's ability to self-regulate. They help children relate with growing competence and expertise. However, what is particularly exciting is to discover that the development of these sophisticated social skills can now be mapped as complex neurological processes. Not only is our psychological development driven by social experience, it also turns out that much of our brain's development is governed by its relationship with the social world, as we shall see in the next chapter.

5
The Empathic Brain

Making sense of the world

The brain sciences are revolutionizing our understanding of how we think, feel and behave. Particularly intriguing is the way the brain develops and organizes itself to make sense of and function well in the world in which it finds itself. Other people are one of the most important parts of the world of which we need to make sense. Social neuroscientists have become interested in empathy. Understanding how the brain perceives and processes social information provides an appealing insight into empathy's behind-the-scenes workings. It is always something of a delight when science and social life throw light on one another. Just as the neurosciences are helping us to make sense of our capacity to empathize, so our lived experience of empathy is providing brain scientists with many creative steers on how to study the wonderful subtlety and sophistication of our social brains.

A self-organizing developmental structure

With advances in scanning techniques, there has been a growing interest in the brain's ability to think about other brains and the mental states that take place inside them. The human brain contains around 100 billion neurons. Each neuron makes thousands of connections to other neurons. The point at which one neuronal connection meets another is called a synapse, across which chemical messages – neurotransmitters – flow. Millions of neurons connect to form millions of neuronal circuits. The human brain is an object of extraordinary complexity.

The newborn baby arrives in the world neurologically 'premature' in the sense that it has most of its development still to do before it reaches maturity and independence. Whereas the young of most mammals arrive with their brains in an advanced state of development, the brains of human infants still have a huge amount of growth to achieve before they reach maturity.

All of this means that infants are peculiarly helpless when they are born. They depend entirely on their carers for their growth and survival. But nature, ever the opportunist, takes advantage of the brain's immaturity at birth.

Programmed to make sense of experience, the infant's brain first needs exposure to experience before it can make sense of it. This exquisite arrangement means that the brain learns to process and make sense of the very world in which it finds itself and has to cope and survive. For human babies, this does not only include learning to see and walk, but also learning language, social skills and cultural norms. It also includes learning to regulate feelings and stress. Thus, observes Churchland (2011: 130), 'The benefit of immaturity at birth is that developing brains can exploit interactions with the environment to tune themselves up to the myriad ways of whatever physical and social world they find themselves in.'

Young brains therefore grow as they engage with the world around them, particularly the world of other people. As babies' brains interact with mothers, fathers, family and friends, their neurons are busy firing away, making thousands of new connections with other neurons every minute. These connections form vast numbers of neural networks able to process particular types of information such as vision, facial recognition, sound, language, motor movements, emotions and social interaction, all with increasing speed and accuracy. With exposure and experience, the world is clarified and begins to make sense.

The richer the environment, the denser and more complex grow the neural connections. Babies who enjoy warm, responsive, well-regulated care become particularly good at processing and making sense of emotional and social stimuli. Gradually, the social outside gets into the baby's psychological – that is, neurological – inside. As we saw in Chapter 4, the ability to make sense of and manage the social world depends on how well the baby is recognized and managed as a complex, independent, psychosocial being.

people don't develop first and create relationships. People are born into relationships – with parents, with ancestors – and those relationships create people. Or, to put it a different way, a brain is something that is contained within a single skull. A mind only exists within a network. It is the result of interactions between brains, and it is important not to confuse brains with minds.

(Brooks 2011: 43)

Social neuroscience

A relatively new branch of the neurosciences – social neuroscience – has been looking at the neural processes that support our ability to recognize and understand other people's thoughts, feelings and beliefs; that is, to have empathy and a Theory of Mind (for example, see Decety and Jackson 2004; Decety and Ickes 2011). The science has also become interested in the related fields of mentalizing, mind reading and empathy (Singer 2006).

Social intelligence relies on complex links and information sharing taking place between many areas of the brain. In particular, emotional and cognitive circuits involved in feeling and thought, if they are to work well, need to enjoy rich neurological connections. For example, the prefrontal cortex, which lies behind the forehead, has many dense pathways that connect it to the brain's more ancient emotional structures. The quality of neurological activity between these two areas – thought and feeling – has a major impact on our ability to mentalize and be socially intelligent. The orbitofrontal cortex, for instance, is heavily involved in social cognition, which requires understanding of both emotional and mental states.

Simplifying matters, it therefore appears that the brain can respond to other people's emotional states in two ways (Eisenberg and Eggum 2011: 73). The first is subcortical, primitive and fast track. We see, tune into and contagiously feel the other's feelings. This is emotional or affective empathy; no thought required. The second is cortical, slower, more deliberate. We might have to make a conscious effort to think ourselves into the other's shoes, but having done that, we can appreciate the world from their emotional point of view. This is cognitive empathy.

There is no simple 'empathy centre' in the brain (Farrow 2007). In fact, many different but interconnected areas of the brain appear to be involved in empathizing. Four discrete neural functions – affect sharing, perspective taking, emotional regulation and self/other awareness – have been found to be necessary before a full empathic experience can be achieved (Decety and Jackson 2004; Gerdes 2011). Each function has a role in such things as reading facial expressions; thinking about one's own and others' feelings; giving actions and behaviour an emotional value; the recognition that the initiating agent of one's subjective emotional experience is the other, not oneself; the recognition of intention and purpose in other people's behaviour; awareness of pain and distress in the self and others; and the ability to infer the other's perspective requiring the intentional suppression of one's own viewpoint. All of these neurological insights are a reminder of what an extraordinary, wonderful and complicated capacity empathy is.

Disorder, damage or disease to any one of the many brain areas associated with emotional processing can upset the 'empathy circuit', to a greater or lesser degree. For example, patients with lesions, frontal lobe degeneration or damage to the prefrontal cortex and right hemisphere of the brain show significant impairments in both their Theory of Mind and empathic abilities (Shamay-Tsoory 2011).

For empathy processing to be at its best, we need to recognize and understand, manage and respond to our own as well as other people's thoughts and feelings. In thinking about someone else's mind we have to be simultaneously thinking about what is going on in our own. When volunteers are placed in brain scanners and given emotional and empathy-related tasks, neuroscientists can 'see' which parts of the empathy circuit are active. Only in extreme cases in which empathy, whether cognitive, affective or both, is very low do we see reduced neural activity. The affective empathy processing circuits of psychopaths, for example, fail to activate when the person is interacting with those in distress.

Mirror neurons

So as we have seen, empathy involves recognition of what is going on in someone else's brain, imagining what it must be like to be in that state of mind, to be emotionally affected by that understanding and to feel the other's feelings. How this might be possible, particularly at the neurological level, has not always been clear. However, recent findings have revealed a type of neuron that is raising some intriguing possibilities about how we might feel the feelings of another, and therefore how empathy, in part, might be possible.

Brain scientists have discovered that a special group of neurons – *mirror neurons* – seem to get fired whenever we observe the behaviour of others (Rizzolatti *et al.* 2002). Perhaps more accurately, it is not so much that specialist neurons are firing, but rather that particular neural networks made up of ordinary neurons become active. Siegel (2007) describes these as the 'resonance circuitry'. Mirror neurons form part of this circuit and they become active when we observe the behaviour of others. Mirror neurons and their circuits 'have been shown not only to encode for intention, but also to be fundamentally involved in human empathy, and also in emotional resonance, the outcome of attunement of minds' (Siegel 2007: 165–6) The significant correlation between empathy and activity in the mirror neuron system suggests that internally mirroring the emotional responses of others might provide a way of allowing individuals literally to feel what others feel (Iacoboni 2008; Pfiefer *et al.* 2008).

When these mirror neural networks fire, they subtly activate similar micro-behaviours in our body. Emotional arousal in particular allows us to resonate with the condition of the other person. These various simulations are automatic and unconscious.

Some of this modern thinking was anticipated by eighteenth-century Scottish philosophers. David Hume, for example, wrote: 'the minds of men are mirrors to one another, not only because they reflect each other's emotions, but also because those rays of passions, sentiments, and opinions may often be reverberated ... No passion of another discovers itself immediately to the mind. We are only sensible of its causes or effects. From *these* we infer the passion: And consequently *these* give rise to our sympathy' (Hume 1978[1739]: 365 and 576, emphasis in original). Adam Smith, prescient in many areas, also recognized this phenomenon over two centuries ago:

> by the imagination we place ourselves in his situation … we enter as it were into his body, and become in some measure the same person with him, and thence form some idea of his sensations, and even feel something which, though weaker in degree, is not altogether unlike them … The mob, when they are gazing at a dancer on the slack rope, naturally writhe and twist and balance their own bodies as they see him do, and as they feel that they must do in his situation.
>
> (Smith 1759: 9–10)

Also unaware of empathy's neurological subtleties, Lipps (1903) and Titchener (1909) similarly recognized that 'motor mimicry' produces an emotional reaction in individuals watching other people in emotionally and behaviourally challenging situations. The emotion generated is consistent with that being observed as the individual unconsciously imitates the behaviour of the other (for example, our muscles tense when we watch someone straining to lift a heavy object). Vocal mimicry is also common. In conversation with others, we very quickly find ourselves adopting the speed, volume and cadence of those around us.

The original mirror neuron research examined the premotor cortex of monkeys (Gallese *et al.* 1996; Rizzolatti *et al.* 1996). Researchers noticed that a group of specialist cells involved in motor movements fired both when a monkey performed a hand movement itself *and* when it simply observed another monkey performing the same hand movement.

Similar neurons were then found in the human brain. We get a hint of this neural circuitry in action when we notice ourselves mimicking the actions of another person, particularly if that person is doing something difficult or stressful such as trying to stretch in order to reach a hold on a rock face, or preparing to leap over a high-jump bar in an athletics competition. This is behavioural resonance. Our brain experiences the behavioural mimicry, which in turn generates the feelings, thoughts and other mental states that the observed behaviours imply. Behavioural resonance, emotional attunement and empathy help synchronize our social behaviour.

Later research found that mirror neurons are also involved when our emotions are aroused and when we observe someone else in a state of emotional arousal. When I see you smile, my mirror neurons respond, giving me a slight, unconscious feeling of happiness too. In this sense, we are able to share someone else's pain or pleasure. If I see you screw up your face in disgust because you have just eaten a rotten plum, the chances are that I will not only sense the disgust but also facially mimic your expression of disgust. Mirror neurons and empathic brain responses allow us to share feelings.

What is interesting to note is that these neurons only get excited when we observe the behaviour of other beings who have minds and mental states similar to our own. The neurons do not fire when we observe the movement of inanimate objects, unless we credit such objects with psychological-type properties. High empathizers tend to be particularly prone to mirroring other people's emotional expressions, vocal tones and body language.

Perhaps even more interesting, the intensity with which the neurons fire varies depending on the intention and outcome of the behaviour being observed. For example, mirror neurons fire more intensely when an observed person picks up a glass in order to drink from it than when a person picks up the glass with no discernible purpose. The goal of the observed behaviour is also being mirrored and therefore, to a degree, experienced.

The ability to understand the intention of others while watching their actions is critical if our social behaviour is to become skilled and competent. In a fundamental evolutionary sense, being able to categorize other people's behaviour as threatening or engaging might make the difference between staying safe or being harmed.

The work on mirror neurons has allowed some of the more enthusiastic scientists to propose a general account of empathy in which, according to Iacoboni (2009: 663), 'the core imitation circuitry would simulate (or internally imitate) the facial emotional expressions of other people. This activity would then modulate activity in the limbic system ... where the emotion associated with a given facial expression is felt by the observer.' He expands on this, saying:

> The observation of your smiling face triggers a cascade of neural activity in my brain, from inferior frontal (mirror) neurones controlling my facial musculature down to anterior insula neurones and to limbic neurones such that I suddenly and deeply feel your happiness. Your happiness is in my body.
> (Iacobini 2007: 316)

Moreover, there is some evidence that those with more responsive mirror neuron systems show greater empathy, suggesting that individual differences in mirror neuron activity go some way to accounting for individual differences in empathy (Pfiefer and Dapretto 2011: 191).

The study of mirror neurons has certainly excited those in the neurological and psychological sciences, but it is still in its very early days and many questions remain. For example, the vexed matter of interpretation means that simple neurological mimicry of another's behaviour still doesn't necessarily reveal their state of mind or intention. Does your smile indicate agreement or disbelief? Is your yawn one of tiredness or boredom? Only context and history can help us make sense of these behaviours. Equally problematic are questions such as: Do I feel angry when I see you looking angry? Do I feel shame when I see your look of shame? Churchland (2011), while acknowledging the significance of mirror neurons, advises proceeding with caution.

Blending and belonging

As a species, we are skilled at 'fitting in'. Socially skilled individuals quickly learn what is expected when they join a new team, attend a funeral or visit the parents of someone they hope to marry. Conventions are noted and copied. Unconscious mimicry of voice and body language helps people blend in. We smile when they smile and look concerned when they look concerned.

Low-level, unconscious mimicry encourages relationships to be warm and reciprocal. Mimicry increases liking, empathy and rapport. It makes us feel more similar. When the other person unconsciously mimics our expressions, intonations and body posture, we judge them more favourably (van Baaren *et al.* 2011). As a result, we become more sociable. Non-conscious imitation also increases pro-social behaviour (Chartrand *et al.* 2005; Baron *et al.* 2006: 390). We are more likely to go out of our way to help someone whose voice, expressions and body language echo our own.

Most of us want to belong. And the more we succeed in fitting in, the more other people accept us and the more relaxed they feel. To be like me means I feel that I can understand you, know you and predict your behaviour. I feel more safe and less wary. It is when people behave very differently, oddly and unexpectedly, that we feel anxious. If I can't predict your behaviour, my levels of stress will rise very quickly. Indeed, it is when people do not micro-mimic us as we interact that we begin to feel slightly uncomfortable. Empathy that leads to non-conscious imitation is therefore the default mode in most everyday encounters (van Baaren *et al.* 2011).

However, we have to look to other areas of the brain for higher-level empathy, empathy that allows us to tune into other people's hopes, beliefs and desires. These higher-order empathic achievements also involve a more sophisticated self-knowledge about the way in which our own and other people's psychological processes work. This suggests that higher-order empathizers are likely to be emotionally intelligent and psychologically reflective. The study of mirror neurons has shown that both cognitive and emotional processes are involved in moments of empathy. However, many other brain regions also become involved as more complex empathic states arise.

Empathy circuits

Modern brain-scanning equipment has the power to give us visual pictures of empathy at work in our heads. Functional magnetic resonance imaging (fMRI), for example, measures blood flow and therefore oxygen and energy use in the brain.

Areas in which oxygen levels are high indicate neurological activity. Parts of the brain involved in processing the senses and the emotions they trigger (known as the limbic system, which includes the brainstem, thalamus, anterior insula, anterior cingulate cortex and somatosensory cortices) become more active whenever we have an emotional experience such as feeling in pain.

But what happens when we observe another person in pain? Singer and her colleagues (2004) scanned individuals who were watching other people in pain. As we might expect from the research on mirror neurons, simply looking at another person, particularly if the observer was closely related, was sufficient to activate some of the very same emotional regions of the brain that become active when we ourselves undergo strong arousal, such as feeling in pain.

So although watching someone in apparent pain does not directly excite our pain senses (therefore we do not actually feel in physical pain), nevertheless we do experience some of the emotions that go with being in pain. Thus, simply observing another's pain is sufficient to give us a strong emotional sense of and identification with the other being in a state of pain. Singer *et al.* (2004) concluded that empathy is mediated by those areas of the brain responsible for processing affective information, but not those directly involved in processing sensory inputs. That is, observing another's feelings can give us a parallel feeling state, but seeing the sensory cause of their feeling does not excite those parts of our own brain involved in processing similar sensations.

People who score high on empathy-rating scales show the strongest activation of their emotion-processing networks when observing other people in apparent pain, particularly in cases where the other is a close friend or partner. Damage to any part of the empathy circuit, whether through accident or disease, typically leads to loss of social cognition and social competence, poor empathy and the inability to perceive and process emotional states in the self and others (Shamay-Tsoory 2011).

There is also the intriguing condition of *mirror-touch synaes-thesia*. This causes individuals to hyper-empathize (Torrance 2011). The more general condition of *synaesthesia* is one in which there is cross-wiring or cross-activation between different senses in the brain that normally remain separate and relatively unconnected (Ramachandran 2003). In the case of synaesthesia, some senses become blurred. About 1 in 200 people has some form of this condition.

One of the more common forms is when an individual experiences a particular colour when he or she sees or hears a specific number. Seeing the number five might, for example, give the individual the experience of seeing blue, while seven creates the sensation of seeing red. The brain's colour-processing and number-processing areas happen to be fairly close to each other, and so in some people sensory cross-stimulation takes place. In other cases, hearing the word 'door' might trigger a taste sensation of, say, strawberries.

To an extent, most of us have some potential for synaesthetic experiences. The use of metaphor in speech and writing – the use of an image to convey a meaning – is the most general form. Ramachandran (2003: 83) gives Macbeth's utterance 'Out, out brief candle' as an example. Words, including those that are onomatopoeic, can also suggest mild forms of synaesthesia – snake, chunky, spiky, feather, fluffy are examples of words that somehow convey the look and feel of the object being described. Sound, vision and even touch become conflated.

Interestingly, synaesthesia has been found to be more common in artists, musicians, poets and novelists – people who use one sensory medium to express, explore and link experiences across a range of other senses, particularly those in which emotions run strong.

Talking about her own 'mirror-touch' synaesthesia or hyper-empathy, Torrance recalls

> standing in my parents' garden in South Africa, aged six, watching butcher birds hang mice on the wire fence. I felt the tug on my neck and spine; it was as if I was being hanged. I remembered crying to my mum, trying to explain what happened. I wanted her to understand that I could see emotions as colours, and feel sounds; that someone else's anger felt like heat running between my chest and stomach ... I was constantly crying – not because something had

happened to me, but because I had seen someone else crying or felt someone else's pain.

(Torrance 2011: 14)

Torrance's synaesthesia is an exaggerated version of the way most of us react when we flinch if we see someone hit their finger with a hammer, or tense when we look at a climber stretch to reach a branch high up in a tree. She eventually learned to enjoy her talent. She can now watch a bird in the sky and feel as if she's flying, experiencing pure joy. This also makes her a sensitive, highly empathic friend. After all, she says, 'I know exactly what it feels like to be them' (Torrance 2011: 14)

Oxytocin and the bonds of love

Most of early brain development – the ability to self-regulate, learning to talk and make sense of the self and others, for instance – takes place in mother–child, father–child and family–child relationships. As we have seen, the quality of these relationships is critical to the development of a whole range of life skills, including self-regulation, the sense of self, the understanding of others and the conduct of social relationships. This caregiver–child relationship shapes many key features of the baby's early brain development. Optimum brain development requires empathic parenting.

In Chapter 4, we noted that babies cannot regulate emotions on their own. It is in relationship with their primary caregivers that they learn to make sense of and manage their arousal. When babies feel aroused and distressed, their stress-response systems become active. As all new experiences and therefore learning are inherently challenging, stimulating and a little stressful, small doses of stress are normal and good for babies. When parents help babies manage small amounts of stress, they are preparing their young brains to tolerate everyday stresses. Regular, repeated and well-patterned experiences of being soothed, contained and comforted by sensitive, interested and responsive caregivers helps babies make connections between positive relationships, feelings of pleasure and well-being, empathy and reduced stress.

The brain and its development are deeply affected by the ways in which stress responses are regulated. In the case of well-regulated babies, both children and parents experience the release of a range of chemical messengers in their brains that promote warm, positive and relaxed feelings. These include oxytocin, dopamine and endorphins.

In passing, it is worth noting that touch is at its most frequent and intense when we soothe babies (although we also see an increase in adulthood when we are first in love). A number of relaxing, mildly sedating neurochemicals (natural opiates), including oxytocin, vasopressin and endorphins, are released in the brain when we are caressed by someone else and whenever we experience the intimacy of a close relationship.

Oxytocin is particularly associated with bonding and its formation. It facilitates birth, lactation and a number of maternal responses to infant behaviour. Tending releases oxytocin, so tending simply feels good. Cuddling babies triggers oxytocin, so cuddling also feels good. Warm, cuddlesome, empathic relationships with carers in infancy have a positive effect on brain development, including the ease with which the brain can release oxytocin when an individual experiences love, trust and closeness. These early, good-quality parent–child experiences give children a lifelong addiction to close, empathic relationships.

From an evolutionary point of view, we can see an extension of caring for infants to caring for family, friends and fellow group members. Over time, mental attunement and social skills spiral out from psychologically based interactions between parents and children to relationships with kith, kin and community. Oxytocin's release in the brain cements relationships; it is 'nature's way of weaving people together' (Brooks 2011: 64). It is released in all positive social interactions, including breastfeeding, positive parenting and falling in love. The mere presence of familiar, loving people helps us feel safe and calm. Positive, well-attuned and well-regulated relationships therefore become attractive, as they are associated with good feelings and states of relaxation. Our biology rewards cooperation, collaboration and good relationships.

Absence of good relationships can send people in search of artificial, but ultimately addictive and harmful ways of getting the same neuro-chemical highs through drugs. And those who are unlucky enough to have a particular gene variant that affects the brain's ability to respond normally to oxytocin have been found to be less empathic, less sociable and less likely to sustain long-term relationships (Rodrigues *et al.* 2009); although we should always remember that single genes do not have specific effects on behaviour, but interact with other genes and the environment in complex ways.

When oxytocin is present, levels of tolerance, trust and generosity increase (Kosfeld *et al.* 2005). When we are among loving family and friends, our level of oxytocin is high. We feel relaxed and safe. The hormone even improves our ability to mind read and empathize with others. People who are exposed to higher levels of oxytocin, whether naturally or administered experimentally, improve their accuracy in Theory of Mind and emotional recognition tasks (Domes *et al.* 2007).

It is critical for the survival of very helpless, immature human infants that their mothers provide care and protection. Oxytocin appears to produce feelings of focus and calm when mothers feed, stroke, rock and gaze at their infants. In evolutionary terms, Churchland (2011: 31) talks of the female mammalian brain being 'maternalized' as it takes the crucial step that leads from self-caring to other-caring, all supported by the release of oxytocin and other hormones during moments of closeness and intimacy.

Also from an evolutionary perspective, mothers with strong caring behaviours of course had more offspring who survived than those whose care was weak and neglectful. Not only do highly responsive mothers have high levels of oxytocin, but their infants (included those fostered as well as genetically related) have similarly high levels. These elevated levels predict that the offspring, too, will in all likelihood become sensitive, caring parents. Infants raised by unresponsive, poorly attuned, neglectful and abusive parents are at risk of lifetime low levels of oxytocin production, and in some cases they are destined to repeat the impoverished parenting that they suffered themselves (Meaney 2003, 2010; Heim *et al.* 2008).

Oxytocin is only part of the story, but it does remind us that complex brain–body mechanisms influenced by genes and environment underlie our social behaviour. In particular, we need to appreciate the powerful role played by social relationships in all these processes.

The brain, stress and empathy

To provide and to be on the receiving end of relationships in which there is empathy and understanding feels like a positive place in which to be. In fact, writes Ciaramicoli in his warm and wise book on empathy:

> Expressing empathy is, in truth, the key to experiencing it, for empathy is one of those realities, like love, forgiveness, or truth, that we 'get' only when we are willing, first, to give it away.
>
> (Ciaramicoli and Ketcham 2000: 37)

Whether the relationship is one between parent and child, romantic partners or counsellor and client, empathy helps lower stress. Its presence helps people feel safe, and when people feel safe they are free to explore, reflect and mentally reorganize. When people feel under threat, they lose the ability to mentalize and empathize.

There is an intimate connection between relationships with parents and carers, the regulation of stress and arousal, and early brain development. The quality of these early relationships in terms of helping infants regulate their arousal and stress lays down physiological and neurological templates for how future stressful experiences will, or will not, be regulated.

As we saw in the previous chapter, parental mind-mindedness and empathy help infants gain an understanding of self and others. Since understanding the self and others plays a critical role in achieving social regulation, children's ability to empathize is heavily influenced by their relationship experiences in early life.

Children who have not enjoyed good-quality care find it difficult to self-regulate and be empathic. Indeed, because their poor relationship skills mean that they find social interaction stressful, and because increased stress reduces empathy, they find themselves entering a vicious circle: relationship stress decreases empathy, which increases interpersonal incompetence, which raises stress, and so on. The inability to self-regulate means that individuals find it hard to understand and empathize with others.

Children who have suffered abuse, neglect, trauma, rejection, and abandonment tend to have low empathy scores, poor self-regulation, relationship difficulties and impaired mental health. Their young brains are constantly overwhelmed by high levels of stress, often caused by the fear and anxiety engendered by the parent–child relationship itself. In these traumatic relationships, infant brains are unable to manage and process stress. As a result, their brains become hypersensitive even to relatively low levels of stress, particularly if experienced during social interaction. This hyperaroused, hypervigilant state can lead to fear, aggression and hyperactivity. The heart rate increases, blood pressure rises and the cortisol level surges.

During these times of emotional and physiological dysregulation, relationships are poorly managed. Empathy is absent. In even more extreme cases of abuse and neglect, the brain stops processing stress-related information altogether in a state known as dissociation. People report feeling spaced-out, numb, detached. In this deeply traumatic state, the body also surrenders. The heart rate and blood pressure drop as the body defensively shuts down.

The brain is at the centre of the stress-response system. When stress levels are intense and chronic, we see a range of neurological problems. Neural networks become attenuated. There are imbalances in the brain's chemistry. And there is both under- and oversensitivity in the way neurological processes function.

This is one reason why empathy matters so much: from the start of life, we require others to help us cope with stress. Our brain requires social experience to develop properly: we influence each other's ability to manage stress in a very real, measurable way. These connections are written into the architecture of our nervous system.

(Szalavitz and Perry 2011: 16)

Empathic parenting calms and comforts children. As a result, their stress systems enjoy optimal regulation. The double blow suffered by children whose parents lack empathy is that their stress systems run high and go unregulated. Heightened stress and raised anxiety shut down our empathy circuits.

Conclusion

Throughout the early years of their development, children's brains are shaped by experience. In terms of developing social skills and emotional intelligence, most experience is interpersonal. The quality and character of close relationships have a powerful and long-lasting effect on early brain development. More specifically, the brain's ability to recognize and tune into other people's thoughts and feelings only comes about when the brain itself has been on the receiving end of experiences in which its own thoughts and feelings have been acknowledged, valued and understood. If children are to develop empathy, they must experience close, loving, empathic relationships with their main carers.

It almost appears as if the brain's physiology is encouraging these empathic processes. Mirror neurons allow us to feel what other people might be feeling. It seems as though nature has given us the biological ability to resonate neurologically with those around us. This ability facilitates intersubjectivity, mind connecting with mind. And neurotransmitters such as oxytocin also seem designed to reward many human virtues, including care and love, empathy and trust. However, there is also great variation in people's ability to empathize. Individual differences in our thoughts, feelings and behaviour have long interested psychologists. We now need to see what they have found when they have turned their gaze to individual differences in levels of empathy.

6

Individual Differences in Empathy Levels

The person, the situation and social behaviour

As with most human qualities and dispositions, whether intelligence or strength, shyness or humour, great variation occurs in the levels of empathy that individuals show, ranging from high to low. The cause of these differences might be innate and biological or the product of upbringing and experience. More often than not, an individual quality or personality trait is the result of a dynamic relationship between genes and environment, nature and nurture, biology and experience. Behaviour, said Lewin (1936), can also be understood as a function of the person and the situations in which they find themselves. Different people in the same situation often act differently. It seems that personality and dispositional factors can, to an extent, predict a person's thoughts, feelings and responses (Leary and Hoyle 2009).

Folk wisdom as well as scientific enquiry suggests that a person's sex or gender is likely to play a part in their ability to empathize, so we shall pay particular attention to this difference. However, other factors have also been considered, including personality, temperament and culture.

Minding about sex

Taken as a whole, men have been found to be less empathic than women. Of course, this does not mean that any one man is bound to be less empathic than any one woman. Some men score very highly on empathy tests, while some women score low. It is just if one considers all men against all women in a population, men will be slightly less gifted in terms of reading other people's emotional expressions or being interested in what they are thinking and feeling (Mehrabian *et al.* 1988; Trobst *et al.* 1994). Women's friendships, for example, involve more self-disclosure and empathy, while men's friendships are often based on doing things together (Vernon 2010: 13), although there are hints that because there is a social assumption that women are more empathic than men, they often find themselves playing to this expectation (Ickes *et al.* 2000; Ickes 2011: 65).

Empathizers and systematizers

One of the leading proponents of the (average) differences theory between the sexes in terms of empathy skills is Simon Baron-Cohen. Deliberately provocative, he begins his book on the subject with the claim: '*The female brain is predominantly hard-wired for empathy. The male brain is predominantly hard-wired for understanding and building systems*' (Baron-Cohen 2004: 1, emphasis in original). We all vary in terms of how empathic we are, from high to low. However, as already discussed, there is a slight skew between the sexes in which women, on the whole, perform better than men. In this sense, and reflecting the sexual bias, empathizers are said to have a 'female brain'.

Men, on the other hand, tend on average to be better 'systematizers'. Systematizing is the drive to analyse, explore, figure out how things work and find the underlying rules and principles that govern how systems, such as machines, organisms, computer programs or physical phenomena, work. In this sense, and again reflecting the sexual bias, systematizers are said to have a 'male brain'.

Thus, on average, we find more men pursuing subjects like engineering, car mechanics, physics, mathematics and computing, while, on average, we find more women taking up subjects such as literature, psychology, social work and counselling. Systematizers often have hobbies that reflect their bias. They enjoy tinkering with old cars, spotting and recording things and cataloguing their collections. Empathizers are more likely to spend their spare time having coffee and chatting with friends, watching TV soaps and acting as volunteer carers.

Systematizers, whether male or female, tend to have good spatial abilities. Empathizers, whether male or female, are better in their use of speech and language. They are particularly good at detecting emotions and the nuances of social interaction.

The evolutionary thinking behind these differences is that in our 'environment of evolutionary adaptedness', men, in their roles and niche, had to be skilled at hunting, predicting, calculating and controlling physical events. Women, in their roles and niche, had to be skilled in matters of nurture, care and the maintenance of close relationships and social integration.

Although systematizers are good at making sense of objects, machines and processes, their understanding is impersonal and detached. However, these skills do not work when it comes to making sense of people in the everyday, relational sense. It is empathizers who are good at understanding and interacting with other people. Making sense of people and tuning into their minds requires you to be personal and involved. It needs you to recognize that you are affecting them and they are affecting you.

In the middle, we find men and women who are reasonably good at both systematizing and empathizing. Baron-Cohen describes this group, and their brains, as 'balanced'.

Empathy and system skills are normally distributed, each following a bell curve. We all lie somewhere on an empathy spectrum, from high to low. Most people's empathic sensitivities lie somewhere towards the middle of this normal distribution, with a modest bias one way or the other. This suggests a strong genetic component to the relative presence of empathy (Anckarsäter and Cloninger 2007).

There is also a normal distribution for systematizing skills. Thus, from an evolutionary perspective, moderate levels of both empathy and systematizing skills appear to be the most adaptive. Having modest skills in both logic and empathy allows most of us to tick along reasonably well as we try to cope with the demands of both an increasingly technological world and the world of people and human interaction.

However, at the extremes of the curve there are a small number of individuals who will have either very high systematizing/very low empathizing skills, or very high empathizing/very low systematizing skills. Given that very high systematizing skills are associated with the extreme 'male' brain and that many people with autism and Asperger syndrome possess advanced systematizing skills (and low empathizing skills), Baron-Cohen (2004) speculates that autism is an example of the extreme 'male' brain (see Chapter 7). This is partly supported by the finding that for every one autistic female there are approximately eight autistic males.

The fact that in any given population we still find people with high systematizing talents suggests that the value of these skills has been, and continues to be, important in the functioning and survival of our species. It is undoubtedly the case that humanity's extraordinary achievements in mathematics, science, engineering and technology is down in no small part to the continued existence of individuals who, although they might be poor at social relationships, are gifted at analysis, pattern recognition, rule spotting, system innovation and technological creativity.

Foetal brain development

Certain social and cultural experiences might account for some of these sex differences, but many scientists have also sought biological explanations (Chakrabarti and Baron-Cohen 2006). For example, differences have been found between the brains of men and women in terms of the way emotions are perceived and processed (Bradley et al., 2001; Hamann and Canli 2004). Female brains have also been found to have 'better empathic abilities ... when assessing the emotional states of other people and their emotional response to the feelings of others' (Schulte-Rüther *et al.* 2008). The front runner for the appearance of either a systematizing or an empathizing brain bias is the level of hormones circulating in the growing baby during specific stages of foetal development. Levels of testosterone affect foetal brain development, particularly during the mid-trimester. Male babies are likely to produce more testosterone than females, although levels can also be increased or decreased from levels of testosterone naturally circulating in the mother's blood supply. Testosterone levels peak again around five months after a birth and during puberty.

Foetal testosterone levels affect the rates of growth of the brain's two hemispheres. Spatial abilities and systematizing skills are associated with the right hemisphere. Language, communication and empathizing skills are associated with left-brain activities.

High levels of testosterone during the middle stages of pregnancy lead to faster growth of the right hemisphere and slower growth of the left hemisphere. Babies who are exposed to lower levels of testosterone tend to experience slightly faster growth of their left hemispheres. Testosterone levels that are somewhere in between lead to the hemispheres developing at roughly equal speeds during these developmentally sensitive stages.

Thus, on average, partly because they produce their own testosterone as well as being exposed to the maternal blood supply, male foetuses are more likely to have this boost to right-brain activity during mid-pregnancy. As a result of their exposure to higher testosterone levels, their brains are set to become 'masculinized'. However, some female foetuses will also experience relatively high levels of testosterone at this particular time, while some male babies will be exposed to relatively low levels. These relative exposures during mid-pregnancy do not affect overall sexual development, just the speed of growth of either the right or the left hemisphere.

So lower levels of foetal testosterone (seen more commonly in females) leads to better levels of language, communication skills, eye contact and social skills – all signs of better empathizing. And if restricted interests are an indicator of in-depth systematizing, these results clearly show that good systematizing abilities are linked to higher levels of foetal testosterone.

(Baron-Cohen 2004: 102)

Social skills and gender

Developmental psychologists have always been keen to test young children on their social skills. Sex differences in these skills appear from a surprisingly young age. Day-old baby girls look slightly longer at faces than do day-old boys. Baby girls make more eye contact than do boys. 'As soon as children develop enough to show signs of empathy and caring, girls show it more than boys. One-year-old girls are even more likely than boys to help others in distress' (Bloom 2004: 31).

In addition, 5-year-old girls tend to perform better than same-age boys on tasks involving Theory of Mind and reading facial expressions. Adolescent girls score higher than adolescent boys on empathy measures and pro-social reasoning skills (Dolan and Fullam 2007: 36). Men talk as much as women, but women are better at taking conversational turns and tend to use a richer emotional vocabulary. And when asked to write down in two minutes as many synonyms as they can for an emotionally charged word, such as shame or anger, women typically outperform men by quite a large margin.

Much of this research is reflected in our experience of how men and women deal with everyday problems and situations. The most commonly cited example is what people typically do when they are lost in an unfamiliar city. Women are more likely to ask a stranger for directions. Men will insist that they know where they are and claim that they simply need to get their bearings.

Personality and temperament

People's empathic responses in particular situations appear to differ depending in part on their personality and temperament. *Agreeableness*, for example, is a construct that recognizes individual differences in being good-natured, likeable, pleasant and considerate in relationships with others. Some people are more agreeable, less irritable and less combative than others. Agreeableness is one of the five major dimensions of personality in the so-called Big Five, which include extroversion, agreeableness, conscientiousness, neuroticism and openness to experience (McCrae and Costa 1999). As might be expected, of all the major dimensions of personality, agreeableness correlates positively with pro-social emotions including empathic concern and a willingness to help others (Graziono *et al.* 2007). Agreeableness and the empathy that goes with it often mean that individuals possessed of this trait are good at resolving conflicts and at promoting cooperation in socially challenging situations. Those low on agreeableness show less empathy and a reduced willingness to help.

People also differ in their desire for acceptance and their 'need to belong'. Those who score high on scales used to measure the need to belong usually say that they have more close friends, use Facebook and have larger social networks (Leary and Kelly 2009). They also tend to be more empathic. 'Need to Belong scores', found Leary and Kelly (2009: 402), 'were related to greater empathic accuracy in that people scoring high in need to belong were more often correct in their construal of what another person was thinking or feeling than those who scored lower.' A slightly different construct – 'sensitivity to rejection' – is also positively associated with empathy, albeit of the primitive emotional kind (Romero-Canyas *et al.* 2009: 469). In this case, the acute awareness of other people's negative feelings actually leads to personal distress in which all connection to the other's perspective is lost. The final cluster to mention in this personality range is that comprising high trait neuroticism, in which empathy tends to be low and feelings of loneliness high (Beadle *et al.* 2012).

Shame and guilt – the self-conscious emotions – have also been examined with respect to empathy. Individuals prone to feelings of guilt tend to be 'other-oriented'. They score higher on seeing things from other people's point of view and the ability to empathize compared to those who are more shame prone (Eisenberg *et al.* 2004; Robinson *et al.* 2007). Shame means that people focus on their own feelings of distress, which inhibits their capacity for empathy.

Conscientiousness is also related to feelings of guilt, but in two slightly different ways. Conscientious people, being conscientious and therefore doing what needs to be done, experience guilt less frequently than those who are more careless and less thorough. However, when highly conscientious people do suffer guilt, they experience it more intensely (Einstein and Lanning 1998). Thus, complex links seem to exist between being conscientious, empathic and prone to guilt. Being aware of the other's perspective and being conscientious generally mean that effort will be put into 'getting things' right. However, if the effort fails, strong feelings of guilt are induced.

Culture and empathy

As many societies are becoming increasingly diverse in terms of ethnicity and culture, there has been a growing interest in cultural differences and empathy, sometimes described as 'ethnocultural empathy' (Wang *et al.* 2003). Rasoal *et al.* (2011: 8) define ethnocultural empathy as '*feeling, understanding, and caring about what someone from another culture feels, understands, and cares about*' (emphasis in original). To the extent that individuals from different cultures perceive and experience the world differently, there is the potential for misunderstanding, prejudice and conflict. For example, cultures often differ in whether it is polite to maintain eye contact or not, acceptable to touch or not, or all right to stand close or not.

A study by Mathur *et al.* (2010) found that levels of empathy for both African-American and Caucasian American individuals were higher when people observed distress in members of their own sociocultural group. These in-group/out-group differences can also be detected at the neurological level, 'suggesting that neurocognitive processes associated with self-identity underlie extraordinary empathy and altruistic motivation for members of one's own social group' (Stompe *et al.* 2010: 45). These findings have major implications for cross-class, cross-cultural and cross-racial relationships interpersonally, professionally and internationally.

Misperceptions and misunderstandings might also arise when professionals, such as counsellors or psychologists, work with clients whose ethnic and cultural backgrounds are very different from their own. Accurate empathy has the potential to mitigate many of these concerns. Ridley and Lingle (1996: 22) believe that cultural empathy 'involves a deepening of the human empathic response to permit a sense of mutuality and understanding across the great differences in value and expectation that cross-cultural interchange often involves.' However, to date, the research on the subject has been limited.

Trommsdorff *et al.* (2007) studied young children's empathic responses in four countries, two in the West and two from South-East Asia. They found that Western children who observed another's distress showed better emotional regulation and elements of empathic concern for the other person. The South-East Asian children picked up on the other's plight, but that was more likely to lead to personal distress, which is less likely to trigger empathic help and concern.

In Chapter 4 we learned that children who develop good mentalizing skills also become effective regulators of their own emotions. People who are able to regulate their arousal in situations where other people are in distress tend to show higher levels of affective empathy, which leads to empathic concern rather than personal distress. This is then followed through with a greater likelihood of responding helpfully.

Cassels *et al.* (2010) explored these arguments by looking at affective empathy in two cultural groups in the city of Vancouver, Canada. One group of adolescents was of Caucasian origin and the other comprised individuals born in Asia but whose families had emigrated to Canada. When subjects were confronted with another person's distress, they found that adolescents and young people raised in the Western culture reported higher levels of empathic concern and lower levels of personal distress than their culturally raised Asian peers. They also found that the empathy scores of subjects with an Asian heritage but who had been born and raised in Canada fell midway between those of the two primary cultural groups.

The dearth of research on empathy and culture means that it is difficult to draw any firm conclusions. There are hints, though, that parenting and caregiving experiences might be playing a part in whatever cultural differences exist in levels of affective empathy (Cassels *et al.* 2010). Nevertheless, the possibility that cultural differences do occur in both levels and types of empathy suggests the need to tread carefully whenever people with different cultural backgrounds meet and interact. Caution and not presuming too much are likely to be particularly important for those who work as counsellors, health and welfare workers.

Thus, in order for professionals to be ethnoculturally empathic and work cross-culturally, Wang *et al.* (2003) recommend that they consider the other not simply as another individual independent of their cultural context, but as someone, like themselves, who can only be understood in terms of and as a product of their cultural context. The insight that all human behaviour, action and psychological activity takes place within a context means that our minds are culturally embedded and, to an extent, socially constructed. 'Since our way of seeing things is literally our way of living,' wrote Williams (1965: 55), 'the process of communication is in fact the process of community.' Making sense of other minds has, therefore, to be seen as an activity that is culturally mediated. There can be no direct meeting of minds independent of and unaided by information about how those involved are embedded in a broader social environment (Stanford Encyclopedia of Philosophy 2008: 11).

On this argument, high-quality empathy is only possible when we understand something of the other person's unique history, personality, social context and cultural milieu. The ability to read the other's behaviour, expressions and body language takes more than simple, albeit sensitive, observation. It also requires that we know something of the other's culture and psychosocial makeup. The lack of eye contact in one culture might mean deference, in another guilt, in a third courtesy, while in a fourth shame. Cultural distance increases the risk of reduced mutual empathy. It could be quite a challenge, for example, for a middle-aged Western white Christian male to empathize with a young, black African Muslim woman about to enter an arranged marriage.

There also needs to be an awareness of how society and the media view and treat individuals from particular ethnic groups. All of us should accept that there are cultural differences, that people from other ethnic groups might well have different traditions, beliefs, outlooks, habits and tastes. Counsellors, social workers and therapists who fail to be ethnoculturally empathic are more likely to have clients who terminate treatment before its proper completion (Karlsson 2005). All of this is a strong reminder that practitioners have a moral as well as a therapeutic obligation to know about and understand the cultural backgrounds and contexts of the clients with whom they work (Lawrence and Luis 2001).

Conclusion

Individual differences in temperament have been associated with differences in level of empathy. The challenge to be empathic increases when we meet people whose class, race and cultural background are radically different to our own. There is neurological as well as psychosocial evidence to support the view that on average men and women differ in their natural empathy levels. Many men, in fact, do score well on mind-reading and emotionally based tasks, while some women outperform men on tasks that depend on good spatial and systematizing skills. These differences between the sexes also crop up in what are often described as 'disorders of empathy', in which the ability to empathize appears to be very low.

The next two chapters consider a number of these disorders, partly for their own sake, but also because the relative absence of empathy throws light on what is required in order for us to maintain everyday social relationships.

7

When Empathy Is Absent or Low

Conditions of low empathy

Good mental health is associated with the ability to empathize with and be attuned to other people. The capacity to reflect on our own and other people's behaviour, thoughts and feelings gives us mental balance, psychological equilibrium. According to Greenspan and Benderely (1997: 193), mental health 'requires a feeling of connectedness with humanity' and a keen sense of empathy. As we have seen in previous chapters, our capacity to empathize varies naturally depending on our temperament, situation and relationship to the other person. However, there are conditions in which individuals find empathizing very difficult, if not impossible.

So what happens when people are not able to empathize? What social consequences follow when individuals are unable to empathize with other people's thoughts, feelings, beliefs and intentions? Given that the smooth running of social life depends on social understanding and empathy, the expectation is that everyday sociality breaks down. The loss of empathy predicts a range of behavioural, emotional and relationship problems. Such losses, however caused, can be a source of distress to patients, family and friends alike.

There are a variety of conditions, sometimes described by the medical and psychological professions as *disorders of empathy*, in which the ability to empathize seems reduced or absent (for example, see Baron-Cohen 2011: 108). These include, among others, autism, Attention Deficit Hyperactivity Disorder (ADHD), schizophrenia, eating disorders, conduct disorder, psychopathy and Obsessive Compulsive Disorder (OCD)

(Gillberg 2007). Other conditions can also lead to temporary reductions in our capacity to be empathic: depression, alcoholism or substance abuse, for instance. Damage to and degeneration of the brain's empathy circuits, as happens in some forms of dementia, can also lead to a loss of empathy.

Chapter 6 described how, in any given population, levels of empathy are normally distributed along a bell curve. We all lie somewhere on this empathy spectrum. In extreme cases, Baron-Cohen (2011) refers to 'zero degrees of empathy', when people have no awareness of how they come across to others or how to anticipate other people's feelings and possible reactions. In these cases, individuals are self-centred and seem oblivious to the idea that there might even be other points of view. They seem not to 'get' relationships. Having zero degrees of empathy

> means that you have no brakes on your behaviour, leaving you free to pursue any object of your desires, or to express any thought in your mind, without considering the impact of your actions or words on another person.
>
> (Baron-Cohen 2011: 29)

Some researchers believe that many of these disorders have a strong genetic origin, although, as ever, gene–environment interactions are also at work (Anckarsäter and Cloninger 2007). The quality and character of the environment can modify the extent to which the genes associated with empathy, or its absence, are expressed or not. Genetic abnormalities, illness, childhood abuse and neglect, and diseases and injuries to the brain can all upset the capacity to empathize and sustain social relationships. Some of these empathy problems arise because of impairment or damage to the prefrontal cortex of the brain, which is in part responsible for emotional recognition, understanding, management and regulation. When the brain finds that thinking about feelings is difficult or no longer possible, empathy disappears; and when empathy disappears, social skills and relationships fall apart.

Socially induced states of low empathy

We have seen that empathy levels vary depending on natural dispositions, experience and circumstances. Other people's displays of empathy can affect and be affected by our own emotional behaviour. Empathy can be overridden by other social psychological factors, particularly the behaviour and expectations of others.

One of the tragedies suffered by those whose faces can no longer express feelings, which is the case in Parkinson's disease, is that other people find it difficult to see, read and understand the mind of the sufferer. Individuals with Parkinson's disease and those with similar conditions in which facial muscles become paralysed have all the normal feelings of joy, anger, sadness and pain, but they are unable to express them facially. The two normal ways of exchanging affective communication and empathy are then in danger of being lost. We feel disconcerted when someone else's face is without expression. It seems odd. It makes us anxious. Without emotional feedback, we lose our social bearings. Those who cannot express feelings reduce the empathic potential of those with whom they interact. Responses therefore become confused and awkward and the sufferer all too easily is cast into a world in which relationships lack resonance and synchrony. 'Our faces display our emotions,' write Szalavitz and Perry (2011: 43), 'but they also shape them.'

Milgram's (1974) famous obedience experiments showed that empathy can be overridden when people conform, follow group expectations and obey orders. In his notorious experiments, ordinary people unwittingly found themselves in an authoritarian environment in which they were asked to administer apparent electric shocks to unseen subjects. The subjects were in fact 'actors' who did not actually receive any electric jolt, but faked pain as if they had. A surprisingly high number of people under the firm direction of the experimenters were prepared to administer very high levels of electric charge, which if they had really been delivered might even have been fatal. Milgram argued that most of us under particular conditions show a remarkable propensity to obey authority, no matter what behaviours are being asked of us, including those that involve responding punitively. In these cases, empathy is either lost or suspended and moral restraint disappears.

Zimbardo's prison experiments also produced sobering results (Haney *et al.* 1973). Here, volunteering students were cast in the role of either guard or prisoner and invited to role-play a simulated prison environment. Those who were in the role of guards began to show alarmingly cruel, non-empathic behaviour during the course of the experiment. The study aimed to see whether, as a result of the roles played, participants would come to behave like real guards and real prisoners. They did. 'In fact, so dramatic were the changes in the behaviour of both the prisoners and the guards that it was necessary to stop the study after only six days, instead of the two weeks for which is was planned ... The roles they played exerted powerful – and chilling – effects on their behaviour, and are indicative of the powerful impact that roles often exert on us in many different groups' (Baron *et al.* 2006: 463).

In these examples, we see how even in normally decent, socially aware people, empathy levels can drop dramatically, leading them to behave in ways that are unfeeling, even cruel. Under pressure or stress, or when we feel flustered, most of us suffer a temporary loss of empathy. We have to get the children to school and we cannot find our car keys. When one of the children anxiously points out that she's going to be late for her first lesson, we react with uncharacteristic verbal aggression. We are preoccupied with our own distress and just do not see or appreciate our daughter's real worry. Under many everyday conditions our 'empathy circuits go down' as we suffer a transient loss of connection with others and their feelings (Baron-Cohen 2011: 116). Nevertheless, only in cases in which empathy circuits are permanently down do we find ourselves in the company of those who suffer disorders of low empathy.

Empathy, illness and psychiatric disorders

Empathy can be low or absent as a result of illness, disease, neurological development or upbringing. For example, sufferers of various psychoses include people who seem to have lost touch with reality, might hallucinate and hear voices, have delusions of grandeur or experience paranoia. Schizophrenia is one such condition. A number of studies have found that patients diagnosed with paranoia have difficulty understanding what other people are thinking. They have an impaired Theory of Mind. Paranoid patients have problems correctly understanding other people's intentions and often, but erroneously, believe them to be hostile (Brune 2005). These difficulties mean that many patients diagnosed with schizophrenia, particularly paranoid schizophrenia, suffer low self-esteem, empathy dysfunctions, Theory of Mind problems and a propensity to jump to conclusions based on insufficient evidence (Bentall 2009: 175).

Baron-Cohen (2011) recognizes two types of 'zero degrees of empathy', one negative and one positive. Under the group in which zero degrees of empathy is negative come psychopathy, borderline personality disorder (BPD), antisocial personality disorder (APD) and people who are very self-centred and have a profoundly heightened sense of their own importance, defined as having a narcissistic personality disorder (NPD). Those with an NPD have difficulty recognizing other people's feelings and subjective experiences. The focus on the self is so intense that it inhibits consideration of the feelings of others. There is some evidence that narcissism is often found in those who abuse children, both physically and sexually (Dolan and Fullam 2007: 43). We consider two of these negative types of low-empathy disorder in the next chapter.

When zero degrees of empathy is positive, Baron-Cohen (2011) discusses autism and Asperger syndrome; that is, individuals who find themselves with a condition that lies somewhere along the autistic spectrum.

Autism

Autism is a neuro-developmental disorder. As there are many variations in the nature and severity of symptoms, modern diagnoses prefer to recognize and describe an 'autistic spectrum disorder' (ASD). The spectrum ranges from profoundly impaired individuals to those with Asperger syndrome, a small number of whom score well on IQ tests, although they still display impairments of communication and social interaction.

With improved diagnosis, estimates suggest that perhaps as many as 1 in every 200 or 300 children lies somewhere along the autistic spectrum. More boys than girls are diagnosed, typically in the ratio of about 8:1.

People who interact with autistic children sometimes feel as if they are being treated as no more than objects. Autistic children's empathy and communication skills seem poor. For example, most toddlers react with upset if an experimenter appears to have hit her thumb with a hammer, hurting herself and yelping with pain. In contrast, autistic children generally show little reaction to the experimenter's apparent distress. Children with autism fail to point to objects to achieve joint attention. They also remain uninterested in other people's emotional attitudes towards objects and events in the world. This can lead to social withdrawal.

Most children diagnosed with autism have major learning difficulties. Although some learn to speak, about half do not. It is quite common for autistic individuals to develop strong and narrow obsessions, fixations and repetitive behaviours. There is a preference for 'sameness' – for routines, the way the furniture is arranged in a room, the foods that are eaten – and any change in routine can cause great distress. Similarly, anything unexpected is likely to be experienced as extremely stressful. A minority of autistic children have IQs that are average and above and some high-functioning autistic individuals achieve extraordinary success in fields such as mathematics and theoretical physics, worlds that are governed by rules and logic.

As they mature, some of those with autism do begin to appreciate that other people are centres of mental experience, people with independent thoughts and feelings. Even so, difficulties in social relationships remain. These empathy-related and interpersonal disadvantages also have consequences for the development of self-awareness and the capacity for self-reflection (Hobson 2007). This can result in a lack of self-consciousness, which might, in part, explain the low levels of embarrassment, social inhibition or shame experienced by many autistic individuals. An autistic adolescent might say out loud that he does not like the sound of someone's voice and that he wants to leave now. A partner with Asperger syndrome might suddenly decide to go outside into the garden to check on Jupiter's path in the clear night sky during a dinner party, without explaining to wife or guests why he is leaving.

> What barely needs stating ... is that empathy is something that happens *between* people. It is something experienced by one person as a mode of relating to another, part and parcel of what it means to have interpersonal relations, and not merely something that occurs in sporadic bouts of fellow-feeling ... So it is that people who relate to children with autism feel the lack of something they expect to be part of their interchange with others; and for the children's part, by all appearances, they seem to lack the feel of what personal relatedness really means.
>
> (Hobson 2007: 127, emphasis in original)

Children and adults who have autism find it difficult to read people's emotional expressions and pass Theory of Mind tests (Baron-Cohen 1987). They find it hard to tune into other people's mental states (their thoughts, feelings, plans), particularly as they might affect their beliefs and behaviour. As a result, people with autism experience problems in seeing the world from other people's point of view. Theirs is a very literal, behavioural world in which there is little understanding of the complexity and subtlety of social interaction.

The brilliant British theoretical physicist Paul Dirac held the Lucasian Chair of Mathematics at the University of Cambridge. He won the Nobel Prize for Physics in 1933 for his work on atomic theory, quantum mechanics and his postulation of anti-matter (see Farmelo 2009 for an excellent biography). It is thought likely that Dirac had Asperger syndrome, mainly because of his taciturnity, social shyness and extreme literal-mindedness. During the early stages of their relationship, his wife Margit wrote him many letters. She complained that his replies lacked feeling. During their long marriage, his behaviour would regularly infuriate her. One day she yelled at him, 'What would you do if I left you?' Dirac thought for a moment and, without any ill intent, replied, 'I'd say good-bye, dear.' His lectures were famous for being very ordered and logical.

However, in the middle of one lecture, someone said, 'Professor Dirac, I haven't understood equation number ten.' Dirac made no response and carried on with his lecture. Puzzled, the audience member asked, 'Professor, why haven't you answered my question?' To that Dirac replied, 'Question? I thought what you said was simply a statement, that you have not understood.' As a question wasn't technically asked, no reply was required.

Children with autism engage in little pretend or shared play. Processing social information seems difficult. Meaningful glances, innuendo, double-entendres, sarcasm, word play and verbal jokes are lost on the autistic mind. They lack mental empathy and 'mind-mindedness', and Baron-Cohen (1995) suggests that they suffer 'mindblindness'.

Not only are individuals who are on the autistic spectrum not very good at tuning into other people's mind states, they also do not seem to reflect and wonder much about their own feelings. This major deficit seriously impairs their ability to develop social cognition and emotional intelligence. An autistic individual might talk rapidly about his interest in bus routes and timetables, without ever looking you in the face or waiting for you to reply, before walking away abruptly. In fact, for most autistic individuals direct eye contact is hard. There is no intention to be rude, just a failure to see how the interaction might be seen and experienced from the other's point of view. For those who are autistic, social interaction is both a puzzle and a problem:

> Imagine what your world would be like if you were aware of physical things but were blind to the existence of mental things. I mean, of course, blind to the things like thoughts, beliefs, knowledge, desires, and intentions, which for most of us self-evidently underlie behaviour. Stretch your imagination to consider what sense you could make of human action … if, as for a behaviourist, a mentalistic explanation was forever beyond your limits.

> (Baron-Cohen 1995: 1)

Thus, for autistic individuals, sharing the world with other people and seeing their perspective is not easy. If the autistic boy is fascinated by train timetables and is inclined to talk about them endlessly, he is unlikely to appreciate that this is a topic of limited interest to most of us. Individuals with autism rarely lie or attempt to deceive, yet their honesty and directness can be both off-putting and appear odd. Being told that we are fat or wrinkly or sweaty is unlikely to endear us to the truth-sayer.

If one is unable to appreciate the complexities and subtleties of the social world, mentalization is difficult. In turn, this means that smooth, coordinated social interactions are not possible. This, in part, explains why autistic individuals find the inherent openness, unpredictability, uncertainty and uncontrollability of the social world distressing, even frightening, hence their preference for the relative safety of the closed, complete worlds of systems, be they timetables, mathematics, machines, technical drawing, computing or software programming.

Baron-Cohen (2004) sees autistic spectrum disorders as examples of the 'extreme male brain' that we met in the previous chapter. These are brains which are very good at systematizing and spatial skills, which look for patterns and order, which search for the invariant rules that underpin any natural or man-made system. There is a preference for routine, predictable environments. These are minds that like things to be unchanging and exact. They don't cope well with unpredictability, nuance and the need to interpret. Consequently, the world of people, other minds and relationships is confusing and difficult. The social world operates on fuzzy, shifting rules. So much of what takes place in the world of people is socially constructed and making sense of it depends on interpretation. All of the uncertainty and apparent arbitrariness of the social world lead emotions and relationships in themselves to be uncomfortable for those with autism and perhaps best avoided.

However, unlike individuals with psychopathy and borderline personality disorder who have zero empathy and lack a moral compass, those with autism, particularly those who do have language skills, tend to be very 'moral'. Their law-abiding behaviour is not solely based on the restraining powers of empathy but on the high value that they give to rules. Laws and rules make the world predictable. Breaching them destabilizes conduct and behaviour and is not to be condoned. So although

autistic individuals have low empathy, find relationships difficult, sometimes treat others as if they were objects and as often
as not ignore those around them, they never behave intention-
ally cruelly or exploit others.

These distinctive characteristics of autism and Asperger
syndrome explain why Baron-Cohen (2011) has been encouraged to see them as examples of 'zero degrees of empathy' that
are *positive*. The marked differences between autism and
psychopathy suggest different aetiologies for the two conditions.

In the case of autism, the brain's empathy circuits are not
functioning well. The causes of the problem seem to point to a
neuro-developmental disorder with a genetic and possibly foetal
hormonal environmental base. This is in contrast to psychopathy and BPD, where postnatal parenting and the family environment as well as genetic vulnerabilities are thought to play a
significant part in the aetiology of the disorder (Caspi *et al.*
2002). 'We are therefore forced to conclude', writes Baron-
Cohen (2011: 86), 'that *different* genes must be at work to
produce Zero-Positive and Zero-Negative states' (emphasis in
original).

Autistic traits do seem to run in families, although they do
not always lead to autism. Many genes affecting different
elements of the brain's empathic circuitry are likely to be
involved. For example, the genetic substrates responsible for the
production of oxytocin receptors have been linked to the disorder (Jacob *et al.* 2007). There is evidence that in autism there is
abnormal functioning in the mirror neuron system (Oberman
and Ramachandran 2007). However, whatever the specific
causes, what we do see in the extended families of many autistic people is a bias, particularly in males, towards systematizing
talents rather than obvious emotional, empathy and interpersonal skills.

Intense world theory of autism

If autism is a low-empathy disorder and if the ability to cope
with the social world depends on the presence of empathy and
mind-reading skills, then we might expect individuals with
autism to find the world of people a puzzling, unpredictable and

therefore stressful place. If a situation is experienced as stressful, one might choose to avoid it, order it or control it.

As we have seen, autistic children prefer routine and predictability. They also dislike any sudden or intense arousal of their senses.

Temple Grandin, a professor of animal sciences who happens to be autistic, says that animals that are potential prey are exquisitely sensitive to the *behaviour* of other creatures. All their senses are highly tuned to behaviours that might, however nuanced, imply threat. Any hint of danger and they flee. Sudden movements or a piece of paper blowing in the wind will easily frighten them. However, Grandin makes the point that these highly developed sensory skills that so readily trigger a flight response are based on picking up behavioural cues that indicate threat, not on cognitive skills that suggest intention.

Grandin (2006) describes her own ultra-sensitivity to the sights, sounds and smells around her. She adds that she is not very good at seeing the world from other people's psychological point of view. She finds social interaction difficult. So although she is a consummate observer of behaviour, she is blind to what might be going in the minds that are generating that behaviour, hence her social awkwardness and the puzzle that the world of other people poses for her.

There have been attempts to understand autism based on the heightened sensitivity shown by most autistic children to sensory stimulation (for example, Markram *et al.* 2007). Autistic children typically feel anxious, aroused and distressed when things are out of place or move suddenly, lights shine too brightly, sounds are too loud, or social situations too noisy and busy. Social interaction in particular can be experienced as a highly stressful sensory overload from which it is easier to disconnect and withdraw. In their helpful review of this research, Szalavitz and Perry (2011: 86) suggest that living in a social world that feels confusing, stressful and sometimes frightening can lead to flight responses. Quiet places are sought and self-soothing behaviours, including rocking and repetition, are triggered in attempts to relieve the stress.

Of course, one of the downsides of this strategy for an autistic individual is that it cuts you off from close relationships. As a result, your brain is starved of vital social experiences. You therefore fail to learn how other minds and the social world works; you might even fail to learn language. This has been described as the 'intense world' theory of autism (Markram *et al.* 2007, cited in Szalavitz and Perry 2011: 90). The 'social brain needs social experience to function' (Szalavitz and Perry 2011: 95). In this analysis, the inability to empathize is a consequence of avoiding social interaction. This theory does not deny that there are severe neurological irregularities in those suffering from autism. However, the model encourages the introduction of supports and interventions to help autistic children feel less overwhelmed by sensory stimulation. This allows them to engage with the social world more calmly and more constructively.

Dementia

Degeneration of and damage to the medial orbitofrontal cortex (OFC) and the right anterior temporal lobe, parts of the brain involved in processing emotions, are also associated with loss of empathy (Shamay-Tsoory *et al.* 2003). Patients with frontotemporal lobar degeneration (FTLD), which involves the loss of neurons in the cortex and insula, suffer from dementia. They also lose the capacity to be empathic (Rankin *et al.* 2006; Fernandez-Duque *et al.* 2010); with that loss, social interaction breaks down catastrophically. Skilled and fluent interaction depends on the brain's ability to link and process emotional and cognitive information. When that ability is lost, relationships become almost impossible. The sufferer's 'old' personality has gone and the individual seems no longer to be his or her self, which is distressing for both family and patient alike.

When people lose their ability to be empathic, and when they can no longer process and regulate their own and other people's emotions, it can also decrease the empathic responsiveness of those responsible for the patient's care. When emotional synchrony and reciprocity no longer exist, there is a constant risk of interactions becoming dehumanized. Health and care workers are very conscious of this risk (Gilson and Moyer 2000). In order to help doctors, nurses and social care workers retain their capacity for empathy in such cases, much has been written on both the nature of dementia and the best ways to remain responsive, caring and connected (for example, Kasl-Godley and Gatz 2000; Bush 2003). Encouraging the development of cognitive empathy, the ability to imagine and see the world from the sufferer's point of view, forms a key part of many dementia care training programmes.

Empathy failures and compassion fatigue

This final section on situations in which empathy levels might be low, although not based on clinical conditions, is yet another reminder that we are all prey to the loss of empathy from time to time. No matter an individual's overall empathic skill, empathy rates vary throughout the day. As we have seen, we are more empathic when our mood is positive. In contrast, we are less empathic when those with whom we interact are unknown, psychologically distant and depersonalized. When organizations talk not of people but of target populations, punters or profits, empathy levels drop.

Emotional concern and feelings of compassion also tend to fall when professionals and practitioners work for prolonged periods with people who naturally evoke empathic concern. Most healthcare and welfare professionals feel empathy for those who are ill, who have been the victims of abuse or who have disabilities that mean everyday life can be a challenge. Nevertheless, such cognitive empathy takes mental effort. In order to focus on the other person's perspective one must overlook one's own. When professionals spend whole days working with those who deserve our empathy, strain mounts and 'compassion fatigue' and 'burn out' can set in (Figley 2002). Compassion fatigue can occur when we have to work with problems that are chronic or people whose suffering is prolonged. It can also set in when we have to work with those whose medical outcomes are not good and not much can be done.

Empathy failures can also occur when professionals work predominantly with those whose own empathy is weak, absent or currently missing. Warring parents in custody disputes, racist offenders and self-pitying divorcees can test even our best efforts at empathy. Counsellors, prison officers and mental health workers whose caseloads comprise only sociopaths, violent offenders and child sex abusers can find it very difficult to maintain much of their natural empathy by the end of a full working day.

It behoves individuals and their organizations to recognize the risks of working with those who are in pain, need and distress. Regular breaks and good supervision might help. Varying the workload and client type might also keep empathy levels high. If workers are to remain empathic, they need employers who are equally empathic and who run emotionally intelligent organizations.

Conclusion

A number of social, biological and medical conditions have been found to reduce empathic sensitivity. Autism remains the disorder best known for its links with problems of low empathy. There is still no consensus on the exact causes of autism and the autistic spectrum disorders. Theories abound, although most agree that autism is most likely a neuro-developmental disorder with a strong genetic load. And whatever genetic hand you have been dealt, it has to be played in the world of people and things in which you find yourself, therefore both genes and environment have been implicated.

The intense study that autism has received is driven by two interests. There is a deep concern for the condition itself and what might be done to help people whose lives are affected. There is also recognition that the absence of empathy causes sufferers huge problems in everyday social life. Their problems help to throw light on the profound importance of empathy in human behaviour and development.

Problems of low empathy turn out to be particularly troublesome when we begin to look at the other major group of empathy disorders, including psychopathy and personality disorders. One of the major differences between, say, autism and psychopathy is that whereas individuals with autism find society a problem, those with psychopathy are a problem for society. It is to such disorders that we turn in the next chapter.

8
Psychopathy and Borderline Personality Disorder

Negative empathy

As we saw in the previous chapter, people who have little awareness of how they are viewed by others have been described as having 'zero degrees of empathy' (Baron-Cohen 2011). When this lack of empathy leads to troublesome and antisocial behaviour, it is defined as 'negative'. Individuals with this type of low empathy can be very self-centred. They seem unconcerned that other people have feelings unless those feelings impinge on their own wants and needs. To be in a relationship with such people can be distressing, problematic and chaotic.

Decety and Meltzoff (2011) observe that violent offenders and those with antisocial behavioural problems lack empathy. They tend to react aggressively to other people's distress. In this chapter we shall consider two types of zero degrees of empathy of the negative, active and hostile kind: psychopathy and borderline personality disorder.

Psychopathy

In any given population, around 2 per cent will be diagnosed as psychopathic or suffering from antisocial personality disorder. However, the figures are slightly different for men and women, with up to 3 per cent of males and only 1 per cent of females falling into these classifications. Prisons, particularly those housing violent and aggressive offenders, contain very high numbers of individuals diagnosed with antisocial personality disorder.

Blair *et al.* (2005), Baron-Cohen (2011) and others see psychopathy as a deficit of empathy. The inability of psychopaths to behave morally arises because even when they observe distress in others, they remain unmoved by it. They have some cognitive empathy, but they lack any semblance of affective empathy. It is as if they are simply not processing certain types of emotional information.

Although there appears not to be any Theory of Mind impairment in individuals with psychopathy, Blair (2007) has found that psychopathic individuals are poor at recognizing and processing expressions of fear, sadness and possibly disgust in other people (although they seem to be less impaired when it comes to processing other people's expressions of anger, happiness and surprise). The inability to recognize, process and respond to cues of fear in particular suggests orbital medial prefrontal cortex and amygdala dysfunctions as key neurological features of the disorder (Cozolino 2006: 274).

Pain observed in others, for example, has no affect on psychopaths. In some cases it might even cause them pleasure. Similarly, if psychopaths cause pain in others, they feel no remorse. Lacking affective empathy, they just do not care. Normally the presence of empathy leads to social restraint and behaviours that are moral. As they have no affective empathy, psychopaths have no moral brakes. They will do whatever they feel is necessary to get what they want in order to fulfil their desires.

Psychopaths have neither social fears nor fellow feeling. These deficits are a recipe for recklessness, violence and exploitation. Possessed of some cognitive empathy – that is, the ability to recognize and figure out what someone else thinks and feels – they can worm their way into other people's minds. They can mislead and manipulate, all without compunction. Psychopaths lie and deceive to get what they want. So although psychopaths might be rather good at understanding other people's intentions, the feelings of others seem to be of no concern. Psychopaths therefore lack not only empathy but also a conscience and feelings of guilt, thus punishment has no effect (Hein and Singer 2010).

Since they suffer an empathy impairment, psychopaths rarely form lasting intimate relationships. The impact of their behaviour on others is of no interest or concern to them. They seem not to think or worry about the consequences of what they do. Some psychopaths are capable of great cruelty. Many harmed animals and pets when they were children. The descriptions 'cold-blooded' and callous are often applied to them because of their lack of emotional concern. They are impulsive, thoughtless and wild. Violence can erupt without warning, triggered by alleged social slights: 'I smashed the broken bottle in his face, 'cos he disrespected me. No one looks at me like that. He deserved it.'

Bloom (2004: 102) quotes a number of psychopaths talking about their murderous behaviour. Their words are chilling. 'I was always capable of murder,' says the serial killer Gary Gilmore, 'I can become totally devoid of feelings of others, unemotional. I know I'm doing something grossly fucking wrong. I can still go ahead and do it.' Kenny Bianchi tortured and killed young women: 'It's like kind of going down the street and you see all these candy stores and you can pick any candy you want and you don't have to pay for it and you just take it. You just do what you want. It's the greatest.' And after being captured, Ted Bundy, another serial killer, couldn't understand what all the fuss was about: 'I mean, there are so many people.'

The thoughts and actions of psychopaths are typically self-centred and self-serving. They see their victims, if they think about them at all, as suckers and losers. It is their own fault they were burgled – they should have locked their doors, installed a burglar alarm – they had it coming. There is a great deal of cognitive distortion. The combination of some psychological intelligence, blunted feelings and an absence of a conscience make psychopaths and sociopaths extremely dangerous.

It might also be noted that as well as the more obvious worlds of crime and violence, a few psychopaths and sociopaths are also found in business and politics. Psychopaths can be successful in terms of wealth and material acquisition, although generally they have a careless attitude to money, which they spend freely while debts go unpaid, and their lack of a conscience is an obvious problem.

The childcare background of psychopaths

There is evidence that there are neurological differences between psychopaths and non-psychopaths, particularly in those areas of the brain responsible for regulating emotions, impulses and social responses (Churchland 2011: 40).

The genes that might be involved in constructing the brain's empathy-based circuits are likely to be many and varied. We appear to be a long way still from unravelling the sheer complexity of both the neurology of empathy and the genes that lie behind it, as well as how different genes get switched on or off in different environments at different stages of development, from conception to full maturity. Nevertheless, although gene–environment interactions are fiercely complex, modern debates about the interplay between nature and nurture are reinforcing the importance of the environment in our understanding of how genes work and get expressed. This picture applies to the development of empathy as much as any other area of human development. We might therefore expect psychopathy to arise when heritable and genetic vulnerabilities meet major environmental risks, the biggest risk being exposure to parental abuse and neglect during childhood (Gunter *et al.* 2010).

The family histories of most psychopaths and sociopaths tend to be characterized by neglect, parental indifference, physical abuse and emotional harm. In particular, rejection and cold, brutal parenting feature in the childhood of many psychopaths (Kohut 1977; Bowlby 1988; Howe 2005). Abused and neglected children find no calm or comfort in relationships. Never having been loved, they find it hard to love or even to feel lovable. Their young lives are ones of almost constant fear and stress.

A lack of emotional empathy and an indifference to other people's feelings develop, which make it easy to harm others, exploit them or devalue them. The feelings of young psychopaths never run deep. You need to feel safe and secure before you can relax and see another's point of view. Abused and neglected children tend to react with confusion, distress or anger when they try to fathom and negotiate the challenges posed by peers and social relationships. These distressed reactions get them into trouble with parents and teachers. They are at increased risk of developing antisocial behaviours and mental health problems from a surprisingly young age. Some also suffer 'internalizing disorders', including anxiety and depression.

Beeghly and Cicchetti (1994) found that children who had experienced severe neglect and abuse used significantly less 'internal state language'; that is, they talked less about their own thoughts, feelings and actions than did non-maltreated toddlers. They were also less able to differentiate between feelings. For example, they were confused between their own feelings of sadness, anger and fear. On top of this, their range of feelings appeared limited and rather blunted. One effect of these affective deficiencies is the inability of many maltreated children to regulate their own arousal or to differentiate, label and understand emotional expressions in other people. In contrast to secure and non-maltreated young children, their ability to tell the difference between other people's facial expressions of anger or fear, disgust or sadness was poor in Beeghly and Cicchetti's study. Maltreated children also tend to see more anger in faces than is actually present. As well as faces that really are expressing anger, they also perceive anger in faces that are neutral or even calm. 'It may be the case', conclude Pollak and Kistler 2002: 9075), 'that physically abused children develop a broader category of anger because it is adaptive for them to notice when adults are angry.'

If this bias and misinterpretation continue into adulthood, it is little wonder that so many people whose histories have been blighted by rejection and violence are so quick to see hostility in others, even when none is present. Main and George (1985) also found that abused and neglected children scored poorly on empathy tests. Those who have not been on the receiving end of empathic parenting seem to find empathy difficult (Main and George 1985).

The life situations of maltreated children elicit negative emotions and promote the development of these nonoptimal expressiveness patterns. It is easy to see how expecting anger from others and not having distress relieved could disrupt

young children's own emotionality. Through their own difficult circumstances, these children feel justifiable fear when
confronted with anyone's anger, see a need for self-defence
where none exists, consider anger an automatic response to
many social challenges, and learn non-empathic responses to
others' distress.

(Denham 1998: 196–7)

When considered overall, abused and neglected children show a
poverty of responses and lack variability and flexibility when
dealing with the routine demands and stresses of social relationships. Their empathy circuits never fully develop and as a result,
emotional recognition and restraint suffer damage. There is now
strong evidence that all forms of child abuse and neglect
increase the risk of mental health and psychiatric problems.
Whenever clinical and psychiatric populations are examined,
there is an overrepresentation of people who have suffered
maltreatment as children (Kaufman and Charney 2001).
Roderick is a case in point:

Roderick was very ill as a baby and spent many weeks in
hospital. His parents were successful businesspeople and
found little time to visit him. When he was at home, he was
looked after by an ever-changing series of childminders,
nannies and nursery school workers. If he did manage to
develop an attachment with a carer, she would promptly
leave and disappear. The breakage and loss of close emotional
bonds were highly distressing. Roderick learned not to invest
in or trust carers. For him, people became a potential source
of hurt, not safety and comfort. Deprived of safe, loving relationships, his capacity to love and care atrophied. His social
brain only learned how to stay safe and exploit, not to relate.
Relationships gave him no pleasure. Other people were only
useful in terms of getting his immediate needs met. He could
read their minds insofar as it helped him get what he wanted,
but he had no interest in what they were feeling.

As a child, Roderick was not popular. He was a bully. In
his teens, he told a girl that he loved her, but when she would-
n't go to bed with him, he sexually assaulted her. He showed

no remorse and told his friends, 'She was asking for it. Anyway, who cares?' As an adult, he quickly made a lot of money running a variety of businesses in the sex trade.

However, he eventually came unstuck when he was caught by the police for setting up a large number of internet scams. He fabricated web pages purporting to represent charities involved in famine and disaster relief campaigns. By the time his scheme was detected, several hundred thousand pounds from well-meaning donors had poured into his bank account. He told his solicitor that he wasn't to blame if people were mug enough to give money without checking where it was going.

Successful social behaviour generally involves both cognition and emotion. Emotions give thoughts valence. Psychopaths suffer a deficit in those emotions that are triggered by an acute awareness, often uncomfortable, of other people's perceptions of us and our behaviour. These are sometimes described as the moral emotions and include feelings of shame and guilt. Such social deficits mean that ultimately most psychopaths do not lead successful lives. 'It is emblematic of the psychopath', thinks Bloom (2004: 112), 'that he can be very successful in the short term, such as a one-off con game, but fails in the long term.'

Borderline personality disorder

While the psychopath is indifferent to other people's emotions, individuals diagnosed with borderline personality disorder (BPD) are highly sensitive to other people's feeling states, but only as these states affect them. They possess an anxious egocentricity, which means that any capacity to empathize is severely reduced. There is no wish to understand the other person's mind, only an anxiety about the impact that the other's feelings and behaviour might have on them.

When individuals relate to others in ways that are highly dysfunctional and disruptive, their diagnosis is generally one of 'personality disorder'. Individuals with BPD present with a complex array of symptoms, such as unstable moods, volatile social relationships and low levels of trust. The lives of people with BPD – around 1 or 2 per cent of the population – seem to be ones of perpetual crisis. Such people certainly present in high numbers on the doorsteps of counsellors and social workers, psychiatrists and psychologists, nurses and doctors. They populate the caseloads of those who work in the field of alcohol and drug abuse. Episodes of depression are common among them.

Those with BPD suffer a pervasive fear of abandonment by idealized others. Therefore, although their need for others is high, trust in those others' emotional availability is low. Anxiety reigns and they are particularly sensitive to any hint of rejection. People diagnosed with BPD feel needy, unloved and vulnerable. They generally see themselves as victims and hard done by. Their relationships are characterized by intense feelings, chaos, confrontation and instability. Their behaviour is impulsive, unpredictable and self-destructive.

The simultaneous feelings of need for and fear of others can be extreme. There is much talk of relationships in terms of 'love/hate'. Other people are seen as either 'for me or against me'. One moment, fervent emotional demands are made on a partner, parent or friend. The next, an aggressive, fearful outburst erupts without warning. Kreisman and Straus (1989) actually titled their book on the subject *I Hate You, Don't Leave Me*. Being alone feels like abandonment. Being close feels threatening, with the ever-present danger of suffocation or rejection. There is no middle ground. The result is relationships that are intense, tempestuous, exhausting, destructive and destined to end in pain and hurt.

All of this emotional lability and relationship chaos point to major impairments in the ability to mentalize in general and cognitively empathize in particular. However, at the core remains a haunting fear of loneliness and abandonment. The deep need to feel loved and safe drives individuals with BPD again and again into unconsidered relationships that might be dangerous or desperate.

Individuals with BPD are hypersensitive to other people's emotions, but in ways that are distorted, misinterpreted and prone to a negative bias. Their interpretation of other people's feelings is therefore self-centred and generally wrong. They overreact, blowing hot and cold. Although in a sense it might be argued that their affective empathy, particularly their ability to pick up on other people's negative emotions, is often heightened, this sensitivity only has a bearing on the BPD person's own concerns, fears and anxieties. They have an interest in why you might be feeling the way you do only insofar as it affects them. This 'primitive' empathy rarely translates into thinking about you and your needs. Their lack of interest in why you might be thinking or feeling the way you do also means that they are very poor at predicting your behaviour. Take Julie as an example.

Julie is an unemployed, 34-year-old single woman. She has a history of overdosing and occasionally self-harms, usually by running a razor blade over the skin of her arms, but only deep enough to draw a few bright beads of blood. She has had many relationships with men, some very short term, others lasting up to a year. She usually meets men in bars, claims to fall in love almost immediately, and before the couple know it, by the end of the week, they find themselves living together. In these cases, Julie quickly begins to think of marriage, having babies and even drawing up lists of their children's names.

During the honeymoon period of these relationships, Julie is bubbly and fun, but also extravagant, often over-the-top and extremely talkative. She cannot bear to be apart from the object of her love, and if and when he does attempt to do anything on his own, she becomes anxious, suspicious and increasingly jealous and angry. She sends dozens of text messages every day declaring her love, but feels deprived and hurt if he doesn't respond to each and every one in a like-minded manner. Partners soon feel overwhelmed. Exasperation turns to anger and on more than one occasion Julie has been the victim of domestic violence. It is at this point that the men leave. Julie pleads with them to return, threatens to kill herself if they don't come back, and then when it is clear that the relationship has ended, she goes into a state of depression, sometimes drinking heavily or taking an overdose, which can lead to a hospital admission. In one or two cases she retaliated, sending poison pen letters to her ex-boyfriend's employer, slashing his car tyres, spreading calumny among his buddies and workmates.

In the aftermath of a failed relationship, Julie typically attempts to reconnect with some of her old girlfriends. Uninvited, she turns up out of the blue, begs for somewhere to stay while she sorts herself out, and then proceeds to place huge emotional and material demands on her friends, who feel that their lives are being turned upside down by her arrival. If they attempt to help and encourage her to move on, she cries, breaks down, self-harms or takes to her bed. Her girlfriends feel manipulated, trapped and very angry. However, it is usually not too long before Julie gets herself up and out of the house to find herself yet another lover, saying to her long-suffering friends, 'This time, it's the real thing. I know it.'

The majority of people with BPD seem to have suffered childhood abuse and neglect, including in many cases sexual abuse. In particular, family disruption coupled with emotional neglect and deprivation feature in most early childhoods. Many parents of children who grow up to develop BPD were vulnerable themselves, living lives of chaos, confusion and violence. Being the victim of bullying also appears to be a typical childhood experience. Whereas psychopaths survived childhood rejection, abuse and neglect by giving up on close relationships, those who end up with BPD reveal childhood strategies that involved repeated switches of behaviour between being aggressive and emotionally demanding and being helpless and submissive. When parental love and protection are unpredictable and in short supply, these wildly fluctuating, albeit highly insecure, strategies make a perverse kind of sense.

Thus, although most people who have experienced early abuse and neglect do not develop BPD, of those who do have the disorder, nearly all describe childhoods of physical and sexual abuse and neglect. This suggests that some people carry a genetic vulnerability to such treatment. However, whether this vulnerability adversely affects neurological and biological development and leads to BPD depends on the quality of the early social environment. Only those who carry the genetic vulnerability *and* who are exposed to the environmental risk of serious childhood maltreatment are in danger of developing BPD. In these cases, early life adversity appears to impair neurological development, particularly those parts of the brain involved in creating empathy circuits.

Working with BPD

One of the potential pitfalls for those trying to work therapeutically with adults who have suffered childhood abuse and neglect, including those with BPD, is that closeness and intimacy, though sought, nevertheless continue to connote potential danger. If your attachment figure was also the source of threat, abandonment and danger, people who behave rather like caregivers are simultaneously experienced as the source of both potential comfort and of danger (Howe 2005; Crittenden 2008).

Counsellors and psychotherapists who show empathy, particularly during the early stages of treatment, can therefore sometimes evoke unconscious feelings of fear in their clients. Expressions of empathy by the counsellor imply getting close and becoming emotionally intimate. If you have BPD, all your previous experience of allowing people to get emotionally close has told you that terrible things can happen. As people get closer, whether lover, friend or therapist, your feelings of fear increase. It is therefore best to defend yourself. Don't get too close; don't let your guard down. This leads to fight, flight and freeze behaviours. Counsellors might be verbally dismissed or attacked. Subsequent appointments might be missed.

A plausible explanation is that emotional closeness evokes memories of unresolved (threat linked) attachment traumas that interfere with patients' metacognitive processes. There are many reasons why a patient can find closeness and 'being understood' a threat, e.g., 'If you get close and get to know me you won't like me', or 'It makes me feel too sad and overwhelmed' (Gilbert 2005).

(Liotti and Gilbert 2011)

Thus, ironically, therapeutic efforts at empathy can make some clients feel that they are in danger. In these cases, emotional closeness can evoke memories of unresolved pain and trauma. Such memories create sudden feelings of danger: 'You might hurt me, reject me, abandon me.' Danger is frightening and feelings of fear demand that safety takes precedence. The higher brain functions involving cognition and reflection take a back seat (Liotti and Gilbert 2011). The ability to mentalize and empathize ceases. Perversely, the therapist's attempts at empathy therefore lead to a reduction in client empathy and mentalization. If warmth, closeness and intimacy signal potential danger, the client's ability to explore the troubled contents of their own mind and the minds of others switches off as he or she goes into safety mode.

Of course, a particularly empathic practitioner will feel this, so they will emotionally back off and keep the interaction more neutral and matter-of-fact. Momentarily increasing the emotional distance allows the client to feel safe. Moving in and out of emotional intimacy takes great skill, but if handled well it will very gradually allow the client to stay longer in those therapeutic moments of empathy and mentalization. The overall therapeutic aim remains one of a mutual increase in empathy and mentalization, but it is often a case of three steps forward, two steps back.

Conclusion

There is a popular view that a 'lack of empathy spells social problems, danger to others, criminality, and inhumanity' (Keen 2007: 10). To an extent this is true. Problems in recognizing and being affected by other people's feelings may result from parental abuse, neglect and rejection. To become empathic, children have to have been on the receiving end of empathy. Abusive and neglectful parents are low empathizers. The high levels of stress experienced by children who suffer maltreatment mean that their stress-response systems tend to be hypersensitive, triggered even by low levels of arousal. Heightened stress flips the brain into fight, flight or freeze mode, states in which reflection ceases, thoughts stop and empathy all but disappears. In extreme cases, children grow up into adults who develop a variety of low-empathy disorders, including psychopathy and BPD.

Many professional groups might expect to work with those whose empathy is low. Counsellors, psychiatrists, clinical psychologists and social workers will routinely find themselves attempting to engage with clients who have mental health and behavioural problems, social needs and personal distress. In all these cases it is important that practitioners themselves are possessed of high empathy skills. However, in order to give strength to this claim, we need to hear a word or two from clients about the importance of empathy in helping relationships. It is no accident that studies that have sought the views of clients and patients themselves have employed research techniques based on the social sciences' interest in empathy. The next chapter therefore takes a look at consumer view studies via the social sciences' exploration of the subjective experience.

9

Social Perspectives and Client Experiences

The problems of interpretation and meaning

The wish to understand human experience from the subjective inside first saw social scientists becoming interested in *hermeneutics* – that branch of knowledge which deals with how we interpret texts, utterances, cultures, perception and all that the human arts and sciences can create as the expression of inner thought. If we are to get anywhere close to making sense of what a text means or a person experiences, we have to know so many other things besides what is seen and said.

For example, when trying to understand the meaning of an ancient script, we need to know something about the times in which it was crafted, the original language in which it was written, the metaphors then in use, the prevailing culture and so on. Understanding, interpretation, meaning, translation – these are never straightforward matters. To make sense we need to know so much more than the words written on the page (or the painting before us, or the religious relic in our hand). To understand a text, we need to know something of the mind of the author. To appreciate a picture, we need to understand the time and place of the artist. These examples bring together two of empathy's original elements: emotional resonance and cognitive understanding. Combined, they allow the observer viscerally and imaginatively to see and feel the other's point of view, their world.

It therefore soon became apparent to many social scientists that the study of people, their behaviour and society was an inherently interpretive act. It was not possible to make sense of things at face value. People and their behaviour first had to be interpreted, and then meaning sought before understanding could be achieved. Moreover, each social scientist would bring his or her own culture, assumptions, language, education and personality to bear on the problem of how to make sense, understand and interpret the other.

And if all this was not enough, it was also apparent that a text written or an utterance made at one point in time would not only be interpreted differently at another point in time, it would have a different impact and set of consequences. Language and art and history carry meaning. They are therefore capable of endless interpretation. Whenever language and people are involved, there is no fixed, eternal truth. All is in motion. As the twentieth century advanced, a hermeneutic sensitivity began to produce layer on layer of interpretive possibility. This was a sharp reminder that the greater the difference and the wider the gap between you and me – in terms of gender and race, class and culture, history and language – the greater is the challenge to be empathic, to understand and to be understood.

Active empathy

Towards the end of the nineteenth century, the work of a German philosopher, Theodore Lipps, led to a major shift in the use of empathy. He saw the concept not only as a way of experiencing art, but also as key to the study of the social sciences. As well as playing a part in the aesthetic appreciation of objects, empathy could also help us resonate with and so explore the minds of other people. If we can 'feel into' the experience of the other person, we can begin to know and understand him or her. By identifying with the other, we get inside his or her world.

Whereas the objects studied by the natural sciences have no inherent meaning, the subjects considered by the social sciences are saturated with meaning. People are meaningful. They are centres of subjective experience with minds full of thoughts, feelings, beliefs, ideas, understandings, intentions and plans. Therefore the methods of study used by the social sciences have to be different if they are to enable us to understand human behaviour, subjective experience and meaningful lives. While scientific instruments measure people objectively, empathy understands them subjectively.

It was this mind-reading potential of empathy that interested British psychologist Edward Titchener. As we have seen in previous chapters, when we see someone looking sad, not only are we likely to mimic their sad expression, our minds also mirror the other's melancholy (Lipps 1903). This 'inner imitation' allows us to experience the subjectivity of the other person. Both Titchener and Lipps felt that empathy required a more active effort on the part of the observer in order to get into the mind of the other. It even required a leap of imagination. The observer, they believed, was 'a willful agent deliberately making an effort to step outside the self and "into" the experiences of others' (Davis 1994: 7).

Early advocates of empathy's power were keen to point out that knowledge of what might be happening in the minds of other people was more than 'inference from analogy' (Stanford Encyclopedia of Philosophy 2008). Inference from analogy suggests that when I observe another person behaving in a particular way (say, laughing and shouting), I note that on the occasions when I have laughed and shouted, my behaviour was caused by a particular type of mental state (say, a feeling of glee when I passed an exam). Since my outward behaviour and that of the other person appear similar (laughing and shouting), I assume that they are both likely to be the result of similar mental causes (a state of joyful glee). However, this way of reasoning fails to recognize the deeper resonance that we feel when the other person's subjective experience is felt and recognized, understood and communicated in moments of true empathy.

The philosophers who gave empathy a particular boost were the phenomenologists, even to the point of accepting that it was simply an irreducible 'type of experiential act sui generis' (Stein 1989[1817]: 10). Max Scheler (1954), for example, considered that we could apprehend other minds as we sensitively observe people's behaviour, expressions, gestures and tone of voice. Schutz (1973: 106) said that 'everything I know about your conscious life is really based on my knowledge of my own lived experience'. But Allport (1938) thought that as well as inference, intuition also played a part. As we share a similar biology and develop our psychological selves as we interact with others, we might also know other people intuitively.

Phenomenology is the study of things just as they appear. We know things through our senses, directly. If we can strip away or 'bracket off' all our socially acquired preconceptions about an object or a person, we will be able to see things as they are, for what they are. Husserl (1964), for example, was interested in how we might recognize and understand 'pure consciousness', a sense of being without all the overlays of social, cultural, religious or scientific meaning. If we see and feel the world 'just as it is', we could work on 'absolute foundations: namely, this perception is, and remains as long as it lasts, something absolute, something here and now, something that in itself is what it is' (Husserl 1964: 24).

Husserl's writings inspired many social scientists to try to capture the world, particularly the social world, at first hand, as it is, stripped of all social expectations, cultural assumptions and acquired meaning. Their methods were a form of 'phenomenological reduction'. If we can recognize and then peel away all the many layers of meaning through which we normally view the world, we can see people and objects just as they appear. These attempts to appreciate how meanings arise, how worlds get interpreted and how social realities are constructed became known as 'social phenomenology'. And one of the tools of the social phenomenologist was empathy.

In his recognition of the debt that the social sciences owed phenomenology, sociologist Alfred Schutz wrote that even Husserl himself began to be occupied with 'the problems of intersubjectivity, of empathy, and of the status of society and community as subjectivities of a higher order' (Schutz 1973: 140). Out of such thinking arose the idea that we can know other minds because all minds develop as they interact with the preexisting world of other minds. Stein (1989) argues that empathy enables us to understand others but also to understand ourselves as others experience us. Thus, explain Coplan and Goldie (2011: xiii–xiv), 'through empathy I come to discern the other's mental sates at the same time gaining self-knowledge by coming to know how the other experiences me.' Expanding on this idea, Stark writes:

Even when we come to integrate our own self – to cut it out of the texture in which it had formed one indistinguishable strand alongside many others – we continue to see it against the background of a surviving, although progressively receding, common consciousness ... It is this fundamental fact which, according to Scheler, explains our knowledge – our direct knowledge – of the psychic life of our fellow humans ... *they* live in *us* because ego and non-ego have both emerged out of a common stream of life-experience.

(Stark 1954: xxxix–xi, emphasis in original)

Thus, if the personal worlds of those around us are to be explored and understood, social scientists had to develop ways of getting at subjective experience. The concept of empathy proved to be very useful in helping researchers develop methods of investigation and tools of enquiry that allowed them to appreciate other people's personal experience. Their efforts were ones of *interpretation* and the search for *meaning* in human action, not the pursuit of lifeless facts or simple explanation.

One field that especially benefited from these new methods of enquiry was the 'consumer' survey. And one service in particular, counselling and psychotherapy, was especially interested in the views of its 'consumers'. The reasons for this were twofold. Some influential schools of counselling and psychotherapy had become very interested in empathy, believing that highly empathic therapists were more likely to be effective than poorly empathic therapists. This being the case, it seemed only reasonable to ask those on the receiving end of treatment what they thought had been most helpful. Thus, empathy featured in both the service delivered and its evaluation.

The rise of the empathic counsellor

Psychotherapy, counselling and other helping professions aim to assist individuals with analysing and making sense of their emotional lives. Counselling and psychotherapy offer a major opportunity for individuals to explore their thoughts, feelings, memories, beliefs, motivations and plans. If the help is successful, patients and clients begin to enjoy better relationships, more adaptive behaviour and improved mental health.

Much of the success of these supports and treatments depends on the ability of the practitioner to be empathic in order that clients, in turn, also become more empathic. The empathic, mentalizing practitioner creates a safe place in which psychological exploration becomes possible. These insights have long been recognized by many of the helping professions' most distinguished scholars, particularly those operating from a humanistic perspective. Sharma (1993), for example, has written a helpful book reviewing the part that empathy has played in psychoanalytic thinking and practice. In her review, she considers how many of the discipline's leading figures have thought about empathy, including Sigmund Freud, Theodor Reik, Wilhelm Fliess and Donald Winnicott. Similarly, as he was developing his work on self psychology, an offshoot of psychoanalysis, Heinz Kohut (1959, 1977, 1985) also gave a great deal of thought and impetus to the part that empathy played in practice. He acknowledged empathy's emotional and cognitive makeup, defining it as both an affective in-tuneness and a cognitive information-gathering process.

Carl Rogers (1951) was also one of the first to recognize empathy's healing qualities. He was an early pioneer of what came to be known as 'psychotherapy process research'. Here, the interest is in how the processes of counselling and psychotherapy themselves might be seen as intimately involved in treatments that are judged effective. His scientific examinations of counselling practice helped Rogers identify what it was about the relationship that contributed to therapeutic change.

Rogers expressed great confidence in the client. 'This confidence arises', writes Hazler (2006: 193), 'from a belief that all people have innate motivation to grow in positive ways and the ability to carry out such a growth process.' The basic premise is that people are inherently good. When we are free, we have a natural, inbuilt tendency to direct ourselves towards a state of wholeness and integration. At heart, and when we are allowed, we all want to be a better person. It therefore follows that clients should be granted a great deal of responsibility for the content, direction and style of the helping relationship. If helped, people become motivated to take charge of their own lives. They find direction and strength. All this is possible given the right relationship, one in which the counsellor or therapist possesses warmth, empathy and genuineness.

The core conditions

For Rogers, these three qualities – warmth, empathy and genuineness – became the 'core conditions' of the helpful relationship (Rogers 1957). These facilitative conditions, if sustained, had the power to help bring about positive change (Truax and Carkhuff 1967). For Rogers, given the right relationship, individuals have the capacity to realize their potential – to self-actualize. When we feel safe and we are encouraged, we not only flourish, but we have a natural tendency to grow and become our true selves.

The 'core therapeutic conditions' were seen as vital if practice was to be effective. Packaged together, these relationship skills comprise the *therapeutic alliance*, also known as the *working* or *helping alliance* (Moursund and Erskine 2004). The effective worker therefore possesses and shows (Gross and Capuzzi 2007):

- Empathy – to see and understand how the world looks and feels from the client's point of view, and *accurately convey that understanding*.
- Respect, acceptance and unconditional positive regard for the other – communicating a belief that the client has the ability to take control of and change his or her own life.
- Genuineness and congruence – counsellors do not play at being helpful people; whatever they do is sincere, authentic and true. Most clients can tell if someone is putting on an act and playing the part. What the genuine therapist says is always fresh and unscripted.
- Concreteness – the ability of the counsellor or therapist to tell it like it is, to see the bigger picture, to identify any distortions in the way the client is describing their situation, to help the client be more realistic.
- Warmth – usually communicated through body language,

including a smile, a touch, a kindly look, a friendly tone of voice.

- Immediacy – the ability to acknowledge and deal with 'here-and-now' factors as they occur in the relationship. The counsellor or therapist must not ignore or avoid the client's anger or fear, sadness or indifference. The relationship and what goes on within it form the subject of interest. This is the medium in which the client or patient changes.

Over recent years, empathy has perhaps received the most attention out of these virtues. As we noted at the beginning of this book, talk of empathy crops up in all kinds of places: in discussions about our evolutionary origins, how the brain grows and develops, how we know other minds, how trust is achieved, what makes us good or bad, and how we communicate our creative insights. But of all enthusiasts, perhaps counsellors and psychotherapists have remained the most keen, the most committed to the potency of empathy (for example, Worsley 2009). Reik (1964: 144) talks of therapists listening 'with the third ear' as 'one mind speaks to another beyond words and in silence'.

The importance, indeed the effectiveness, of the relationship and empathy in the practices of all the helping professions has received much philosophical as well as empirical support over recent years (for example, Bohart *et al.* 2002). There are now a number of meta-analytic reviews of the research evidence that confirm the relationship as a key component of therapeutic effectiveness, independent of the specific type of treatment (Norcross 2002). And in their powerful review of therapeutic changes that work and of which factors have been shown empirically to be effective and beneficial, Castonguay and Beutler (2006) examined three key variables: the relationship, treatment techniques and participant characteristics. They report that the quality of the therapist's relationship with his or her client was critical in predicting therapeutic outcomes.

Specifically, the researchers found that therapy is likely to be beneficial if a *strong working alliance* is established and maintained during the course of treatment. Therapists who work *collaboratively* with clients do well. The interpersonal skills of the therapist were also found to predict higher rates of positive change. Supporting earlier findings, the three principles most associated with good outcomes in terms of the therapist's interpersonal skills were that therapists should relate to their clients in *an empathic way*; therapists should adopt an attitude of *warmth* and *acceptance*; and therapists should adopt an attitude of *congruence* and *authenticity* (Castonguay and Beutler 2006: 359).

In his spirited review and analysis of psychiatric and psychological treatments, Bentall asserts that 'if psychiatric services are to become more genuinely therapeutic, and if they are to help people rather than merely "manage" their difficulties, it will be necessary to rediscover the art of relating to people with warmth, kindness and empathy' (2009: xvii). As so much of human distress is the result of unhappy relationships, it might be no great surprise that psychological healing is most likely to take place in relationships where there is acceptance, understanding, empathy and kindness. But do clients agree?

Client, patient and consumer studies

It took a while for social scientists to take an interest in people's daily lives and everyday experiences. However, once the value of hearing about 'life as lived' was realized, researchers began to talk to all kinds of people about their experiences of being a factory worker, drug user, criminal, housewife, doctor, nurse, slum dweller. One branch of this research sought the views of those who had been on the receiving end of various services, including the clients and patients of therapeutic services. What was it like to be treated by your doctor? How do you view social workers? What are your experiences of being in counselling?

Asking clients and patients for their views on the counselling and treatment experience has been a focus of research for more than half a century. In study after study, the same findings keep appearing. Patients and clients comment less on the techniques of the particular therapy being employed, and more about the personal qualities of the therapist and the relationship created (Howe 1993). The same holds true for the clients of social workers, the patients of health professionals and the consumers of most personal social services. This does not mean that the techniques being used by practitioners are irrelevant. Rather, what is memorable for patients and clients is the manner in which the technique is delivered.

Thus, one of the interesting aspects to emerge from these studies is the near universal finding that irrespective of the type of help sought – medical, psychological, personal, behavioural, marital – service users place great value on the relationship. Patients of doctors, psychiatrists and psychologists, clients of counsellors, psychotherapists and social workers, all say the same. It is not merely a case of what is done; how it is done is equally important. A good professional or therapeutic relationship predicts positive outcomes independent of the practitioner's theoretical orientation (Bohart *et al.* 2002; Ridley and Udipi 2002).

Warmth and friendliness, honesty and trust, feeling connected and safe, being kind and showing compassion, acceptance and validation, exchange and dialogue, collaboration and partnership – all these are mentioned by 'consumers' as good when they are present in the professional relationship. Before they feel able to engage, most clients simply want to feel safe and comfortable.

One of the most important experiences reported by clients and patients is feeling understood. Only when clients feel that the therapist or counsellor, doctor or clinician is genuinely interested in them and their condition (and not in evaluating them) are they prepared to engage. Counsellors and therapists who ask too many questions in the early stages, or who are over-eager to interpret, are experienced by clients as lacking empathy.

Not until patients feel acknowledged do they commit themselves to the relationship. People seek help when they feel that they are not handling either themselves or their situations effectively. Life, somehow, is not being lived well. Those who then go on to seek support say this of their experience of being helped: first accept me, understand me, and make me feel safe and then, and only then, can we move on. Clients want to collaborate and feel empowered. They want their self-esteem to be raised. They want to feel hope.

Most astute clinicians recognize the importance of these messages. Freud thought about therapy in terms of 'love and work'. Bowlby (1988) talked of establishing a safe haven, to which you can always return, before sailing out into the therapeutic seas – a secure base from which to explore your thoughts and feelings. Shaver *et al.* (2010: 79) believe that when help and care are working properly, they benefit the person being cared for by solving a problem, increasing feelings of safety and security, or bolstering the individual's own coping abilities. Such relationships make clients feel less isolated.

Feeling understood

Clients are most likely to comment favourably on therapists who they feel understand them, and who actively continue wanting to understand them. One of Fitts' research respondents talks of how her therapist

> climbed into my shoes to see how things looked to me ... My reaction to the first session was surprise ... just plain surprise! I was so utterly surprised to find out that someone was really and truly *understanding* what I was trying to say. I always have such difficulty saying what I want to say.
>
> (Fitts 1965: 26–7, emphasis in original)

Mark recalls his experiences of being in psychotherapy:

> The early sessions were characterised by my feelings of discomfort and embarrassment. What I found, however, was a person who was listening to what I was saying and seemed to understand some of the pain I was experiencing. A feeling of space began to emerge in the sessions; a sense that I was an important person in the relationship, and that I had some control over the discussion and the pace of it.
>
> (Woodward 1988: 92)

Most respondents in consumer-based studies value being given 'time and space' to talk, to feel relief, to reflect, to consider, to make connections. Sue felt that she had been rejected as a child by her parents. In adulthood, she suffered addiction problems and poor relationships. Eventually, she sought therapy:

> It was in a sort of office building but once you got in, it was very cosy ... and I walked in and burst into tears and cried for five minutes and then she began asking what the problem was and I came out with loads of stuff like my relationships and then to cope with what was going on, I was an alcoholic and an addict and bulimic ... I felt just so relieved. I cried the whole way through and she was really sweet and understanding. It was the first person who didn't tell me to do anything.
>
> (Edmunds 1992: 59)

And of course, sharing experiences with fellow travellers always promotes strong feelings of empathy, as this mother describes:

> They helped me get over the depression by bringing me together with other mums, who's got other problems, and you realize that you're not the only person in the world with a problem. We used to have small groups for talking about our problems. I think in a way the other mothers are more understanding, because most of the social workers haven't been through a lot of the things that they've been through.
>
> (Phillimore 1981: 22)

In short, clients want to feel understood as well as accepted.

Everyone has won and all must have prizes

As we noted earlier, one of the more curious findings to emerge out of these studies is that so often, at least from the client's point of view, it is not so much the particular therapeutic technique that is felt to make a difference, but the more general qualities of professional helpers and the relationship with which they delivered their technique. This appears to be particularly true of the 'talking cures'. The hypothesis that all schools of counselling and psychotherapy are equally effective has been likened to the Dodo in Lewis Carroll's *Alice's Adventures in Wonderland* (see Smith and Glass 1977; Luborsky *et al.* 2002). The Dodo organized a mad race without a clear start or finish. When Alice asked how would they know who had won, the Dodo replied, 'Everybody has won and all must have prizes.'

Certainly, the more committed therapists are to their brand of treatment, the more effective they appear to be, but it doesn't seem to make too much difference what brand they espouse. This is not to say that some aspects of some techniques associated with particular types of treatment are not predictive of positive change; indeed they are (Castonguay and Beutler 2006). Rather, the way a particular therapist approaches and practises that skill or technique can be as important as the skill or technique itself.

There is the additional finding from meta-analyses of many outcome studies that for any given type of psychotherapy, some therapists consistently outperform others in terms of effectiveness (Wampold 2001), and that this is due mainly to the formation of a strong therapeutic or helping alliance (Dunn and Bentall 2007). Commenting on these analyses, Bentall (2009: 260) notes that the 'extent to which the therapists could relate effectively with the patients, rather than specific psychotherapeutic techniques, seemed to completely explain the positive effects of treatment'.

So the way the psychotherapist, psychiatrist, clinical psychologist, counsellor or social worker does it matters. In other words, it is not so much the technical *specifics* associated with a particular therapeutic school, whether psychoanalytic or Gestalt, strengths based or family systems, person centred or cognitive behavioural, but more the *non-specifics* of the relationship generated by the therapist or helper that makes the difference. These non-specifics might include the extent to which the therapist smiled when appropriate; how much interest she seemed to show in the client; how kind, warm and compassionate he was; how personable was her manner. When these non-specific elements are present in the therapeutic relationship, the quality of life led by clients and patients gradually improves. When they are absent and the therapeutic relationship is judged not to be good, outcomes are poor.

Good relationships, it seems, are a universal therapeutic good, and may yet turn out to be the single most important ingredient of effective psychiatric care.

(Bentall 2009: 260)

Through empathy the therapist participates in the two-person relationship; and empathy is the single most important human and technical tool at the therapist's disposal.

(Strupp 1996: 137)

Although these views might be tempered with the acknowledgement that some techniques, with some problems, do seem to be more effective than others, nevertheless, even in these cases the quality of empathy determines the quality of the relationship, and the quality of the relationship, whatever the technique, is critical to the outcome (Bohart *et al.* 2002, Castonguay and Beutler 2006). Most schools of therapy recognize this. Strong collaborative and empathic bonds have to be established before therapeutic techniques can be delivered.

Taking all these research findings to heart, many researchers go on to argue that instead of selecting aspiring psychotherapists, counsellors, psychiatrists, doctors, nurses or social workers solely on their intellectual merits, their scores on tests that measure empathic accuracy should also be taken into account (Schmid Mast and Ickes 2007: 415; also see Mearns and Thorne 1999: 44–8). If effective help and therapy do require high levels of empathy, it seems only reasonable to assess the empathic accuracy of would-be helping professionals (Greenberg *et al.* 2001).

Conclusion

Counsellors and psychotherapists were among the first professionals to recognize the healing properties of empathy. They lost no time in trying to put empathy firmly into their practice. They were also early advocates of researching the views of those who had been on the receiving end of their services. Over the years, studies exploring client views have confirmed the value and importance of empathy in the therapeutic relationship. Empathy scores on two counts. When present in the therapeutic relationship it is strongly associated with positive treatment outcomes. It also predicts client satisfaction with the therapeutic experience. With these endorsements, little wonder that counsellors and psychotherapists have been keen to unravel and apply empathy's secrets, as we shall see in the next chapter..

10
Empathic Communication and Helping Relationships

Being empathic

Most counsellors who write about empathy attempt a definition of the concept. Carl Rogers, for example, constantly refined his ideas about what he thought empathy was. To be with another and enter their world without prejudice requires counsellors to put aside their own views and values. Rogers saw the empathic counsellor

> entering the private, perceptual world of the other ... being sensitive, moment by moment, to the changing felt meanings which flow in this other person ... sensing meanings of which he or she is scarcely aware ... communicating your sensings of the person's world.
>
> (Rogers 1980: 142)

There is research to suggest that counsellors differ in terms of whether they tend towards empathy that is based on thinking and cognition, or empathy that values affect and feeling, and that these differences reflect underlying personality types (Churchill and Bayne 1998). However, it is generally presumed that the most empathic counsellors and psychotherapists are those who are at ease with empathy being the product of both thought and feeling. They don't get too hung up on whether or not empathy must be seen exclusively as either an experiential state or an intuitive process, recognizing that its presence is most likely to be the result of an open, alert, fluid, attuned and responsive state of mind. Hennessey (2011: 81) says that in such moments of empathy, 'the worker's "inner world" is in contact with the "inner world" of the client ... but this empathic entry into the perceptual life of the other person does not mean losing sight of your own world.' There is a simultaneous awareness of both the thoughts and feelings of the self, and the thoughts and feelings of the other.

Empathy's values and virtues

Elliott *et al.* (2004: 112) claim three functions of empathy in therapy: it promotes a positive working alliance; it helps clients explore, examine and elaborate their experiences and assumptions; and it helps clients contain, manage and regulate their emotions.

Perhaps the most basic function that facilitates the working alliance is empathy's ability to help clients feel safe, supported and heard. The meeting between counsellor and client then becomes a safe place for those whose lives seem threatened, anxious, troubled or uncertain. Clients feel sufficiently secure to admit their vulnerabilities and fears. And once acknowledged, vulnerabilities and fears can be explored and examined. Elliott *et al.* (2004: 119) give the following example of empathy in practice:

> *Therapist*: I see that you're crying. (gently) Can we stay there a minute? (pause) It hurts when you talk about your Dad? It's just so painful to recall those memories.
> *Client*: (crying) Yes.

Mearns and Cooper (2005) self-critically describe a session between Dominic, who had problems with binge drinking, and his counsellor, Dave Mearns, one of the book's authors. Here is part of the session:

> *Dominic 20*: [Long pause] ... [looks directly at Dave] ... I don't know what I am about ...
> *Dave 20*: [Looks *intensely* at Dominic and moves towards him, speaking slowly] That sounds like a lot, 'you ... don't ... know ... what you're ... about ...'
> *Dominic 21*: I'm so full of crap.

Dave 21: ... and ...

Dominic 22: I don't know whether to believe myself or not.

Dave 22: Say more Dom.

Dominic 23: I'm just so full of crap.

Dave 23: You don't know whether to believe yourself or not
...

Dominic 24: I think I'm serious ... sincere. But, *really*, I'm
only a drunk ... a fuckin' drunk.

Dave 24: You think you're serious ... and sincere. But you're
really only, a fuckin' drunk.

Dominic 25: Yes.

Dave 25: A fuckin' drunk – that's all you are.

Dominic 26: [Tears welling up].

(Mearns and Cooper 2005: 80–82, emphasis in original)

Empathy requires that therapists steep themselves in the world
of the client in order to see and understand matters from the
other's point of view; to understand the 'private logic' of the
other (Egan 2010: 13). Empathy requires active listening.
However, in order to listen well, we must first quiet the busy
chatter of our own thoughts and the restlessness of our minds
(Heidegger 1992[1927]; Agosta 2010). Effective practitioners
want to feel and understand the world of the other. This requires
curiosity and effort. Out of these experiential processes
empathic attunement emerges, defined as follows:

> To be truly empathic, the therapist first lets go of or sets aside
> previously formed ideas or formulations about the client.
> Second, the therapist actively enters into and makes contact
> with the client's world. Third, the therapist resonates with the
> client's experience, experiencing it for himself or herself.
> Fourth, the therapist selects what seems most crucial,
> poignant, or touching for the client. And finally, the therapist
> takes hold of this particular aspect of the client's experience
> and expresses it back to the client.
>
> (Elliott *et al.* 2004: 115)

The simplest empathic responses generally take the form of
'You feel ... because', for example 'You feel guilty because you

misled her about your gambling debts.' There is no evaluation, no moral judgement, just a straightforward recognition of a feeling and the possible reasons for it.

Empathic communication involves putting these various understandings into words and checking that the understandings are correct. The empathic process is therefore two-way. 'Empathic listening', says Egan (2010: 138), 'leads to empathic understanding, which leads to empathic responding.' Those who wish to help not only listen but respond:

> They respond by sharing their understanding, checking to make sure that they've got things right, probing for clarity, summarizing the issues being discussed, and helping clients challenge themselves in a variety of ways. Of course, this is not a one-way street. Helpers respond to clients in the give-and-take of the therapeutic dialogue.
>
> (Egan 2010: 162)

All these processes are, in themselves, curative:

> Empathy is a process of co-constructing symbols of experience. Clients' process of symbolizing their experience in awareness promoted by empathic responding to their internal experience appears to us to be a universal core ingredient of the therapeutic process. Being able to name an experience first makes the previously implicit explicit, thereby providing an improved sense of facilitation and comprehension of how one knows what one is experiencing. This in and of itself provides some clarity and relief from earlier confusion.
>
> (Bohart and Greenberg 1997: 5–6)

Of all the helping professions, counsellors have perhaps been the most assiduous in their efforts to understand and practise empathy. And of the many schools of counselling, person-centred and self-psychology practitioners have possibly given empathy the most thought and attention. Heinz Kohut (1990: 82), for example, defined empathy as *vicarious introspection*, enabling the analyst to think and feel himself or herself 'into the inner life of another person'.

Empathy

Empathy is not just a useful way by which we have access to the inner life of man – the idea itself of an inner life of man, and thus of a psychology of complex mental states, is unthinkable without our ability to know vicarious introspection ... what the inner life of man is, what we ourselves and what others think and feel.

(Kohut 1977: 306)

Counsellors, psychotherapists and analysts, such as Kohut, have thus given much thought to empathy's likely makeup. They have tried to understand what it might be like to be on the receiving end of an empathic relationship. And they have developed ways of training people to be more skilled in their use and understanding of empathy in order to enhance and enrich the therapeutic process (Clark 2007: xiii).

The models and makeup of therapeutic empathy

The basic skills shown by empathic counsellors and psychotherapists offer no surprises. Put aside bias and preconception, have an open mind, ask open-ended questions, listen well and listen long, slow down the thoughts and feelings of the self and the other, tune into and pay attention to one's own and the other person's physical feelings and facial expressions, let stories unfold, and share and communicate what is being understood – these are all part of routine empathic practice (Ciaramicoli and Ketcham 2000: 46, 65). Whenever we find ourselves in quieter, safer, gentler and more open places, we can stop and think. Our defences drop and, knowing that we are not alone, we dare to let in those thoughts and feelings that we have resolutely, fearfully and angrily kept outside and beyond our reflective reach. Sometimes just listening well can be enough.

Katz (1963), Lide (1966) and Zanger (1968) have each developed similar models of empathy. The models typically involve a four-stage process: close observation and identification, incorporation, reverberation, before a final detachment and stepping back. In these models, the therapist must experience *what* the client is feeling (identification), feel the client's experiences *as if it* were his own (incorporation), evoke those life experiences of his own that may aid in understanding his client's experiences (reverberation), and engage in objective analysis using methods of reason (detachment).

(Lide 1966: 148, emphasis in original)

Barrett-Lennard (1981) attempted to formulate his own version of these elements to create what he called the Empathy Cycle. Very similar to earlier definitions, his, too, was made up of four steps: the client expresses his or her experience; the therapist feels a resonance with the client's experience; the therapist expresses and communicates the felt empathy and understanding; and the client receives the therapist's empathy so that he or she becomes aware of being understood. The cycle repeats again and again throughout treatment.

According to Clark (2007), and based on Rogers (1964), empathic understanding in counselling and psychotherapy involves three ways of knowing: *subjective*, *interpersonal* and *objective*. In terms of treatment and practice, these types of empathic understanding can loosely be translated as an *experiential* mode, a *communication* mode and an *observational* mode. In his excellent and comprehensive analysis of empathy in counselling and psychotherapy, Clark (2007) develops these multiple perspectives on empathy and its practice in considerable detail. We shall look at each one in turn.

Experiential mode of empathic understanding

Experiential or *subjective* modes of empathy involve the counsellor resonating or feeling with the client's inner experience and sense of self. Rogers (1951) believed that it was essential for the practitioner to grasp the client's 'internal frame of reference' as he or she perceives it. In order to experience and enter the world of the other without distortion, all preconceptions, diagnoses, assumptions and expectations have to be put aside. The experience is that of the other, not that of the counsellor. I recognize and understand your shame even though I do not experience feelings of shame myself, for instance. Rogers therefore defined empathy as being able 'to sense the client's private world as if it were your own, but without ever losing the "as if" quality' (Rogers 1957: 99).

Thus, with more than a hint of the phenomenologist about him, Rogers sees empathy not only as a process but as part of the counsellor's function to assume, 'in so far as he is able, the internal frame of reference of the client, to perceive the world as the client sees it, to perceive the client as he is seen by himself, to lay aside all perceptions from the external frame of reference while doing so' (Rogers 1949: 86).

If the other is to be known and understood as a subject, as the centre of his or her own experience, then the techniques of therapy will get in the way. Too much reliance on theory and technique puts the therapist at the centre instead. Empathy only becomes possible when we drop our preconceptions and enter the other's world.

Therapeutic techniques can objectify the other in what Buber (1958) calls an *I–It* relationship. In this kind of relationship, the counsellor defines the client. The client is cast within the constructs of the therapist's theory, alienated from his or her own being. Clients are denied the chance to define themselves and their own experience. Empathy, in contrast, is a way of understanding the other as the subject of his or her own experience in an *I–Thou* relationship. For Schmid (2003), 'the therapist's Otherness is called forth by the Otherness of the client, and this requires deep, empathic understanding of the very essence of the client's experiencing' (as described in Mearns and Cooper 2005: 39). 'Close your books', said Ciaramicoli's mother when he was being clever and trying to assess his father, 'and open your eyes' (Ciaramicoli and Ketcham 2000: 170).

Spinelli (1989), again influenced by phenomenology, understands how difficult it is ever fully to know another person. The nearest we can get is to put aside – to bracket off – all our ideas, preconceptions and expectations of the other and listen without prejudice. We must not explain or interpret. We have to concentrate on getting a full description, one without distortion or bias. Listening – listening hard and listening well – is fundamental to empathy.

The ability to tune into the other's perspective requires what psychologists call *effortful control*. Part of this involves the ability to inhibit a dominant response and also, if necessary, activate an apparently less pressing but nevertheless appropriate response. Children with high effortful control are good at regulating their arousal. They rarely develop behavioural problems. Therapists who possess high levels of effortful control are good at cognitively empathizing with their clients, and equally good at not getting caught up by the feelings of the other. It is no good picking up the other's pain if it only leads to your own distress. Therapists who become emotionally dysregulated are no longer available to recognize and regulate the emotions of their clients. Thompson and Thompson (2008) quote Rhian's recollections when she first began working as a counsellor at a GP surgery:

> When I first became a counsellor I found it very difficult indeed. I felt for every client and started to take on board the pain and confusion they were expressing to me. Steadily I could feel myself becoming overloaded with all the emotion. When I raised the issue with my supervisor she was very helpful and reminded me of the importance of empathy not sympathy. She made me realize that I had allowed myself to slip into a sympathetic way of working rather than an empathetic way. It was a tough job making the transition, but I recognized that I had to – I couldn't go on the way I was; it would have done me a lot of harm and would also have meant that I was less help to my clients.
>
> (Thompson and Thompson 2008: 41)

Understanding the other person from within the frame of reference of his or her own experience is extraordinarily difficult. It is demanding, both cognitively and emotionally. But to the extent that it provides a feel and a glimpse of the other's world, it generates a powerful experience for both parties. Nevertheless, empathy remains an aspiration and a thrilling possibility:

We can never know precisely what another person is thinking
and feeling ... Our guesses come from our experience and,
since no two people ever have exactly the same experience,
no two people ever see anything in exactly the same way.
Thus we each live in our own individual world of meaning.
Empathy is always a leap of the imagination.

(Rowe 2011)

Not until the inner world of the other is grasped can it be
communicated. Not until it is communicated can the client feel
understood. And feeling understood by the other represents a
moment of relief, a time of connection. Empathy therefore
represents a way of being with the client. Every nuance of the
other's body language, tone of voice and spoken word is
observed and therefore felt. The experience is visceral. The
empathic counsellor senses that these resonant experiences are
telling him or her something important about the other's
thoughts, feelings, beliefs and defences. In this case, we meet
Penny who is a psychotherapist working with Taz:

Penny felt her body tighten and tense, and her heart rate
increase as she watched and listened to her client, Taz, growing angrier by the second as he complained about the court's
decision that he could only see his daughter once a fortnight.
Although Taz could be quite likable, he could be scary when
he got angry. But Penny sensed that her tension and firming
of the lips was more to do with the pain and helplessness that
lay behind Taz's rage rather than the rage itself. He'd lost
most things that he valued in his life – his partner, his daughter, his flat – admittedly through his own lack of patience and
thought, but Taz was hurting and Penny knew this as she
looked with some intensity into his eyes.

Dekeyser *et al.* (2011) also suggest that although psychotherapy
is essentially a cooperative, two-way conversational process, at
the same time it is felt in the body. They describe this in terms
of Cooper's (2001) concept of embodied empathy and give the
following example:

Nick was an unemployed chef who came to therapy to deal with depression brought on by losing his job. In session three, he described what his work was like for him at its best and what he missed about it. As the therapist listened, he let himself be carried away into the client's experience: he felt a tickling, tingling sensation in his stomach; he remembered the feeling of his own similar successes (rising sense of excitement, accompanied by a sense of feet firmly planted on the ground); he 'ran a movie in his head' of the client striding out of the kitchen, head held high, accompanied by a sense of pride and happiness. He noted how his fantasy matched Nick's upright posture and firm position in the chair, and how he shifted into a firmer position himself. During his description, Nick felt that his therapist was interested and – even though the therapist had not said anything – he experienced support and an invitation to dig deeper into his description.

(Dekeyser *et al.* 2011: 113–14)

Mearns and Cooper (2005) refine much of the thinking and practice described in this section in what they refer to as 'working at relational depth' in counselling and psychotherapy. This captures the full beauty and potential of the relationship in therapeutic practice. They define relational depth as follows:

A state of profound contact and engagement between two people, in which each person is fully real with the Other, and able to understand and value the Other's experiences at a high level.

(Mearns and Cooper 2005: xii)

A feeling of profound contact and engagement with a client, in which one simultaneously experiences high and consistent levels of empathy and acceptance towards the Other, and relates to them in a highly transparent way. In this relationship, the client is experienced as acknowledging one's empathy, acceptance and congruence – either implicitly or explicitly – and is experienced as fully congruent at that moment.

(Mearns and Cooper 2005: 36)

Communication mode of empathic understanding

When counsellors take an *interpersonal* perspective, they strive to ensure that their experiential understandings are also *communicated* to clients, so that clients can be 'felt with', can feel recognized and be understood. Sometimes, perhaps more often than not, the communication need not take the form of words. In the example above, Penny did not say anything to Taz, at least straight away. The look on her face, the concentration in her eyes, the forward posture of her body said it all. Spoken too soon, words might have destroyed the connection. The accurate communication of empathy, of the experience as felt, is critical if the client is to feel recognized and understood. 'Thank God, somebody heard me. Someone knows what it's like to be me' is how Rogers (1958: 16) described being on the receiving end of an empathic response. In the experience of being understood, we can find ourselves in a calmer place in which it feels safe to reflect, ponder and think about feelings.

In the hands of an unskilled practitioner there is the constant danger of merely parroting what the client has just said in the belief that to echo is to empathize, to reflect is to reassure. Many counsellors have quite rightly been mocked for this habit. 'I feel really anxious about joining the group. I get knots in the stomach thinking about it,' said Rosa. 'You feel really anxious and get knots in your stomach,' responded George, her therapist. If said too often and too mechanically, this form of response is unlikely to be either empathic or helpful. It could even be quite annoying.

The belief that the technique of repeating what the client has just said, sometimes described as reflection, is empathic and a communication skill is therefore unlikely to hold true. It even led to a despairing cry by Rogers (1980: 139) that the misuse of reflection had 'led to appalling consequences and complete distortion of client-centered therapy'. He saw the overuse of reflection as mechanical and dehumanizing. Nearer the empathic mark is the following exchange between Terry and his client, Steve.

Steve: Hell, I'm scared what the doctor will say when he gives me my test results. What if, you know …

Terry: If it is cancer.

Steve: Yeh. Yeh.

Terry: Well, that would be a shock, I know. It must be worrying. I can see it's really worrying you.

Steve: It keeps going through my head.

Terry: It must be hard to think of anything else at the moment.

Steve: True. True. But when I take a deep breath [Steve takes a deep breath] and try to think it through, a step at a time, then you know …

Terry: [also breathes in deeply, nodding] OK, OK. Yeh. It slows things down, gives you space to think and get your head around it.

Steve: And then I can get it a bit more in perspective, get a bit more of a handle on it. So then, if the worst does happen, then I guess I know [takes another deep breath] I'll just have to face up to it, get on with it … but it's still scary! [said with a resigned smile].

Observational mode of empathic understanding

The *observational* or *objective* mode of empathizing seems to be the most instrumental and cognitive, and therefore the most distant from empathy's original conception. Empathy here becomes a method of observation and a way of collecting diagnostic data.

In the observational mode, the counsellor's empathy helps him or her understand something of the client's ways of thinking, feeling and being. This understanding gives the counsellor information that helps inform the diagnosis and clarify any theoretical model of the client's psychological functioning that the practitioner is hypothesizing might be helpful. The ideas emerging from this process assist the practitioner with interpreting the client's thoughts and feelings. These interpretations can be shared with the client.

Some psychoanalysts believe, with some force, that a practitioner who openly tries to make sense of the patient in partnership with that patient actually strengthens the therapeutic bond and so deepens empathic understanding (Hill 2004). In this sense, strong therapeutic alliances support interpretation, and interpretation strengthens empathy.

> It was Kohut's belief that the extent of a therapist's theoretical knowledge of psychological dynamics is directly related to the accuracy of employed interpretations. In turn, more accurate or deeply accurate interpretations provide 'proof' to the patient that the practitioner empathically understands his or her experiencing from a broader perspective.
>
> (Clark 2007: 144)

Coupled with wider knowledge of the client's life, the practitioner's use of observational empathy helps him or her to build a working model of the other that deepens conceptual and empathic understanding. 'This tentative patient or client model evolves over a period of time and serves as a functional guide for treatment directions' (Clark 2007: 11).

A counsellor, for example, might recognize that a client's low self-esteem leads to self-effacing but ultimately self-defeating behaviours with strong underlying feelings of anger and resentment. Or in the case of cognitive behavioural therapy, empathy helps the practitioner step into the patient's world. This exploration might assist the clinician in recognizing more clearly the patient's cognitive distortions. This understanding allows the clinician to challenge the distortions and negativity more effectively. It also points towards more adaptive ways of thinking and behaving.

Similarly, a solution-focused practitioner might respond empathically, saying 'You feel disappointed with yourself that you drank quite heavily yesterday', quickly followed by 'But remember, earlier this week you didn't have a drink on either Monday or Tuesday, which I think is pretty impressive. Let's see what you did on those days that helped you not to have a drink.'

Pulling his thoughts together on therapeutic interventions and empathic understanding, Clark (2007) offers the following examples in which it is clear that *thinking with* rather than *thinking for* the client is the preferred response:

A client states, 'I have so many things that I'm mixed up about. I can't even begin to get at it all.' In response, a therapist conveys a minimal level of empathic understanding, 'What you need to do is to draw up a list of things that are bothering you and address each item in terms of priorities.' In another response that manifests a more optimal level of empathic understanding by validating the client's experience, the practitioner relates, 'It seems that there is so much that is troubling you, and even thinking about where to begin seems overwhelming.'

(Clark 2007: 77)

Goal-corrected empathic attunement, mentalization and feeling safe

In her studies of effective helping and therapeutic work, McCluskey (2005) has developed an interesting mix of empathy and attachment theory. She describes the process of effective interaction as *goal-corrected empathic attunement*. According to attachment theory, vulnerable infants display *careseeking* behaviours directed at *caregivers* whenever they feel distressed, confused and upset. Similarly, adults who are in a state of upset, need or confusion are likely to seek support, help and comfort from others who are perceived as 'stronger and wiser'. Clients want to be understood, recognized and regulated. The adults who might provide such support and guidance might also be described as caregivers. At the time of referral, therefore, clients behave as careseekers, and therapists and counsellors occupy the role of caregiver.

Although they are seeking comfort and understanding, most clients will bring their defensive strategies with them and continue using them, at least until they feel a degree of safety. These strategies will have served them well, at least in trying to survive difficult, hurtful relationships. The strategies only become dysfunctional when they are employed in other, everyday relationships – with friends, teachers, employers, romantic partners, therapists.

Helping clients to let go of established, but typically dysfunctional, strategies and yet feel safe is one of the key goals of the early therapeutic relationship. If clients don't feel safe, their careseeking systems and the defensive strategies that have developed will remain active. Clients might continue to be aggressive, subdued, distant, dismissive or disorganized.

In the first instance, the emotionally aroused state of the careseeker (child or client) needs to be regulated. When the child or client is feeling regulated and contained, they can then turn their mental energies to exploration. In the case of young children, exploration loosely equates with play and constructive social interaction. In the case of adults, including patients and clients, exploration might involve reflecting on a worry, thinking about a relationship, or analysing a piece of dysfunctional behaviour. However, exploration and reflection are only possible when the initial goal of careseeking behaviour is met; that is, emotions are regulated and distress acknowledged and contained.

Rennie (1998) reminds us that clients are often most anxious and uncertain before they finally commit themselves to being helped. Empathic responses are therefore particularly important at the outset. He offers the following example of what a counsellor might say to a hesitant client:

> I'm sensing that it's a little difficult for you to be here, now that you've actually arrived. It could be that you don't know what to say, or that you don't feel safe in saying anything. I can understand how it must be difficult, coming to a stranger like this.
>
> (Rennie 1998: 112)

When a caregiver successfully attunes to and connects with the state of mind of their client, the client's careseeking system temporarily switches off. When the careseeking system is 'off', feelings of relief appear, immediate feelings of anxiety reduce and the exploratory system becomes activated. When the exploratory system is activated, clients think with less distortion and reflect with more honesty. So just as babies who feel secure are able to devote their mental energies to play, exploration and interaction, so clients who feel secure feel safe enough to explore – their thoughts, feelings, behaviour, relationships, past, present and future. Thus, the aim of empathic attunement is always to support and facilitate the client's exploratory system (McCluskey 2005).

Similar thinking forms the basis of Liotti and Gilbert's (2011) paper on what facilitates a therapeutic relationship. When individuals experience anxiety, threat and stress, their ability to think, reflect and mentalize cuts out. Under conditions of perceived anxiety and threat, the older evolutionary fear system switches on. In turn, this triggers activation of the attachment system leading to fight, flight and freeze behaviours. These defensive reactions inhibit higher-order cognitive processes. Stopping to ponder and think is too slow, too risky. Fast, quick-acting, non-reflective fight or flight behaviours in the face of immediate dangers are the most adaptive – better safe than sorry.

> In contrast, *feeling safe* because of the protective availability of an attachment figure, who is perceived as capable of protecting against the danger and signals low threat, may foster mentalization. These considerations suggest that attachment *per se* is not the only evolutionary underpinning of mentalization: rather, attachment processes may allow for the recovery of mentalization, in the presence of danger, through the contact with the attachment figure that is able to provide help and guidance and activates a renewed *sense of safeness and soothing.*
>
> (Liotti and Gilbert 2011: 10, emphasis in original)

In this sense, counsellors and psychotherapist, health professionals and social workers can act as transitional attachment figures (Crittenden 2008). The therapeutic relationship then offers the prospect of a safe place from which clients might recover the ability to mentalize, reflect and explore.

> Indeed, psychotherapy is often regarded as a way of exploring one's thoughts, feelings, motivations, and memories in the dialogue with an empathic interlocutor ... The safeness created by the therapists' empathy, and ability to understand and repair ruptures can enable openness of attention and

explorative behaviour in patients, allowing for optimal exercise of their mentalization abilities both in regard to their own
and other's minds.

(Liotti and Gilbert 2011: 13)

However, it must be remembered that many clients, particularly
those who have suffered hurt and rejection in their early lives,
might not trust the safety of a relationship with anyone who feels
like an attachment figure, including counsellors and psychotherapists. All their experiences of close, caregiving-type relationships are that they are unpredictable, unreliable and perhaps
even dangerous. Conflicting feelings are evoked of wanting to
get close, be loved and be protected *and at the same time* fearing
intimacy and feeling vulnerable and in danger. The simultaneous triggering of approach and avoidance, attachment and
defence behaviours in the psychotherapeutic relationship can
provoke powerful feelings of conflict and stress (Prunetti *et al.*
2008). Clients who suffer such conflict are likely to approach
counselling in a very wary, defensive state of mind.

In these difficult cases, therapists have to exercise considerable patience. Their empathy has to be calibrated. They are
likely to suffer many attacks and rebuffs before clients can
begin, very gradually, to build feelings of safety and trust. Thus,
there is the irony that for some clients 'the re-creation of safe-
ness in the therapeutic relationship can reactivate attachment,
which in turn reactivates complex of memories [sic] that may
stimulate a fear of dependency, vulnerability ... or the expectation of being harmed by any potential caregiver ... As one
patient said, "I don't like to feel safe (or cared for) because then
I let my guard down – that's dangerous"' (Liotti and Gilbert
2011: 20). When working with clients who react in these ways,
empathic counsellors might have to tone down their caregiving
behaviour, at least for the time being, in order for clients to
recover feelings of safety and control.

Once the client feels safe, many practitioner behaviours
might facilitate his or her willingness and ability to explore
(McCluskey 2005: 141). A look of interest and concentration
might do. Facing the client squarely, adopting an open posture,
maintaining eye contact and actively listening all convey

concentration and interest (Egan 2010: 134). Simply leaning forward into the client's space can suggest wanting to be 'in there' to see and feel what is happening. Feelings might be named and explored. Eye contact at key moments can give a strong message of concern and wanting to understand. Matching one's own body movements to those of the client sets up synchrony. Responding with energy and vitality when the client appears to be saying something interesting and important creates attunement.

Staying in touch

The effective counsellor is therefore one who remains present, involved, engrossed and connected with the other person. Those who are anxious and in need seek help from people who are emotionally available, responsive, attuned and anxiety free.

When the counsellor reacts defensively, with anxiety or irritation, their caregiving capacities switch off. These losses of goal-corrected empathic attunement might be fleeting or prolonged. They might be a characteristic of a counsellor across most cases or just a reaction to some clients, some times.

'I have noticed', writes McCluskey (2005: 10), 'that as clients bring in what they consider to be affectively significant material they often tend to glance at the face of the inter-viewer, then look away.' They are looking for affective information and reassurance from the counsellor or psychotherapist that it will be safe to proceed, safe to say more, safe to reflect and explore. When clients feel safe, understood and contained, they often become more lively and involved. Egan (2010: 169) gives a nice, although ordinary enough, example of empathy in action. A student enters the counsellor's room with his shoulders hunched, his eyes cast down and his speech rather halting:

> *Client*: I don't even know where to start. [He falls silent]
> *Helper*: It's pretty clear that you're feeling miserable. Maybe we can talk about why.
> *Client*: [after a pause]. Well, let me tell you what happened ...

In cases in which the client fails to express a relevant emotion, empathic helpers often react with the emotion that they feel is not being fully displayed. A counsellor might react with a strong look of surprise or sadness. A therapist catches an underlying emotion, say of anxiety or fear, and brings it to the surface (McCluskey 2005: 27). In these cases, the practitioner is not actually responding with the same level of emotional intensity as that shown by the client, but is tuning into an emotional expression that the client is defensively unable to express, or even experience.

Professionals of whatever discipline have to retain their curiosity and interest. This is demanding work. It takes effort. It is not easy to see the other without theoretical distortion or moral bias, to apprehend the other just as he or she is. The phenomenological stand that requires the practitioner to 'bracket off' all assumptions and preconceptions about the client takes a lot of skill, but when clients feel that the professional is really trying to understand them and their world as they are living and experiencing it, then deep connections are made. There is engagement. Work can begin.

Conclusion

Counsellors and psychotherapists have long recognized the value and importance of empathy in their practice and its role as a key constituent of the helping alliance. Having acknowledged empathy's importance, counsellors and psychotherapists, probably more than any other profession, have examined it, deconstructed it, operationalized it, practised it and evaluated it. Empathy's presence helps client feel safe – safe enough to explore and examine difficult feelings and painful memories. For help and support to be successful, empathy has to remain an ever-present companion along the therapeutic road. However, if those in the helping professions are to maintain an empathic stance and uphold a therapeutic alliance, they, too, must feel understood and supported. Like their clients, they must also feel safe enough to go exploring the rough terrains and troubled waters of other people's minds.

We have therefore found good evidence that empathy works. But *why* does it work? To find answers, we need to weave together many of the insights so far gathered, including how we develop the capacity to be empathic in the first place.

11
Why Empathy Works

Forming and reforming psychological selves

This book has been making the case that empathic practitioners, whether clinical psychologists or counsellors, psychotherapists or social workers, are valued and appreciated by their clients and patients. Studies also suggest that for any given theoretical technique, the more empathic the practitioner, the more effective their treatments and interventions. Why might this be so? What is it about empathy that does not merely facilitate the conduct of successful relationships but also helps bring about personal change?

This chapter attempts to answer these questions by bringing together many of the ideas discussed in earlier chapters, which looked at the growth and development of empathy in children, and the evolutionary benefits of a being a mind-reading, empathizing, very sociable species.

In the early years, significant others provide children with empathic relationships in which they feel recognized, loved and understood. Out of these relationships children's *psychological selves form*. To the extent that empathy is present in therapeutic relationships, and to the extent that clients feel recognized and understood, loved and regulated, they, too, have the opportunity for their *psychological selves to (re)form*. The rest of this chapter fleshes out this claim.

Feeling understood

Being understood by someone else brings people closer together. And as there is a desire in most of us to feel understood, we seek relationships that offer the prospect of being close. Feeling understood also provides feelings of relief and relaxation (van Kaam 1959). Johnson (1971: 24) picks up this theme and argues that 'Empathy is a way to understand. The process of being understood does heal.' Rogers (1986: 129), too, concluded: 'To my mind, empathy is in itself a healing agent. It is one of the most potent aspects of therapy, because it releases, it confirms, it brings even the most frightened client into the human race.'

Relationships and regulation

At times when our emotions are running high or our mind is in a muddle, we seek out other people. The need to connect, communicate and be understood when life gets difficult seems universal. This begins in childhood. Young children are not able to regulate their thoughts, feelings or bodies on their own. Doing so is only possible in the context of a caregiving relationship. The value of close relationships at times of need continues throughout our lives. Because empathy allows us to pick up and react quickly to other people's emotional states, it is essential to the smooth running and regulation of social relationships (de Waal 2010). Indeed, the 'importance of the matrix of empathy in which we grow up cannot be overestimated' (Kohut 1977: 66).

Many psychotherapists and counsellors whose roots lie in the developmentally based sciences are clear that effective help can only be understood in terms of how parent–child interactions lay down the psycho-neurological mechanisms that help us to understand others, and to be helped when others understand us. High empathizers tend to be good regulators of their own and other people's thoughts and feelings. People prone to respond with intensity and distress to other people's feelings are not good at regulating either their own or other people's emotional arousal.

As we saw in the previous chapter, McCluskey (2005) is particularly interesting, as she explores how distress activates the *careseeking* systems of infants. In response to their 'dysregu-lated' babies, the *caregiving* systems of sensitive and empathi-cally attuned parents become activated. Mothers and fathers act as external regulators of their infant's feelings, physiology and behaviour. Children use their parents' 'state of mind' to help them organize their own thoughts, feelings and mental processes (Siegel 1999: 121). For this to be successful, babies need caregivers who are emotionally attuned, psychologically available and empathic. Experiences in these early years create templates that we continue to use throughout life whenever we feel distressed or needy. In effect, as we have already discussed, counsellors and therapists are being cast in the role of caregivers when faced with the careseeking behaviours of distressed clients.

Dismantling defences with empathy

Many clients experienced relationship problems with their parents during childhood. They bring to the therapeutic relationship the defensive distortions and adaptive strategies that helped them survive these difficult childhood experiences. So although distress activates clients' careseeking systems, their experiences of caregivers is that they can't always be trusted, they might hurt you, deceive you or abandon you. Clients and counsellors alike bring these 'internal working models of the experience of relationships' with them as they engage in the helping relationship (Heard and Lake 1997).

The empathic counsellor or therapist, doctor or social worker therefore has to understand that clients' adaptive strategies will come into play every time their careseeking systems become active and whenever clients meet people who occupy the role of caregiver.

> When clients come to therapy, they carry the unconscious expectation that they will be treated as they have been treated before. One of the therapist's most essential acts is to thwart these negative expectations with kindness, empathy, and patience. Kindness pulls the rug from under the defenses we have learned to use to protect ourselves from feelings of rejection and abandonment. Put another way, compassion, warmth, and love have the power to change our brain.
>
> (Cozolino 2006: 315)

Empathic practitioners appreciate all of this. They proceed slowly and with care. They back off when they sense that emotional closeness is being experienced as intrusive and frightening. They express emotion and give voice to feelings when they lie hidden or confused in the mind of the client. They contain arousal. They regulate distress. And if they are particularly aware, empathic counsellors will know that their own defences and adaptive strategies will be triggered during the stresses and strains of the therapeutic encounter.

Even good-enough parents get things wrong when they interact with their young children. They sometimes ignore or misunderstand them. They might get cross or behave unfairly. These 'mis-attunements' leave the child in a state of unregulated arousal. However, one of the key characteristics of secure parents is their ability to recognize and repair these disruptions in the otherwise attuned, empathic relationship. The *repair* often involves recognition and acknowledgement of the parent's mis-attuned behaviour with some discussion of why it happened ('Mummy was annoyed with herself because she burnt the toast and got cross with you as well, which wasn't fair, was it?'). Children can learn as much from the way parents acknowledge, explain and deal with these disruptions in which there are breakdowns in communication and losses of empathic attunement as they can from smooth-running, well-regulated interactions.

And so it is with therapists and clients. Therapists and counsellors will get things wrong. Attunement and understanding get lost. There is constant rupture followed by repair. It is the practitioner's manner of dealing with these disruptions that can be as important as displays of high empathy. Relationship repair can be as effective as relationship flow.

The formation and reformation of the social self

We return to the developmental sciences for the best clues to why empathy continues to be so important in the successful conduct of human relationships. Whether it is with family or friends, therapists or counsellors, at times of anxiety and agitation we need to connect with others. The basic thesis is that because our psychological selves formed in the context of close relationships, it is to close relationships that we return when we need to feel understood, regulated and reformed. Individual selves emerge out of the social matrix. The self does not precede the other; rather, the world of others precedes the self (cf. Mead 1934; Scheler 1954).

Infants' sense of self and psychological coherence develop as they interact with others who relate to them as burgeoning, autonomous new beings. As we have seen, babies' brains are programmed to make sense of experience. Thus, if one of the key experiences to which babies are exposed is *being made sense of* by empathic others, *the sense of being made sense of* actually brings about the independent psychological self. If other people interact with you as if you have a mind, the experience of being treated as mindful helps the brain organize itself into a mindful state, a mind with its own thoughts, feelings, beliefs and intentions. In such ways the 'social outside' helps constitute the 'mental inside'.

To be understood is to learn to understand. Without close relationships, minds do not form. And because the brain is plastic throughout life, capable of making new connections and networks, meaningful close relationships continue to have the potential to change brains and change selves.

These developmental processes and outcomes are particularly successful when close relationships feel safe, supporting and empathic. Close relationships that do not feel safe and lack empathy distort and disfigure the self that forms. Children who have suffered abuse, neglect and rejection often do not feel safe, recognized or understood in close relationships. As a result, their sense of self lacks a degree of coherence and completeness. The longing to feel safe and be understood are still there, but the defences that have built up to keep hurt and danger at bay mean that is harder for others to get close. This poses particular challenges for friends, lovers and therapists alike. The relationship is still the place where positive changes will happen, but it will take much longer to establish feelings of safety and trust.

Talking cures

For a relationship to exist, information between the relating parties has to be exchanged, whether verbally or non-verbally.

Language, including body language, carries information as individuals communicate. Language is the medium in which our thoughts, actions and interactions gain their meaning. Language therefore creates the possibility of a subjective, reflecting, meaningful self. And as our psychological selves form in the context of close relationships, they emerge out of the flow of language and the exchange of meaning.

It is in the use of language that we continue to maintain, make sense of and redefine experience. Our sense of self and the meanings we give our experience can therefore change as we relate, debate and change our language. If we allow it, and feel sufficiently safe, we can immerse ourselves in an evolving discourse in which our thoughts, feelings and beliefs form and reform.

So it is, then, that as our selves form in the world of others, it is to that world that we must return to change. The social formation of the self in childhood explains how we continue to be able to connect and communicate with others; why we seek out empathically based relationships at times of need, distress and dysregulation; and why such relationships and what takes place in them continue to have the power to change us, ontologically, psychologically, emotionally and neurologically. Making sense is a shared, dynamic, reflexive business.

Our capacity to change when we meet an empathic other recognizes that the social comes before the individual, and meaning before being. 'Our like-mindedness and capacity for mutual understanding are therefore secured by the public character of linguistic meaning' (Cupitt 1990: 161). Relationships in which it feels safe to talk – to describe and narrate – hold the possibility of rethinking, refeeling, redefining and reforming the self.

Empathic attunement offers people a powerful opportunity to describe their experience. Description gives experience shape and form. And so description can be seen as a creative process. This is how the cultural and literary theorist Raymond Williams writes about it:

> It is, in the first instance, to every man, a matter of urgent personal importance to 'describe' his experience, because this

is literally a remaking of himself, a creative change in his personal organization, to include and control his experience. This struggle to remake ourselves – to change our personal organization so that we may live in a proper relation to our environment is in fact often painful ... the impulse to communicate is a learned human response to disturbance of any kind. For the individual, of course, the struggle is to communicate successfully by describing adequately ... For unless the description is adequate, there can be no relevant communication ... Genuine communication depends on this absorbed attention to precise description.

(Williams 1965: 42–3)

We therefore communicate, in part, to make sense of both ourselves and others. To the extent that empathy facilitates description and its communication, it plays a key role in the creation and maintenance of the psychosocial self. If language is the medium in which individual selves form, clients who wish to reform their psychological selves have to immerse themselves in talk. This is what clients do in therapy. They talk and tell their story. Talking cures.

Moira agrees. Now in her 40s, in her early 20s she had reluctantly placed her baby for adoption. Talking to no one, she had lived with the grief and pain of the loss in silence. Eventually, she sought specialist counselling:

For the first time in twenty years I talked freely which I found a great relief. Talking to the counsellor made me remember things that I hadn't thought about for a long time. I think I had pushed them to the back of my mind. It was upsetting at the time but I had felt as though a great weight was lifted from me, and the guilt I suffered for years did not seem so bad.

(Howe 1989: 22)

Controlling the meaning of one's own experience

Individuals who feel that their experiences lack meaning and that their lives are not under their control are at risk of poor mental health and existential distress. Practitioners who help people find meaning and recover control do so by way of relationships that are thoughtful and empathic.

The empathic relationship helps clients to make sense of, and gain *control* of, the meaning of their own experience and the meaning that others give to that experience. In his book on person-centred counselling, Rennie (1998) argues in similar vein: 'I have addressed the importance of understanding and helping clients to understand the meaning of their experience,' he writes. 'This is empathy and empathic responding' (Rennie 1998: 73).

The depressed woman laid low with feelings of shame, guilt and low self-esteem might come to recognize that she is blameless for the sexual abuse she suffered as a girl. As she slowly begins to understand what happened to her, who was really to blame and how the trauma has distorted her life, she gradually learns to take control of her own feelings. Control helps us all to cope and feel less stressed. It reduces the need to build defences. Feeling in control empowers and raises self-esteem. We are then returned, strengthened, to the sustaining power of the community of others.

Some of these therapeutic successes are captured by Edmunds in her interviews with men and women, some of whom felt trapped in difficult and violent relationships, some of whom had problems of addiction. In their interviews, they reflected on their positive experiences of being in counselling. John, for example, had suffered a harsh childhood. Like his parents, he too became an alcoholic:

> as I went through the process I understood how ineffective my mother had been and why she was like that because her childhood was lousy and so I realized that to blame her was not the issue. So the process allowed me to let go of the anger that I experienced about my mother and the damage that she did unwittingly. I can't change what happened but I can change me and how I perceive it.
>
> (Edmunds 1992: 27)

As a child, Pamela had been physically abused by her mother and sexually abused by a friend of the family. Counselling helped her to make sense of the experience. This increased her confidence and allowed her to feel that she was regaining control of her life:

> Everything my mother did to me as a child I also did to my children. I took on her mannerisms, her make-up and her way of doing things ... So, when I was fifteen when she died at the age of forty-one, my age now, I didn't connect the two. So when I was forty-one I knew this was the time to go, but I didn't connect it ... [but] at the end of that session I felt ten feet tall. Absolutely brilliant because I knew then that my life was going to change and take on a new meaning ... I knew I was going to get answers and those answers were going to be good enough to help me understand ... I can change myself. I can't change others ... and it's working.
>
> (Edmunds 1992: 63)

Relationships and the plastic brain

It therefore appears that empathy, perhaps along with other virtues such as love, warmth and kindness, creates a relationship in which thoughts and feelings can be recognized and regulated. It is in such environments that clients feel safe, safe enough to think and change.

Hyperaroused and overstressed brains find it difficult to process information, learn and reorganize their neural circuitry. When brains are in low-stressed states – or rather, optimally stressed states – they are able to process information, make sense of experience, consider choices and learn new and better ways of dealing with the world. Relationships that nurture are ones in which brains can begin to change (Siegel 2007; Szalavitz and Perry 2011). There is exciting evidence that high-quality therapeutic relationships allow new neural connections to be made.

> *Empathic attunement* with the therapist provides the context of nurturance in which growth and development occur. By activating processes involved in attachment and bonding, as well as moderating stress in therapy, empathic attunement

may create an optimal biochemical environment for enhancing neural plasticity.

(Cozolino 2002: 62, emphasis in original)

Empathic relationships help clients to tolerate and regulate arousal and affect. Emotional regulation is key to successful therapy. Under conditions of increased safety and lowered stress, brains and their neural circuits can connect and grow. Empathy allows brains and their owners to develop richer, better-connected and more integrated neural networks and processing circuits. When brains are able to process information without distortion, cognitive flexibility rises, reflections improve, behavioural options increase and responses become more creative. This is a definition of mentalization (see Chapter 3) in which brains are firing on all cylinders. It is also a definition of sound mental health.

Conclusion

Our young psychological selves form in the context of relationships in which others recognize and communicate with our own burgeoning psychological being. The parents' capacity to observe and enjoy their child's developing mind helps bring about the child's mind. It also achieves the wonderful trick of children getting to know and understand their own self by getting to know and understand others. Empathy plays a key role in psychological development and the formation of the mind-sighted, mind-reading, mindful self.

Throughout life, when minds feel troubled, hurt and fragmented, empathic relationships retain the power to soothe, heal and mend. Empathy works because in part it is how we came into psychological being in the first place, and it is how we nurture and sustain our psychological health throughout life. Counselling and psychotherapy offer refined and focused versions of the empathic relationship. They help clients recover their equilibrium so that they can return to the community of others. As their own empathy skills increase, clients become more socially relaxed and emotionally regulated.

Psychologists have observed that people who are able to tune into the thoughts and feelings of others are more inclined to act cooperatively and more selflessly. As we shall see in the next chapter, psychologists describe such behaviours as 'pro-social'. Philosophers, too, have recognized that moral behaviour also depends on people's ability to tune into and be affected by the thoughts and feelings of other people. It is now time to expand our horizons and look at the relationship between empathy, morals and pro-social behaviours.

12
Empathy, Morals and Pro-social Behaviour

Living well together

Moral principles underpin much of what makes for a good society. Moral concerns generally involve notions of fairness, reciprocity, respect, care, compassion and avoidance of causing harm. By sponsoring shared living, these virtues also support survival and success. Churchland (2011: 9) sees morality providing a framework for effective social behaviour. Its origins are complex and lie in a range of human needs and practices including *caring* (rooted in attachment to kith and kin and care for their well-being), *recognition of others' psychological states* (rooted in the benefits of predicting the behaviour of others) and *problem-solving in a social context* (matters of how we should distribute scarce goods, settle land disputes and punish miscreants).

It is in our efforts to live well among others that behaviours arise that we describe as moral. A successful social life requires moral codes and values, otherwise living well together is difficult. The inevitable conflict between self-interest, desires and the welfare of others therefore has to be negotiated if social life is to be made possible and social problems solved.

Discussion about morals has to acknowledge the possibility of tensions arising between reason and emotion. Reason may tell us what is going on and what might be done, but it is emotion that drives us to act. Passion tells us what we want, while reason tells us how we might succeed. In this sense, morality develops out of our emotional lives. We learn to moderate our wants and desires as we recognize and come up against the wants and desires of others. To behave well, we

147

must understand the passion in others as well as ourselves. In acknowledging other people's feelings, we recognize what should be done and what shouldn't be done. Moral codes develop as we balance our own rights and responsibilities against the rights and responsibilities of others. And it is the presence of empathy that ensures that the moral scales are not unfairly tilted.

Sympathy, empathy and morals

The moral philosophers of the eighteenth century believed that what they then referred to as a sympathetic stance helps us to appreciate the condition of the other, both cognitively and emotionally. We need to *know* the experience of the other and to *feel* their happiness or pain. Knowledge and experience of the other mean that compassion is possible, and compassion encourages behaviour that is likely to be moral. Indeed, early uses and definitions of sympathy by Hume (1978[1739]) comfortably overlap with modern ideas about empathy.

> No quality of human nature is more remarkable, both in itself and in its consequences, than the propensity we have to sympathise with others, to receive by communication their inclinations and sentiments, however different from or contrary to our own.
>
> (Hume 1978[1739]: 206)

Adam Smith (1759) also argued that an experience of 'fellow feeling' was the result of our ability to imagine the world of the other. Sympathy, he felt, encouraged people to be better citizens. Whatever 'is the passion which arises from any object in the person principally concerned, an analogous emotion springs up, at the thought of his situation, in the breast of every attentive spectator' (Smith 1759: 10). Thus, in order to think about what makes a behaviour moral, we also have to wonder about other minds and how we might know them. This creates the link between our capacity for empathy and our moral sensibilities.

Moral principles

Two moral principles in particular have close ties to the presence of empathy: caring for others, and principles of fairness and justice. The more we recognize and understand the other person's point of view, the more likely it is that our dealings with him or her will be fair, compassionate and moral. Alongside this, Immanuel Kant was particularly impressed with humankind's potential to behave rationally. He felt that if we can agree on a set of universal moral principles to govern our dealings with each other, including fairness and justice, our cognitive strengths should allow us to proceed rationally in complex social situations. For example, we might judge a society's moral condition by the way it treats the vulnerable and elderly, and the disadvantaged and distressed. The presence of fair play and justice would be likely to define the kind of world in which most of us would want to live. We could argue, therefore, that an empathic *and* rational citizenry would increase behaviour that is caring and just, and that caring and just behaviour makes for a good society.

Over the centuries, most societies, religions and traditions have recognized the wisdom of treating others as you would have them treat you. Such wisdom encourages interpersonal relations that are caring, protective and fair. Every single one of the major traditions – Confucianism, Buddhism and Hinduism, as well as the monotheisms of Judaism, Christianity and Islam – have taught that empathy has a spiritual dimension in which our own suffering is related to that of others.

Perhaps the most powerful statement of this moral injunction is to be found in the Jewish Torah: 'Do not do unto others as you would not have done unto you.' Armstrong (2005a: 306) believes that this is even more demanding than Jesus's 'Do unto others as you would have done unto you', as it requires that we refrain from doing harm to others. We therefore need to look into our own hearts to discover what distresses us, and then refrain from inflicting similar pain on other people.

Rules that apply to everyone, rather than work just for the self, allow actions to be justifiable and moral. Who could conceive of being a slave as anything but unpleasant? Who would not feel outrage if they were disallowed from voting on the grounds of sex or skin colour? Notions of fairness and equality of treatment follow such indignation. It is out of such principles that we can generate ethical standards, principles of justice and systems of law.

However, in order for these principles to lead to welfare action and just behaviour, we also need empathy and imagination. Care ethicists reject the idea that the ethical life runs solely on the notion of autonomous individuals and abstract rules. Empathy is necessary in order to develop an understanding of others and to decide what is the best action to take in real-world situations (Held 2006; Slote 2007). You may not be old yourself, but you can imagine what it must feel like to be frail, infirm and dependent. The hope might be that other people – as private citizens or state-supported professionals – could imagine what it feels like to be old and vulnerable. The empathic feelings induced should encourage responses that are caring and protective.

Empathy therefore increases the likelihood that I will wait patiently as you walk your frail body slowly across the road or happily pay my health and welfare contributions to support the old and needy. Empathy makes it more likely that I will not begrudge the taxes I pay to support the social care services. Ehrlich and Ornstein (2012: 7) even challenge us to think of taxes as an expression of society's empathy, our willingness to be concerned and do something about the condition of others.

Hoffman (2000) has long been interested in the relationship between empathy, emotions and our moral development. He suggests that people in a moral conflict may weigh the impact of alternative courses of action on others. 'This evokes', he says, 'images of others' being harmed by one's actions; these images arouse empathic distress and anticipatory guilt; the images and empathy affects activate one's moral principles. The concurrence of empathy and principles creates a bond between them, which gives the principle an affective charge' (Hoffman 2000: 239).

For example, you see an oafish man teasing without mercy a boy who has a stutter. You know that this is wrong. The boy is in distress. The man's behaviour is unwarranted, cruel and unfair.

You feel the boy's humiliation. Your hackles rise. Not only do you feel that standing by and doing nothing would be hard to live with, but your sense of injustice is inflamed, so you challenge the aggressive man. Whatever the outcome of your intervention, at least you reacted. You experienced empathic distress. And you knew that a moral principle was being violated. It would seem reasonable to surmise that the boy felt supported and that your integrity remained in tact.

Of course, in more extreme cases, the combination of empathic distress and holding moral principles can lead to actions that show great courage. People who recognized the inhumanity of slavery and campaigned for its abolition, individuals who protected Jews knowing that Nazi soldiers would kill them as well as the fugitives if found, citizens who exposed their government's use of torture against innocent people knowing that they risked being tortured themselves, all experienced powerful links between empathic arousal and moral outrage. Empathy has the power to activate moral principles. Our ability to imagine and feel the world from the other's point of view is likely to temper our feelings, curb unbridled wants and encourage reciprocity.

However, there are behaviours that lie beyond the straightforwardly moral. These are behaviours that appear to be simply selfless, behaviours that do not seem to benefit the perpetrator in any way. This brings us to the subject of altruism and pro-social behaviours, in which empathy, once gained, is seen to play a central role.

Altruism, behaving pro-socially and regard for others

Acting selflessly, without apparent regard for one's own wellbeing, has traditionally been viewed as heroic, even saintly. Curious about how such selfless acts might be understood biologically and psychologically, scientists began to cast their eye over human acts of kindness, bravery, altruism and behaviours that were described as pro-social.

Altruism and *pro-social behaviours* are those acts carried out by individuals for the benefit or welfare of others without gain to themselves. You are running late at work, so I am happy to pick up your children from school. I see you stuck by the roadside because your car has run out of petrol and I stop to give you a lift to the nearest filling station and back. You donate a kidney to a complete stranger knowing that people who suffer renal failure lead restricted and often painful lives.

As there are individual differences in people's capacity for empathy (see Chapter 6), so people differ in their inclinations to act pro-socially (Penner and Orom 2010). Many people, for example, on seeing pictures of strangers who have been the victims of famine, tsunamis or earthquakes will be moved to give money. As in most matters of behaviour, our willingness to consider the welfare of others without gain to ourselves is determined in part by our genetic inheritance and in part by our upbringing and environment (Knafo and Israel 2010). There are dispositionally pro-social people out there, born to be good, raised to be moral. And one of their hallmarks is high empathy.

> Predispositions to respond empathically to others' distress, feel a sense of responsibility for others' welfare, and engage in other-oriented moral reasoning are associated with prosocial thoughts and feelings. Studies of both helpful and heroic individuals suggest that these thoughts and feelings are probably most likely to result in actual prosocial behaviour among individuals who are socially dominant and have a sense of self-efficacy or personal control.
>
> (Penner and Orom 2010: 69)

Many studies appear to support the suggestion that empathy, pro-social behaviours and care-oriented moral reasoning are indeed related (for example, Eisenberg *et al.* 2001). Less empathic individuals are less likely to be selfless and other-oriented. The more someone is empathically aware of another's plight, the more likely it is that they will help, and the more quickly they are likely to help. But different people faced with the same situation vary in how intensely they experience empathic distress. As a result, the propensity to respond varies. Not everyone, it appears, is prepared to put themselves out or risk their lives for others should the need arise. Indeed, some people become so upset as they empathically imagine the other's distress that they are rendered helpless, unable to respond.

Altruism or egoism?

The more psychologists thought about altruism and pro-social behaviour, the more they realized that it might not be a case of simply appreciating the other's perspective and behaving decently. Empathy does not necessarily lead to sympathy or pro-social behaviour. For some people, simply holding very clear notions of equality, fairness and justice can lead to altruistic and pro-social behaviour. Empathy need not be involved. In these cases, judgements based on reason and moral principle rather than empathy, whether cognitively or emotionally inspired, lead to acts of altruism. People who protect, hide and smuggle to safety persecuted minorities are just as likely to be driven by moral outrage as by empathic concern (for example, see Oliner and Oliner 1988).

Another line of argument is that an appreciation of other people's distress motivates us to do something about their plight, not simply to make their lives better, but to alleviate the unpleasant feelings that their upset condition is causing us. We help, therefore, to rid ourselves of discomfort, whether of distress, guilt, embarrassment or even annoyance. We might even help just because it makes us feel good or expect a reward (an honour, promotion, praise). Feeling pleased with oneself or expecting reward and recognition is unlikely to pass as altruism, even less as the actions of a moral player. Apparent altruism in this analysis is egoistic; a self-serving, self-interested response.

In a series of experiments, Batson (1991) set out to explore the empathy–altruism thesis. He believed that it is our ability to empathise that encourages us to act altruistically, not a selfish drive to rid ourselves of the bad feelings we might experience when we see other people in a state of need or distress. Even though we might experience an empathic response, whether or not we actually end up acting altruistically will depend on other factors. If the personal cost of acting altruistically is very high, we might not follow through with the selfless act. For example, although I am acutely and distressingly aware of your terrified state, jumping into a swollen, fast-flowing river to save you from drowning might be judged altogether too risky. I experience *empathic distress*, but it does not lead to behaviour that attends to your safety or well-being.

But as I stand on the bank dithering over what to do, I see my companion leap into the raging waters, attempting the rescue that I chose not to carry out. He also sees the terror in your eyes, but at the same time has an immediate sense that he couldn't live with himself if he did nothing. In my friend's case, egoism appears to have slipped back in, even though it produces 'altruistic' behaviour. To class such bravery as 'egoistic' seems rather harsh, but to the extent that the action is in part a response to his anticipated feelings of guilt, then it has a degree of self-interest attached to it.

Nevertheless, Batson found that when levels of empathic feeling are high, people do seem much more likely to act altruistically, even in situations where it is relatively easy to walk away and not respond at all. *Empathic concern* arises when an individual recognizes someone else's state of need and is motivated to do something about it without discernable benefit to the self. Although it is undoubtedly the case that some acts of apparent altruism are egoistically motivated, there is considerable research evidence that true altruism based on empathic concern is possible and does happen (Batson 2010). Moreover, people who do respond find that their feelings of empathic distress reduce more quickly than those who continue to observe but do not actually help.

The conclusion is that pro-social behaviours happen, even if some commentators cast them as enlightened self-interest. Altruism is part of human nature. When needs arise, many individuals are prepared to promote the well-being of others without apparent gain, material or psychological, to the self.

However, although Batson presents a strong case for empathy leading to altruism, his thesis does not necessarily connote moral behaviour. It is true that the more people are encouraged to imagine themselves being in a similar situation to another person, the higher their empathy, and so the greater the chance of altruistic behaviour. But the extent to which we identify with the plight of others can be confused by other, less worthy aspects of our natures.

Empathy, similarity and difference

Batson (2010) observed that the more *similarities* there are between people, the higher their empathy and the more likely it is that they will act altruistically. The more alike people are in terms of gender, education, culture and economic status, the higher are their empathy–altruism scores. The more people identify with a particular group – family, work, ethnicity, class, age – the more likely it is that they will view fellow members of the group favourably and the more likely it is that they will act pro-socially (Dovidio *et al.* 2010).

Empathy therefore rises and falls depending on whether the other is 'one of us' or 'one of them', a member of the 'in-group' or not. This might not always make for sound judgement or lead to a moral consensus. The more alike the other is and the greater their need, not only will it raise our feelings of empathy, the more likely it will be that we willingly share resources with them. We tend to like what we know and find little comfort in the strange.

If acting morally suggests following universal norms of just, fair and proper conduct, the other's culture, gender or education should make no difference either to our judgement or our behaviour. The relationship between empathy and moral behaviour is therefore not straightforwardly simple if it can be shown that our compassion, selflessness and sense of fairness are affected by the degree to which we feel socially, economically and biologically similar to the other. For many philosophers, a morality based on empathy and altruism alone would be too fickle. The only safe way to proceed if moral behaviour is to be consistent and universal is to identify sets of rational principles by which human behaviour and social life can be governed. Empathy is too unpredictable a feeling on which to base a moral code.

We are therefore left with two tricky thoughts. First, perhaps behaving morally does not require us to be empathic. We do not have to be mind readers to be moral agents. All we need to do if we are to behave in ways that are moral is recognize, accept and follow codes of moral conduct that are universal.

Second, empathy, with or without its moral implications, does sponsor understanding, compassion and pro-social behaviour, but the degree to which we are able to be empathic is relationship specific. All too often there is an 'in-group' bias (Hoffman 2000). The more we identify with the other's characteristics, the less prejudiced and the more empathic we are likely to be. Conversely, the more unlike and different we are to the other, the less likely we are to empathize. This looks like discrimination, even if it does hark back to the primitive strategies that help explain our evolutionary survival. The familiar is safe; the different and strange might be dangerous.

Imagining the other

One way out of this slightly troubling position is to note one of Batson's other findings: the more we are encouraged to imagine what it must be like to be someone else in a particular situation, the more likely it is that our empathic sensitivities will heighten. Cognitive effort (thinking what it must be like to be that other person in that particular situation) therefore can increase emotional empathy. This is a more self-conscious, cognitive, perspective-taking kind of empathy. When I stop and imagine what it must be like for you to be racially taunted in the city in which you were born and raised, the hurt, injustice, distress and anger also become mine.

It is also useful to know that prejudice might be reduced if we encourage members of one group, whether defined by sex, race or religion, to put themselves in someone else's shoes. A number of experiments in improving inter-group relations have shown that when individuals in one group are invited to think about and empathize with the experience of people in another 'out'-group, inter-group prejudice, adverse judgment, bias and hostility decrease. For example, Finlay and Stephan (2000) presented white students with essays ostensibly written by black college students describing their personal experiences of discrimination.

In discussing the results, Dovidio and colleagues (2010: 395) write that the study 'revealed that Whites who were instructed to empathize with the Black person (by imagining either how the writer of the essay would feel or how they themselves would feel in such a situation) showed lower levels of bias in their evaluations of Whites versus Blacks compared with those in a control condition who were instructed to attend objectively to the details of the essay.'

Such exercises in empathy can improve understanding and harmony between men and women, black people and white people, Christians and Muslims, non-disabled and disabled people, the old and the young. Based on raising empathic awareness, people's willingness to act morally can be improved when people are asked to take the perspective of the other. This is nicely observed in President Kennedy's 1963 speech (quoted in Frady 2002: 120) defending civil rights action:

> If an American, because his skin is dark, cannot eat lunch in a restaurant open to the public, if he cannot send his children to the best public school available, if he cannot vote for public officials who represent him, if, in short, he cannot enjoy the full and free life which all of us want, then who among us would be content to have the color of his skin changed and stand in his place? Who among us would be content with the counsels of patience and delay?

Imitation and intimacy

Much empathic feeling is emotional, automatic and involuntary. It seems hard-wired into our makeup. I shudder when I see you grimace as a large splinter is removed from your foot. Or, without realizing it, I feel more positive about a new acquaintance who is unconsciously and subtly imitating my body language.

Unconscious mimicry, imitation and the evocation of positive feelings are particularly strong when two people meet and feel attracted to one another. The more two people like each other, the more they imitate each other's facial expressions, voice intonation, speech rhythms and body language. And the more they imitate each other's body language, the more they are attracted to one another. These subtle, usually unconscious imitations of others' motor behaviour increases feelings of friendliness and intimacy between both the imitator and the person whose behaviour is being imitated (Iacobini 2007). Specifically, people who have good empathy and are able to take others' perspectives seem particularly prone to mimic the behaviour of others non-consciously (Chartrand and Bargh 1999). Counsellors who clients judge them to be empathic, for example, are more likely to mimic their client's body language non-consciously (Maurer and Tindall 1983).

Similarly, people who tend to 'self-monitor' and be more aware of the effects of their behaviour on others also tend to be both more empathic and more likely non-consciously to mimic other people's behaviour (Cheng and Chartrand 2003). High self-monitors are good at tuning into other people's thoughts and feelings. There is also evidence that people from collectivist cultures that have more *inter*dependent self-construals (the case in many Asian societies) are more likely to mimic the behaviour of others than are individuals raised in cultures that have more independent self-construals (van Baaren *et al.* 2003).

Lakin *et al.* (2003: 147) argue that unconscious mimicry, 'or the tendency to adopt the behaviors, postures, or mannerisms of interaction partners without awareness or intent, might have played an important role in human evolution by allowing individuals to maintain harmonious relationships with fellow group members'. They go on to suggest that people who mimic the behaviour of others increase their chances of being liked. Non-conscious mimicry therefore acts as a *social glue* that binds people together and increases social harmony. Human beings have a fundamental need to belong and be accepted (Baumeister and Leary 1995). Automatic mimicry is therefore adaptive.

Development of pro-social behaviours

As a psychologist, Hoffman takes a developmental approach to the study of empathy. It takes four or five years for a child to begin to show signs of cognitively based empathy; that is, the ability to see the situation from the other person's point of view and react congruently. In contrast, babies are only capable of emotional contagion. They pick up on the emotional climate around them, but show no clear sense of who is feeling what. Put a baby among other babies who are crying and more likely than not the baby will start to cry herself. A young toddler upset by observing another toddler's distress will seek comfort from his mother. This 'egocentric empathic distress' occurs when the young child sees the other's distress but lacks a clear distinction between self and other.

It takes several years for young children to differentiate clearly between self and other. A distinct sense of self is necessary before young children can show a sympathetic reaction to another's distress. It is not until children reach the age 3 or 4 years that they begin to realize that other people have minds of their own and independent views on situations. An appreciation of the other person's unique perspective helps explain their thoughts, feelings, actions, beliefs, desires and behaviour. For example, although 4-year-old Roxie was sad that her best friend, Megan, was grumpy and wouldn't play with her, she explained to her mother, 'Megan doesn't want to play with me because she's cross that her daddy wouldn't let her ride on her brother's scooter.' So faced with a crying child, a baby cries in tandem, a 2 year old simply stares, while a 4 year old shows empathic concern, perhaps offering comfort.

It takes several more years before children achieve the most sophisticated levels of empathy. Here, individuals are role taking, imagining how they would feel if they were in the other person's shoes (Hoffman 2000). It is at this developmental stage that pro-social behaviour and empathy-based compassion become possible. Hoffman's position on moral action represents an attempt to combine our emotional and cognitive capacities, to recognize the value of both our empathic and our rational characters as we attempt to negotiate the choppy waters of human relationships.

For example, children who score well on tests of social understanding have also been found to have a good grasp of basic moral principles (Dunn *et al.* 2000). Most competent social actors take account of other people's thoughts, feeling, beliefs and intentions. An 8 year old witnessing another child bully his way to the front of the queue and then being rewarded with the last remaining prize from an unwitting adult would not only judge the situation to be unfair, but would empathize with the distress and sense of injustice felt by the bullied children who missed out. A good deal of the fictional literature written for 7,

8 and 9 year olds concerns issues of what is fair and not, and what is wrong and not. In most of these stories, although the hero suffers unfairly in the short term, her fair, thoughtful and virtuous behaviour gets rewarded in the long run.

Empathy therefore has the power to act as a universal pro-social motivator in matters of welfare and justice (Hoffman 2000: 273). Seeing another person unfairly tricked out of money, or witnessing a bully steal a boy's watch, arouses strong fellow feelings of outrage and injustice. And if sufficiently aroused, empathic morality often leads to action. The trickster might be challenged, the bully tackled, the victim helped.

Conclusion

If our behaviour is to be judged as altruistic, pro-social and moral, it is likely that it involves both affective and cognitive empathy. The division between these two types of empathy is not hard: one often triggers the other. If we imaginatively *think* about the other's plight we are likely to *feel* their distress. And when we feel the other's feelings, we are more likely to think about and reflect on the way the world looks and feels to them.

There are many everyday opportunities to develop and maintain empathy. Indeed, empathy is promoted whenever we reflect on the human experience, read a novel, act in a play or watch a movie. The recognition that a strong empathic sensibility, whether emotionally or cognitively inspired, tends to make us more moral, socially attuned, pro-social and community minded has encouraged many people to seek its promotion in both children and adults. The next two chapters review some of their efforts.

13

Promoting Empathy in Children

Encouraging children to be empathic

If lack of empathy increases the risk of poor mental health and diminished social well-being, and if prevention is better than cure, then it is clearly better to promote empathy in the young. With this in mind, many social commentators and educationalists advise early exposure to empathy, whether it involves being on the receiving end of empathic responses or encouraging children to show empathy themselves. The advice, and the practices that support it, is targeted at parents, nursery staff and teachers.

The trouble with many current approaches to children's development and education is that emphasis is given to the rational at the expense of the emotional, to the individual and not the relationship. In his bestselling book *The Social Animal*, David Brooks (2011) describes society's obsession with intellectual understanding rather than social understanding:

> We still have academic fields that often treat human beings as rational utility-maximising individuals. Modern society has created a giant apparatus for the cultivation of the hard skills, while failing to develop the moral and emotional faculties down below. Children are coached on how to jump through a thousand scholastic hoops. Yet by far the most important decisions they will make are about whom to marry and whom to befriend, what to love and what to despise, and how to control impulses. On these matters, they are almost entirely on their own. We are good at talking about material incentives, but bad about talking about emotions and intuitions.

> We are good at teaching technical skills, but when it comes to the most important things, like character, we have almost nothing to say.
>
> (Brooks 2011: xiv)

Empathy, as we have shown throughout these pages, develops as babies interact with empathic and attuned parents. Empathy struggles to emerge when children miss out on love and understanding. Empathy is stunted when babies suffer neglect and rejection. In their report on the nature and origins of violence, Hosking and Walsh (2005: 10) write, 'Empathy is the single greatest inhibitor of the development of the propensity to violence. Empathy fails to develop when parents or prime carers fail to attune with their infants.'.

If empathy encourages behaviour that is caring and just, then what kinds of parenting and education help empathy develop in young children? First, it is important to help children recognize, understand and discuss emotional states in the self and others. Children should be helped to reflect on other people's inner states and experiences. They need to experience being on the receiving end of empathy and being empathic themselves (Kennedy 2008). Parents should talk with their children about their own and other people's feelings. Children need to be encouraged to make amends when they have hurt or upset someone. Missing out on these experiences leaves children low on emotional intelligence and at risk of being self-centred and aggressive.

At home with empathy

Hoffman (2000) has been a strong advocate of empathy-based moral education. He believes that parents and teachers have many opportunities to help their children see other people's point of view, feel their distress and understand its causes. For example:

> Another child drops her ice cream, looks sad, and is on the verge of tears. Maya's father sees his four year old daughter looking with some interest at the other child's plight. 'Maya, what's happened? Why's that little boy looking so sad?' Or:

'Oh dear. Do you remember when you dropped your bottle of cola? Do you remember how you felt?'

Similar opportunities to foster empathy occur when children are pretend playing. Without being too intrusive, a parent might subtly ratchet up the emotional challenges: 'Oh look! There's only one piece of chocolate left. Which dolly is going to have it?' Similar ideas and opportunities can be transferred to the school and nursery setting. As well as planned empathy-based learning, most days in the classroom throw up moral issues. Although it demands quick, nimble thinking, teachers can take advantage of what can be learned when teasing or cheating or queue jumping take place.

Parenting that is strict and authoritarian, brooking no discussion, does not help children develop empathy or social understanding. This is a reminder that although children have the genetic and neurological potential to be socially skilled, whether or not empathy and social understanding develop depends heavily on the quality of their environmental experiences, including parenting and family life. Nature needs nurture.

Here is a recipe offered by Bloom (2004: 151) for creating children who are 'generous in their moral perspective':

1. Increase contact with other individuals.
2. Interact with others in circumstances where cooperation leads to mutual benefit.
3. Expose children to stories, real and imagined, that motivate them to take the perspective of distant others. The more children read, the more they learn about others. And if they are also encouraged to write about themselves and others, the potential for empathic understanding and connectedness increases even further. Reading and writing helps children to see 'them' as 'us' (for example, see Roessing 2005). Children whose parents regularly read them stories tend to be better psychologists and more skilful social players. When parents read to children, not only do they tell the story but they invite children to enter the minds of the characters. 'Why do you think the fox was frightened by the mouse?' 'How do

you think Charlotte is feeling now that her mummy has gone?' Encouraging children to take the perspective of the other promotes empathy. If there are pictures accompanying the story, invite children to identify facial expressions and body language. Ask them to think about what a particular look might mean. Promote empathy.

4. Expose children to the moral insights of previous generations.

And likewise, Sroufe offers his thoughts on the same subject:

How do you get an empathic child? You get an empathic child not by trying to teach the child and admonish the child to be empathic, you get an empathic child by being empathic with the child. The child's understanding of relationships can only be from the relationships he's experienced.

(Sroufe 1989, cited in Karen 1998: 195)

Szalavitz and Perry (2011) are also eloquent and compelling on this subject. They remind us that no one learns to be empathic unless they have been on the receiving of empathic care. Empathy develops in relationships characterized by love, shared understanding and reciprocity. 'Empathy – fully expressed in a community of nurturing interdependent people – promotes health, creativity, intelligence, and productivity' (Szalavitz and Perry 2011: 288). Video and computer screens are not empathic. Relational poverty poses the real risk of creating societies that are 'empathy lite' and all the more dangerous for it.

When bonds loosen and relationships become instrumental, compassion ebbs away. Social life becomes less caring and more brutal.

Infants and toddlers need touch, warmth, presence, things even the most interactive computer cannot provide. Babies cannot develop the foundations of empathy without frequent, nurturing contact with a few consistent caregivers. Social development requires multiple repeated face-to-face interactions.

(Szalavitz and Perry 2011: 230)

If we are to produce caring, empathic children destined to become good citizens, we need to support those who raise them. Caring for mothers, argue Szalavitz and Perry, is therefore a good first step in creating a healthy society. Empathic parents tend to create families in which emotions, in the self and others, are comfortably recognized, acknowledged, thought about and responded to.

Here is an example. Jade, 5 years old, is playing in the porch and still hasn't put her shoes on ready for school. Her mother is getting somewhat cross and exasperated:

Mum: Jade, hurry up! Put your shoes on. We're going to be late for school.

Jade: Can I bring Emma home for tea tonight?

Mum: You still haven't put your shoes on! I'm sorry I'm getting all cross, but you know how upset you'll be if we miss the beginning of class. I don't want you to be upset, so let's get a move on! (*said briskly but with a smile*).

Jade: Sorry, mummy. But I was really hoping Emma could come round for tea.

Mum: I know you were, love, but let's get your shoes on and we'll talk about it on the way to school when we're not feeling so rushed.

Jade: OK, mum, but I still hope you'll say yes.

Mum: Aagghh! (*gives Jade a quick exasperated but friendly shake and a hug*)

Empathy in the pre-school years

The pre-school years are the best time to foster children's emotional, social and empathic competence. Peer relationships offer a particularly rich opportunity for children to learn emotional intelligence and develop pro-social behaviours. It is while playing with peers that children have the chance to talk, communicate, take the other's perspective, play and pretend, give scope to their imagination, share, take turns, control their anger and impatience, resolve conflicts and sort out social problems, and decide what is fair and just. Teachers and therapists, as well as parents, can play a key role in helping children learn from these experiences. Linking pre-school-based programmes with parent-focused early interventions, particularly in the case of at-risk children, is especially desirable.

It is also the case that one of the best predictors of later social adjustment is the ability of children to get on well with their peers (Sroufe *et al.* 2005). Children need time, space and support to engage in pretend play. Pretend play gives free rein to the imagination in which children can explore what others might think, feel and do in all kinds of situation and circumstance, especially those that might be difficult or distressing. For example, a child might imagine what happens when a dolly can't find her mother, a car crashes or a teddy misbehaves. Playing with other children is vital for healthy social and emotional development.

Bierman and Erath (2008: 601–2) outline four approaches to help young children develop social competence and perspective taking:

- Provide children with instructions. Model socially competent behaviour. Read children stories or show them videos to help them recognize, understand and think about thoughts and feelings, beliefs and behaviours, intentions and outcomes. The overall goal is to teach children general strategies for behaving with competence and sensitivity in social situations.
- Provide children with opportunities to try out new social skills. Play, games, making and building things, role-plays and drama encourage children to see the world from other people's point of view.
- Feedback and discussion of people's behaviour helps children think about what might be going on in other people's minds and the complexities of social interaction. Discussion can be about what happened when there was an argument in the classroom, what was going on in a story or who did what and why in a role play. Adults 'can help clarify subtle social cues by eliciting feedback during ongoing social interactions, to help young children understand the impact of their behaviour on their own feelings and the feelings of their peers. By enhancing the child's self-monitoring and social awareness, the goal is to promote empathic and

socially responsive behavioral choices' (Bierman and Erath 2008: 602).

- Learning to be socially competent can only take place in classroom settings that feel safe and supportive, ordered and predictable. When there is conflict or disagreement, interventions should be firm but fair, followed by reflection and discussion. Flexible approaches to social problem solving are encouraged. Children are helped to consider various options and evaluate the pros and cons of each before deciding which might be best. Dolls, puppets and the like can all be employed to help children understand the world from many points of view.

Social and emotional learning in schools

Empathy mitigates aggressive and prejudicial behaviours. It encourages positive social behaviours. Creating classroom environments that are based on cooperation rather than competition increases children's empathy and pro-social behaviour (for example, Aronson and Patnoe 1997). To ensure that children have a positive attitude to school, teachers need to be empathic (Feshbach and Feshbach 2011). Children taught by empathic teachers feel accepted and understood. If they are better motivated, they are more likely to achieve.

Working with young school-age children, Feshbach and Feshbach (1987) helped them participate in a number of empathy-promoting exercises. For example, the children were asked to think about what presents would make members of their family happiest. They were encouraged to think about how the world might look and feel from a small cat's point of view. The children also listened to stories and were then asked to retell and role-play them from the perspective of different characters. Their performances were video-recorded and then discussed. At the end of the training, most children had improved their empathy scores. It was also found that their self-esteem and generosity increased, while aggressive behaviours had decreased. An unexpected finding of such exercises, for both children and adults, was that they also appeared to improve cognitive flexibility and creative thinking, and even their academic ability.

Seeing the world from different or unusual points of view promotes an original turn of mind. Aronson *et al.* (2005: 423) give the example of Richard Feynman, a Nobel prize-winning physicist. When he was a boy, his father would challenge his intellect by, for example, asking him to pretend that he was a tiny creature living in the carpet. Such 'games' excite children into seeing things from unusual points of view. Feynman was famous for his brilliant ability to understand and explain the complexity and weirdness of the world at the quantum level, using images and ideas that could be grasped even by those who struggle with the abstract world of mathematics.

In England and Wales, the government-backed 'Social and Educational Aspects of Learning' (SEAL) programme 'is a whole-school approach to promoting the social and emotional skills that underpin effective learning, positive behaviour, regular attendance, staff effectiveness and the emotional health and well-being of all who learn and work in schools' (DCSF 2007: 4). Most schools, both primary and secondary, are involved (DfES 2005). Empathy is one of the five key skills being promoted (the others being self-awareness, self-regulation, motivation and social skills). Cognitive empathic skills are woven into many aspects of classroom life and subject learning. For example, children might be asked to imagine how people in history, in a different culture, in a difficult classroom situation or who were slaves might view and feel about their world, and why this might be so. By helping children to think empathically whenever interesting and complex social and emotional situations arise, the hope is that their emotional intelligence and social skills will increase and that school life, including academic performance, will improve.

Mary Gordon, an educator and child advocate, has also developed a widely adopted programme whose aim is to nurture empathy and emotional literacy in young children. She calls it *The Roots of Empathy* (Gordon 2009). She believes that failures of empathy lead to indifference, cruelty and even violence. There is an observed negative relationship between empathy and aggression. The higher the empathy, the lower the likelihood of behaving aggressively. The lower the empathy, the more capable people are of violence.

Gordon's strong belief is that empathic, socially intelligent children are less likely to be aggressive and more likely to be caring, compassionate and concerned. 'Teaching children emotional literacy', she says, 'and developing their capacity to take the perspective of others are key steps towards collaboration and civility' (Gordon 2009).

The Roots of Empathy programme is made up of three key components. First, children have the opportunity to talk about their own and other people's emotions. Enriching children's emotional vocabulary helps them develop a more subtle appreciation of feeling states. Second, children are encouraged to see things from other people's points of view. And third, the classroom itself becomes a place where caring, acceptance, tolerance, respect and perspective taking can be recognized, talked about and practised.

In the presence of an instructor, some of the learning in the Roots of Empathy programme takes place as children watch a baby interact with his or her mother, live in the classroom. The babies, of course, begin to interact with the children themselves. The children discuss the baby's behaviour and likely thoughts, feelings, wants and frustrations. Session by session, they begin to see the world from the baby's point of view, sensing what it must be like to be dependent and vulnerable, excited and frustrated, puzzled and intrigued, anxious and overjoyed. The instructor often asks the children, 'If the baby could talk, what do you think she would say to us?' (Gordon 2009: 71).

One of the key reflective skills that children develop is to think about why the baby might be crying, given that babies do not cry wilfully or for no reason at all. Although caring for a crying baby can be stressful, putting yourself into the child's body and mind helps you see, feel and experience things from the infant's point of view. Babies can only communicate through behaviour. So although their behaviour might be demanding, it might be seen as meaningful and reasonable under the circumstances – I'm hungry, tired, wet, ill, frightened.

Children are also encouraged to make comparisons with their own experiences. While they are thinking about why the baby is smiling or crying or feeling sleepy, they are also developing a 'vocabulary of feelings' to help them recognize and understand their own and other people's emotions (Gordon 2009: 61). In particular, children are helped to think about other people's intentions and the states of mind that might lie behind them.

In another exercise, children are given a picture of a girl who is sad. They are asked to reflect on the potential reasons for her feeling low. Answers range from 'She's upset because other kids are teasing her' to 'She's sad because her dad just lost his job' (Gordon 2009: 119). By observing behaviour, naming emotions, reflecting on the nature of their own and other people's feelings and discussing feelings with others, the children in the Roots of Empathy programme learn to develop their mind-reading skills.

Children are helped to realize that they have a responsibility to one another. There are tasks and exercises in which children learn to understand what it feels like to be frightened or hurt or humiliated. Rather than attack difference in others, they learn how to tolerate it. The promotion of empathy also helps children develop more cooperative and collaborative behaviours. The ability to work and communicate with others, and the wisdom that values *interdependence* (rather than independence), is recognized as a key social skill. And as this wisdom grows, so aggression, bullying and discrimination shrink. Learning and understanding take place as the children collaborate and work together. In these sessions, there is no place for competitive learning. The emphasis is on thinking together, understanding one another and socially constructing new knowledge.

Finally, music has also been shown to help children improve their empathic capacities. A Finnish study reported the outcomes of a 12-hour programme in which children sang, played instruments, listened to music and talked about lyrics that had an empathic flavour. Making music is famous for its ability to bring people together and to increase their feelings of care and warmth. At the end of the programme, the researchers found significant increases in the children's level of empathy and pro-social behaviour (Hietolahti-Ansten and Kalliopuska 1991; Kalliopuska amd Ruokonen 1993). There is harmony in music.

Conclusion

Scientists and philosophers tell us how important empathy is for the well-being of society. There are many forces that still have the power to hold back the tide of empathy. Instrumental learning, winning at all costs, the celebration of money, the fear of the other and the exaggeration of difference are all inimical to empathy's civilizing presence.

Developmentalists and educators advise how to promote empathy in the young, at home and in school. There has been a gradual realization that our children's emotional education is as important as their intellectual learning. And what is true for children is also true for adults. Educationalists, employers and therapists are beginning to promote empathy in the college, the clinic and the workplace, as we shall see in the next chapter.

14
Promoting Empathy in Adults

Empathy training

Group learning is a powerful tool. It is used to generate under-standing and wisdom, not just for schoolchildren, but also for doctors, nurses, counsellors, psychologists, judges and social workers as they discuss cases, consider assessments and think about procedures. Safe groups of fellow travellers sponsor chal-lenge, innovation and insight. They provide opportunities for collaborative learning (Brufee 1999). Empathic, emotionally intelligent work environments have a good track record of increasing creativity, improving problem solving and raising productivity (Goleman 1999).

A number of studies have considered the impact of empathy training on the behaviour of aggressive individuals. The training typically involves looking at films or role-plays of mean, selfish, aggressive or violent behaviour and discussing it from the victim's point of view (see Björkqvist 2007 for a brief review). The findings generally support the effectiveness of such train-ing, which works on the principle that increases in empathy lead to decreases in aggression.

Baron-Cohen (2011), too, offers a list of treatment interven-tions that might be used to improve the empathy capacities of those who are particularly deficient in the skill. With colleagues, he has developed a number of resources to help children and adults with autistic spectrum conditions improve their ability to recognize emotions and 'mind read' (for example, see Golan *et al.* 2006, 2010).

Empathy training has also been introduced into the prepara-tion of counsellors and therapists, nurses and doctors, social workers and care workers (Marangoni *et al.* 1995; White 1997; Siegel 2010; Watson and Greenberg 2011). Trainers sometimes make a distinction between basic empathy and trained empathy (Alligood 1992; Morse *et al.* 1992). Basic empathy is that which develops as we relate with others throughout life. It has a high affective or 'feeling' component.

Trained empathy, on the other hand, has a higher cognitive component. When practitioners are encouraged to think about another's perspective, when we are asked to imagine and visualize what it might be like to be someone else, when we read about others' lives, we develop an intellectual grasp of their world. Thinking about the lives and histories of other people is likely to improve cognitive empathy. But in order to be able to do this, we must be interested in their lives, their stories, their experiences.

> Obtaining an inside view and a clear sense of clients' narratives may be as important for therapists' processing in the session as it is for clients. By listening to detailed, vivid, and clear stories, therapists are more likely to be able to be empathic to their clients' experience and come to a better understanding of their worldviews. To enhance empathic resonance, therapists can ask clients for the details of situations to get a better sense of the contexts of clients' lives, or they might suggest systematic evocative unfolding – helping clients to 'play a movie of a scene' – so that situations come alive for both participants in the session.
>
> (Watson and Greenberg 2011: 130)

The notion of cognitive empathy probably has the greatest relevance to health, social and psychosocial carers. Indeed, some counsellors advise caution over relying solely on affective empathy, particularly when working with clients from different cultural or racial backgrounds (Steward *et al.* 1998). In order to avoid false feelings of understanding, good knowledge and a strong sense of the client's lived world are likely to improve cognitive empathy. In these cases, cognitive empathy is likely to create fewer therapeutic pitfalls. Empathy is therefore improved when we make a cognitive effort to see and imagine the world from the other person's point of view. This might be achieved by trying to take the role or perspective of the other. In this process, we attempt to construct in our minds the other person's imagined mental state (Hogan 1969), the 'attempt by one self-aware self to comprehend unjudgmentally the positive and negative experiences of another self' (Wispé 1986: 318).

Reflection and analysis of therapeutic sessions, client feedback on their thoughts and feelings and videotapes of worker–client interactions have all been found to help improve practitioners' empathy scores. The combination of video and audio feedback has been found to be especially effective, particularly material that requires listening to what clients actually say about their experiences. Role playing and role taking, for example in helping counsellors work with clients from different cultural backgrounds, have also been found to be helpful (Scott and Borodovsky 1990; Irvin and Pederson 1995).

In this example, a trainee counsellor is asked to imagine what it must feel like to be Sue, who is suffering mild depression:

> After enjoying a year's travel, Sue's youngest child, Masie, has just decided to stay in Canada, keep her job and apply for citizenship. Sue's often mentioned she feels close to her daughter and has talked bravely about how easy it is to fly from the United Kingdom to Vancouver. Although her older children live not too far away in a nearby city, for the last few years and since her husband died, home life has involved just Maisie and Sue.
>
> Sue is coming up for retirement and has suddenly found herself feeling low, uncharacteristically tearful and that life has lost its meaning. The counsellor has been encouraged by his supervisor to imagine himself in Sue's situation, thinking about her recent history, and to picture himself, like Sue, returning home from work, contemplating the evening. Such affective role taking does appear to increase people's empathy and ability to connect and communicate. Ideally, the counsellor should try to imagine Sue both in terms of her character and personality (dispositional attributes) and the situation in which she currently finds herself.

Reading has also been found to improve professional empathy. For example, a study by Shapiro *et al.* (2004) looked at the change in self-reported empathy scores by medical students who read, discussed and reflected on fictional literature in which there were issues of illness and distress. Qualitative data from this study 'indicated that student understanding of the patient's perspective became more detailed and complex after the literature-based intervention' (Shapiro 2007: 480).

These findings support the broader argument that literature has a significant part to play in the empathic practice of good medicine and, in all likelihood, in the practices of many other helping professions (Halpern 2001). Stories help to 'contextualize' patients and their worlds. In allowing patients to tell their stories, to personalize their illnesses and pains, their hopes and fears, doctors may not only feel something of the other's world, but come to understand it. And with understanding come sensitivity, perceptivity and probably efficacy.

Being open to the patient's story is a constant corrective to sticking rigidly to the medical narrative. Practitioners who approach patients with only one story in mind, the medical story, are in danger of failing to hear what is going on. Key symptoms that lie outside the medical narrative are simply not heard. They are beyond the medical plot line; they remain invisible. 'Thinking with stories is, like empathy, an achieved mutuality and relatedness' (Spiegel and Charon 2004: ix)

Similar issues crop up when the elderly are nursed and cared for. It is easy to forget that the frail person sitting before you was once a young child, a cheeky adolescent, an ardent lover, a married woman, a caring mother, an inspiring teacher, a keen gardener, a patient grandmother. Inside our heads, most of us never age. It is only when we look in the mirror that we see the passage of time.

In her wonderful book *The Warmth of the Heart Prevents Your Body from Rusting*, the French psychologist Marie de Hennezel meditates on the art of ageing. She is saddened by the all too frequent mechanical indifference and the lack of empathy shown by many of those who look after people who are old:

> People habitually fail to look at the old, to really look at them. Carers need to realise that they are not really looking at the person they are caring for, but are avoiding the patient's gaze

by looking up, into the distance, or aslant, before turning away to get on with their work.

(de Hennezel 2011: 107–8)

'What we must do', she says, 'is value qualities that have not been prized in the past, such as gentleness, touch, and presence, and encourage carers to display a humane approach in front of their colleagues' (de Hennezel 2011: 110). Care that is gentle, care that is humane, has to be empathic. To care well we must know the other and their story, even though the present world and its horizons might be no more than a worn-out body and bed. To care well we must have a sense of knowing the experience of the other, what it must feel like to be stiff and slow, to be dependent, to feel in pain.

Empathy and the everyday

There has been increasing interest in how we can routinely improve our empathic capacities. Many ordinary, everyday activities involve us thinking about and appreciating the views of others. Indeed, we appear to have a natural desire to understand other minds. Our curiosity gets us reading novels, seeing plays and watching TV soaps. We have an appetite for gossip. And the more talented of us explore character, invent worlds and create stories. In fact, a good imagination and the ability to empathize seem to go together. Over 200 years ago, the famous nineteenth-century essayist William Hazlitt wrote:

> a sentiment of general benevolence can only arise from an habitual cultivation of the natural disposition of the mind to sympathize with the feelings of others by constantly taking an interest in those which we know, and imagining others that we do not know.

(Hazlitt 1998[1805]: 14, quoted in Keen 2007: 49)

Those who believe that the world is a better place when empathy is present are also keen to promote a range of empathy-enhancing pursuits, many mundane and informal. Telling stories and listening to stories are empathy saturated and empathy dependent. Book reading and book clubs, role making and role taking, creating art and performing art are all recommended as ways of becoming more empathic.

The idea of developing our empathy skills is a relatively modern notion. However, it is rather nice and entirely appropriate that many of these empathy-promoting pursuits involve the arts and being creative. After all, the concept of empathy was fashioned to explain and understand our response to beauty and the idea of an aesthetic experience.

Creating art

As we saw in Chapter 2, the very idea of empathy was the result of German philosophers thinking about and trying to understand art and beauty. The empathic experience ran in two directions: from object to art via the mind of the artist, and from art to observer via contemplation of the work of art. In order to render the inner truth, meaning and beauty of the object of contemplation, the artist has to get inside that object and experience it from within. He or she then has to communicate the experience in the form of a work of art. The viewer's appreciation of the work of art depends on his or her ability to see and feel the work as seen and felt by the artist.

The aesthetic experience is one of empathy, in which the viewer resonates with the work in such a way that he or she sees and feels something of both the thing rendered and the mind of the artist who rendered it. Thus, to be involved in art, either as artist or viewer, is to be part of an empathic experience in which perception, understanding, meaning and interpretation are changed.

Seen in this way, aesthetic empathy has the power to change our understanding of life and its meaning. It has the potential to be therapeutic.

A Jewish art student, Friedl Dicker-Brandeis, was interned in one of Nazi Germany's concentration camps, Terezin, north of Prague. Inspired by the teaching of several major Bauhaus artists, including Paul Klee and Vassily Kandinsky, it was while she was at Terezin that she began to run art classes for many of the camp's children.

In a moving paper describing Dicker-Brandeis's life and work, Wix (2009) develops the idea and value of aesthetic empathy in teaching art to children and adults. For Dicker-Brandeis, making art was a way to claim experience, it was a way to know a thing at first hand:

> Her words, her teaching, and her artwork all point to faith in image making as a way to access personal courage, truth, imagination, and beauty. She knew that even if the lives of Terezin's children ended in the gas chamber – perhaps especially if that was their destination and for the majority of them it was – art could strengthen her students through accessing their own images, perceptions, experiences, and intuitions ... The children learned from Dicker-Brandeis to hold fast to who they knew themselves to be by repeatedly engaging artistically with the realities they had to endure, one way or another.
>
> (Wix 2009: 154)

Dicker-Brandeis used her teaching to enhance children's relationships with themselves, to participate sympathetically with the world. It was her way to help the children psychologically survive their experience, whatever their eventual fate. She felt that empathy, personal meaning and a shared humanity could be found through art. In 1944, Dicker-Brandeis was transferred to Auschwitz, where she was killed on 9 October. Her legacy is a life lived beautifully, an inspiration to those who continue to recognize the value of art and creativity when working therapeutically with both children and adults (Wix 2009).

Reading fiction

Of all the books published each year, fiction outsells all other categories. And of all the fiction sold, romantic novels and crime thrillers head the list. Biographies are also bookshop favourites. Stories have always been a powerful way of communicating things that matter to us. 'It is partly through engaging with story telling in its literary, theatrical, and cinematic forms', believes Fairbairn (2009: 191), 'that we learn about what it is to be a person, or more accurately, about what it is to be different kinds of person. When we are moved by a play or a film or by a novel, we are moved because we begin imaginatively to live the lives of the characters we are watching or reading about.'

There has been a long-held belief that reading literature – novels, poems, plays – improves empathy and social competence, and makes us more moral. Testing this belief, Mar *et al.* (2006, 2008) did indeed find that reading fiction predicted good scores on a variety of empathy tasks. Reading fiction was also positively associated with enjoying good social networks. Johnson (2012), too, found that reading fiction was positively associated with empathy and pro-social behaviour. 'The great instrument of the moral good', wrote the poet Percy Bysshe Shelley, 'is the imagination; and poetry administers to the effects by acting upon the cause' (Shelley 1973: 750). The storyteller hopes to give the reader an emotional experience. The empathic reader will connect with the characters' feelings of joy or guilt or sadness. To live, writes the author Candia McWilliam (2011),

> we must imagine how it is to be another. This is where fiction, though it is not a utilitarian art, or anything so simple, cannot but come in. We need urgently to know how other people feel … Fiction is what takes us into the understanding of people who we are not.
>
> (McWilliam 2011: 224, 281)

All of this is sometimes referred to as *narrative empathy*. By stimulating and extending the imagination, goes the argument, we begin to develop a better understanding of other people's worlds. We gain insights into their thoughts and feelings, desires and motives. We have the opportunity to explore the experiences of people very different from ourselves – opposite genders, other races, contrasting cultures, foreign faiths, the good and the bad. We particularly like stories in which there are emotional crises, conflicts, confusions and moral dilemmas.

Gardiner (1989) considers the way authors offer and represent 'otherness' to their readers. Reading (and writing) helps us to see ourselves as others see us (Lessing 1987). It can even help readers change the way they see themselves. Gardiner is particularly interested in the way women authors write about these matters, and how readers become 'eavesdroppers' on the mental worlds of a book's characters. In her study of the novels of Jean Rhys, Christina Stead and Doris Lessing, she develops a 'politics of empathy':

> to change people's minds, new information is not enough; they must be moved to feel the plight of others, especially the oppressed, as their own. Perhaps more important, they must be moved to see that plight in a way that calls for change. This rhetorical effect implies psychological empathy. For these writers, then, women's fiction becomes a privileged arena for moral action and creating psychological prerequisites to historical change. Through their fiction, the authors establish those strategies of identification and distanciation that lead us to empathize with their characters and texts and so imagine changing their and our social worlds.
>
> (Gardiner 1989: 18)

Identification with a character can be particularly strong when the author writes in the first person. As we engage with characters and follow plots, our minds are opened to new 'experiences, dilemmas, time periods, places and situations that would otherwise be closed' (Keen 2007: ix). 'Art', wrote the novelist George Eliot (1963[1856]: 271 cited in Keen 2007: 54), 'is the nearest thing to life; it is a mode of amplifying experience and extending our contact with our fellow-men beyond the bounds of our personal lot.' And the author Sue Monk Kidd says that she wants to 'jolt the reader's heart. I want my words to open a portal through which the reader may leave the self, migrate to some other human sky and return "disposed" to otherness' (Kidd 2005: 9, quoted in Keen 2007: 124).

Skilled language users are also fond of employing metaphors. Metaphors enrich the way we use language. They introduce playfulness and subtlety, inviting listeners and readers to think flexibly and with imagination. Metaphors allow more nuanced thinking. They invite us to see the world from other points of view. Those who do not appreciate the use of metaphor often find communication and social relationships

difficult. For example, adults with autism find metapł
They have a literal view of the world.

Reading therefore helps increase empathy and altruism, ...
makes us better citizens (Nussbaum 1997). Or, as Pinker puts
it, our gift for empathy and capacity for 'storytelling has made
the human species "nicer"' (quoted by Keen 2007: xviii).

It is often argued that the more we see and feel things from
the other's point of view, the more difficult it is to do them
harm. If you are unlucky enough to be taken hostage, one strategy is humanize yourself to your abductors. 'The goal of
humanising oneself is to make the kidnappers view the person
as a human being, not simply as an object ... the way to human-
ise yourself is attempt to establish some kind of rapport with
one's captors' (Alvarez 2007: 66). Human beings are more likely
to harm others the greater the psychological (and of course
physical) distance there is between the would-be killer and his
or her victim. Distance, particularly emotional distance,
decreases empathy. The enemy soldier who is the same age as
you and a father like you simply becomes a depersonalized,
unknown, often unseen target. This dehumanization and deper-
sonalization of the enemy, of course, are how armies train
soldiers to kill. So if you are captured, individualize yourself. Be
known, and maybe as a result you will save your life.

If, on the other hand, you want to hurt and harm people, you
need to believe in their difference, their otherness. When people
have strong feelings of who is 'us' and who is 'not-us', who is
friend and who is foe, they can conjure great empathy for their
own 'kind' and strong feelings of hate for those who are 'not
them'. Storytelling about the terrible deeds and depravities of
those who are our enemies is a powerful way to desensitize and
distance us from the others' humanity and increase the chances
that we will harm them should they come our way. Stories can
therefore increase our feelings of empathy for those we get to
know and see from their point of view, and decrease our feelings
of empathy for those who are rendered as other, alien and
dangerous (Fairbairn 2009).

We can also turn things around and note that people who are
not interested in other people or what makes them tick are
unlikely to be great readers of fiction (although they might be

consumers of non-fiction; Mar *et al.* 2006). So although reading might improve people's empathizing skills (though not necessarily boost their altruistic tendencies), it is high empathizers who are more likely to be avid consumers of novels and biographies. Given a reading choice, low empathizers might turn to something more factual, impersonal or mechanical. If they read at all, low empathizers are more likely to look at car manuals, computer magazines or books cataloguing world sporting records.

There is also a strong case that empathy is likely to improve further as a result of reading when readers share their reading experience with others. Reading groups, book clubs, discussion and role playing are likely to augment and deepen the reflective process. Thinking about character and plot with other people reveals the complexity and subtlety of our psychological makeup. Conflict and ambiguity, ignorance and dilemma, constraint and choice, nature and nurture create endless psychological possibilities. If we are to empathize with and make sense of other people, our appreciation of these and many other factors has to be sharp. Novels, poems and plays act as grindstones on which our empathizing skills become ever keener.

Writing fiction

It also seems to be the case that if writers are going to be any good at their craft, they must be good empathizers. Dunbar (1996) believes that the ability to imagine and enter the worlds of other people, even if they are fictional and do not actually exist, is an extraordinary business. Theory of Mind allows us to think about how someone, real or imagined, might respond to particular situations.

> In other words, we can begin to create literature, to write stories that go beyond a simple description of events as they occurred to delve more and more deeply into why the hero should behave in the way he does, into the feelings that drive him ever onwards in his quest.
>
> (Dunbar 1996: 102)

It was not until the eighteenth century that we began to see the proper emergence of the novelist in full psychologically reflective mode. Story writing became increasingly immersed in the experience of the subject as authors began to explore their characters' inner worlds. The big themes of life were contemplated as they were lived and experienced. Life's conflicts, dilemmas, hopes and beliefs were examined as characters engaged, related and muddled along. As readers, we see each character interacting more or less well with other characters, but we are also privy to their innermost thoughts and feelings. There is a strong case to be made that the modern mind itself is the product of art's increasing interest in the interior world of the other (for example, Armstrong 2005b).

Reviewing the writing of Virginia Woolf, Keen (2007: 59) recognizes that 'a writer's empathic exertions must extend to both "the dark places of psychology" and the broad field of other people's experiences, for no material is barred. "Everything is the proper stuff of fiction, every feeling, every thought," writes Woolf (1925[1919]: 215).' There is evidence that novelists, for example, score higher than average on empathy tests, and particularly high on activities that involve fantasy, daydreaming and perspective taking (Taylor 2002–03). In order to create plausible characters, writers have to get into the minds of their fictional people, who might be good or bad, black or white, male or female, young or old.

'My second novel', said Silko (n.d.), 'has some pretty outrageous villainous characters, and I have to admit, I was right inside them.' But whether people are good at writing novels because they are high empathizers, or whether writing novels improves the author's ability to empathize, is less certain, although one would strongly suspect that natural mind readers are more likely to create believable characters.

For a newspaper feature article, 'I will have to make it up', a number of leading novelists were asked about the secrets of their craft, including how they invented and wrote about their characters (Guardian Review 2011: 4–5). An empathic mindset was seen as critical in answer to the question: 'What sort of relationship exists between writers and the people they create on the page?'

P.D. James: How it works for me is best described in the opening of *Devices and Desires*. The book begins with the murder of a young girl, I think she was called Brenda ... She gets a lift with two women drivers, but they can only take her part of the way; they leave her at the end of this country road. She never reaches the bus because the murderer is there on that road. When I was writing that passage I was Brenda, feeling first of all the relief that she was going to be on the bus and then the realisation that there was this murderer, and then an increasing fear and unease ... I was just Brenda.

Ian Rankin: Where do all these characters in your books come from? They come from inside your head ... It's not really putting on someone else's clothes; it's putting on someone else's skin, their mind, their body ...

Hilary Mantel: Where do you pull your characters from? You have to create them out of your own self ... To create the protagonist of a book you really have to be prepared to live through them, and for me the process is physical as well as mental: I don't know quite how to put this, but I am so intensely engaged with my characters that their physicality passes into mine ...

Affective role taking

There is a great deal of evidence that encouraging people to put themselves in someone else's shoes and imagine what they would think and feel in that situation improves empathy (for example, Stotland 1969; Archer *et al.* 1979). Novelists, actors and psychologists have long known that simply mimicking an emotional expression can help you feel and understand that emotion. Adopting a look of anger or pouting the lips in pretend disgust gives us a direct feel of the emotion imitated, and what it feels like in the body as well as the mind.

There is in fact a subtle difference between inviting people to imagine how the other person feels in a given situation (imagine-the-other), and asking people to imagine how they would feel if they were in that situation (imagine-the-self). Imagining the self to be in the particular situation that another finds himself or herself in tends to lead to better empathy. Improvement is observed not merely in the level of empathy achieved but also in the ability of the individual to communicate that understanding, and even their willingness to respond helpfully.

It is worth remembering that we tend to see ourselves as possessing many more complex, subtle and contradictory traits than those we see in other people. Whereas I might see myself as generous but careful with money, close acquaintances might emphasize my economic caution, which, they tease me, borders on the stingy. In our explanations of others, we simplify their personalities; in our accounts of self, we try to get across what interesting and complex individuals we really are. It is a healthy reminder that when working with others, they are unlikely to see themselves as one-dimensional, diagnostically defined or simply explained.

It follows, then, that role playing, acting in plays, dancing expressively and taking part in many other kinds of performing art have the potential to make us more empathic.

Conclusion

Any activity that encourages us to get inside the head of a character or explore the experience of another helps us to see the world from someone else's point of view. Those who paint or draw, write or read, act or observe have the chance to employ and enlarge their empathic skills. Societies may value instrumental learning, but if those societies are to be fair, decent and good, they also need to embrace the arts and humanities. Empathy is lived rather than learned. Emotional literacy is therefore every bit as important as technical competence. If we are to live well together, we need to ensure that our stocks of empathy are in good supply.

15
Living Well Together: Empathy and Social Cohesion

Social relationships

What part might empathy play in the conduct of social relationships? Are marriages more successful if partners have and show empathy? Do friendships facilitate empathy, and does empathy sustain friendships? Are people more creative, indeed more productive, in work environments in which colleagues tune in and empathize? Most of us gain when we seek to work things out together, collaboratively. Without these shared understandings, life would become isolated and brutish.

> Because other people commonly have needs, desires, and goals which differ from our own, and because attainment of their goals is frequently incompatible with ours, a powerful tendency toward conflict is inherent in all social life ... Or, more accurately, the result can be such a conflict-filled existence if no mechanism, such as empathy, is available to interrupt this sequence.
>
> (Davis 1994: 178)

Sharing feelings with others both maintains and helps establish close relationships. People often say that they feel closer after an emotion has been shared. Sharing increases people's sense of social belonging and reduces feelings of isolation and confusion. Empathy helps reduce tension and forestalls conflict. Giving voice to feelings when in a relationship with an empathic other helps make sense of the emotion, gives meaning to the experience, and so assists the individual with feeling more in control.

There is also evidence that those who are more prepared to be open, use self-disclosure and empathize in close and intimate relationships are better liked than those who are more reticent and withholding (Reis and Shaver 1988). Fellow feeling seems to bring about companionship. Compassion between friends is likely to seal their intimacy. Being interested in and paying attention to the other person are important. Doing so can be affirming. We all need to be recognized and valued.

To understand and be understood is therefore deeply attractive, even seductive. It is comforting to sense that the other person is trying to see the world from your point of view, attempting to understand you and your 'frame of reference'. It is not simply that empathic partners sponsor good relationships. It is also the case that those on the receiving end of empathic understanding tend to feel well disposed to the other and the relationship that exists between them. If empathy is to facilitate relationships and promote cooperation, it must be expressed and perceived, communicated and received. In this more dynamic sense, empathy has to be a property of the relationship, not just of the individual.

Furthermore, if empathy encourages help that is selfless, then family, lovers and friends are where we would expect altruism to be at its height. Close social relationships are where we see human concern, kindness and sympathy at their most intense, and where we find care and cooperation at their best. We are often at our most empathic when involved in the emotional lives of partners, companions and close colleagues. Simply being there can be a great comfort. Nothing need be said.

If empathy oils the wheels of social life, then empathy is especially important in those areas of social life on which we depend most frequently. Without some sharing of understanding, without some seeing the world from the other's point of view, without some give-and-take, close relationships would very soon stop being close. Love and companionship would slowly crumble. Cooperation and setting about life together as a team, as workmates, as fellow travellers would hold no force. Empathy helps keep the relationship show on the road.

Partners, family and close friends also tend to know a good deal about each other's past histories and present lives. The depth and quality of empathy increase as we hold information about each other's highs and lows, hopes and fears and future plans and intentions. Your tendency to be self-deprecating and evasive in matters of success and opportunity might be irritating, except I know that you were raised in a poor neighbourhood by a strict, dismissive father who ridiculed any pretensions that you might have had. I know that you like to have your achievements recognized, but that any plaudits have to be low key and not too effusive.

Empathy benefits

Davis (1994: 183) recognizes four types of social behaviour in which the presence of empathy undoubtedly seems to help. First, individuals who are good at perspective taking, seeing and acknowledging other people's feelings and point of view help keep social conflict at bay. Or if conflict is present, they are good at managing it. When both individuals in a couple score high on perspective taking, they argue less, resolve conflicts quickly and enjoy a relationship that might be described as democratic.

Second, empathy tends to produce better, more accurate and more constructive communication between people. High empathizers are used as confidants by others. They make good work colleagues.

Third, empathy makes people more considerate. Tact is never very far away. Tempers tend to be even. Reflecting and empathizing make us more compassionate, cooperative and helpful. Seeing how matters might look and feel from the other's point of view is also likely to make us more tolerant and forgiving (Gilbert 2005).

And finally, high empathizers are more likely to evaluate their relationships positively. They express satisfaction with the relationship they have with their partners (Johnson 2004). They have friends and people befriend them. They get the best out of other people at work and other people get the best out of them. One of the risks faced by low empathizers is a lack of close friends, loneliness and isolation.

Those gifted with high empathy therefore help the social world go round. The skill is good for family life, business dealings, decision making and problem solving.

Empathically accurate perceivers are those who are consistently good at 'reading' other people's thoughts and feelings. All else being equal, they are likely to be the most tactful advisors, the most diplomatic officials, the most effective negotiators, the most electable politicians, the most productive salespersons, the most successful teachers, and the most insightful therapists.

(Ickes 1997: 2)

Ella, for example, in her weekly meeting with Oliver, a newly qualified counsellor, is aware that he is very upset about a client, Martin, who has terminated treatment after only four sessions. Oliver had thought things were going well between them. He cannot understand why the client suddenly stopped coming, without explanation. He is agitated and has talked about whether he is really cut out to be a good counsellor. His first words on meeting Ella are:

Oliver: I just didn't see it coming. I thought it was going reasonably well. If I can't spot an unhappy client, what am I doing in this business?

Ella: It feels bad to wonder if, maybe, you might not be a good counsellor.

Oliver: I feel confused.

Ella: (*picking up on his agitated body language*) This has hurt you. You look helpless and cross.

Oliver: (*with a hint of annoyance*) I put so much thought ... and feeling into this case. I was even beginning to feel quite pleased with myself. How wrong can I be?

Ella: Feeling rejected is painful. You feel upset because you thought things were going so well. You felt confident. Then that confidence was undermined when Martin didn't continue.

Oliver: Yes, too true. So I wonder what happened. Where did I screw up?

Ella: That sounds like a good question, so let's have a look at things. Martin is your fifth client since you joined us. Your first four cases all went well, very well. So Martin's reaction, particularly as you felt things were going well, is both a surprise and, I guess, a bit of a blow.

By this stage, Oliver is a little calmer. He is more willing and able to begin thinking about what happened rather than remaining caught up in his feelings of confusion and hurt. In the rest of the session, Ella helps Oliver to reflect critically on his work with Martin, never losing sight of the fact that he has been wounded by his client's apparent rejection. Oliver and Ella get into a discussion in which they review and analyse what happened and think about any lessons learned. Throughout, Ella has an implied but unstated belief that this is only a setback that really needs to be kept in perspective.

Effortful control and cognitive empathy

We have seen that when an individual reacts in a distressed fashion to someone else's upset state, they suffer what Batson *et al.* (1987) describe as personal distress. Although there is a similar emotion taking place in the person who is observing the other's distress, the emotion is not other-oriented. Individuals who are not very good at regulating their own arousal in emotionally charged relationships therefore tend to be low in empathy.

Individuals who are emotionally and physiologically well regulated, including secure and reflective people, are much less likely to suffer personal distress and much more likely to be empathic (Liew *et al.*, 2003; Eisenberg 2010). They possess good cognitive empathy that helps them see and imagine things from other people's point of view. Well-regulated people are said to possess *effortful control*, a dimension of temperament. Eisenberg says that effortful control 'involves the abilities to shift and focus attention as needed; to activate and inhibit behavior when required, especially when one does not feel like doing so; and to use other executive functioning skills needed to integrate information, plan, and modulate emotion and behavior' (2010: 133).

People who possess effortful control, who have strong willpower (Baumeister and Tierney 2011), are better at focusing on the other's condition and therefore better able to be both empathic and sympathetic. We see examples of empathy when the state of the other that triggers the empathic feeling is, on first sight, not in fact the most glaring feature of the situation or circumstance. Take the following case:

Michelle is visiting her best friend, Ruby, who is in hospital. Ruby is dying of cancer. She knows it. All her family and friends know it. It is now mid-spring and she has been given three or four months to live. Ruby has lost her hair and a lot of weight and doesn't look too good. But if truth be told, Ruby is getting a bit fed up with the solemnity that increasingly surrounds the visits made by many of her family and friends. Recognizing her visitors' distress, discomfort and loss of words, Ruby feels that it is becoming her responsibility to lighten the mood and help those who come to see her feel at ease! She could do without all this sombreness.

By temperament, Ruby is naturally cheerful and chatty. The one visitor she really does look forward to seeing is Michelle. The two women have always shared an interest in gardening and they talk about the new season, what Michelle has planted and how this or that shrub or tree is doing. They share tips and plant wisdom. They laugh a lot. The one thing they don't talk about, unless Ruby raises it, is the pain, the disease and its progress. Michelle, who has known Ruby for many years, seems to know exactly how to tune into Ruby's mood. Ruby never worries about having to make Michelle feel better. In fact, Ruby often says after Michelle has visited that their time together beats any tonic. For an hour or so, she can forget about time, disease and mortality. She said, 'With Michelle, I can just be me. I'm not the cancer. I'm not the patient. I'm not the cause of other people's sadness. It's lovely.' And as she talks about Michelle, she cries, cries with the joy of love and friendship.

Holding society together

Societies based solely on rational principles are in danger of forgetting that our shared emotional nature also has the potential to bind us together in our shared fate. Rational thought is lifeless without empathy's humanity. However, empathy without reason is equally suspect. In order to respond to feeling the feelings of the other, empathy requires rationality:

empathy that opens us up to the plight of the other can be felt as the call of conscience. Empathy allows the other to call us into question in our positing of the world. Having raised this call, however, empathy cannot evaluate it. It cannot tell us if the call is legitimate. Neither can it inform us how we are to respond. Only reason can provide this service. It gives 'sight' to empathy, allowing it to transform itself into practical action.

(Mensch 2011: 24)

For Rorty (1979, 1989), our shared embodied nature is a more powerful 'glue' for holding societies together than is abstract reason. As living beings, we all need to eat, drink and sleep. We share our vulnerability, sensation of pain, ability to be humiliated, love for our children and family, and feelings of grief (Weber 2011: 27). It is the vulnerability of the flesh that unites us. Our solidarity depends on our capacity and willingness to feel for others (Weber 2011: 30).

It is therefore not so much philosophically rational arguments that hold us together, but shared visions, hopes and dreams. That is why, Rorty believes, poets, writers and those blessed with imagination are more likely to be the heroes who inspire new worlds and better ways of living than are dry philosophers and drab political theorists. Literature helps us to see and feel the world of the other. Literature can therefore boost empathy and empathy can increase the richness and density of our social connections. Substituting literature for philosophy opens our imaginations to the lives of others as they are lived. 'For the liberal ironist, skill at imaginative identification does the work which the liberal metaphysician would like to have done by a specifically moral motivation' (Rorty 1989: 29). And so we are back to the empathy-enhancing powers of literature that we met in the previous chapter.

Equality and inequality, selflessness and selfishness

Successful people are often the most socially and emotionally intelligent. As we have seen, they are 'other-oriented' rather than always 'me-oriented'. Pop philosophies that celebrate love of the self forget that well-being involves other people. Our psychological self is the ongoing product of our relationships with friends, family and colleagues.

Societies that promote self-interest and only reward those who are aggressively self-seeking exist in a state of tension. They are often characterized by great inequality. The gap between rich and poor is significant. Even in societies that are rich overall, if economic inequality rises and the gap between those at the top and those at the bottom is too high, social problems increase and overall mental health decreases (Wilkinson 2000; Wilkinson and Pickett 2009). The ability to empathize also decreases as social differences stretch. Very unequal societies end up being the least empathic and the most unstable.

Societies that promote unbridled individualism, although they might be seen as rich and support many wealthy people, nevertheless tend to have high rates of crime and social tension. Overall levels of physical and mental health also tend to be relatively poor. This analysis raises many awkward political, moral and mental health issues. It implies that empathy, altruism and optimal mental health lessen as societies grow more individualistic, market driven, self-seeking, self-promoting, intolerant and insensitive to the needs of the weak, vulnerable and unsuccessful.

The opposite is also true. Even if a society's overall wealth is not high, if the gap between the relatively rich and poor is not too great, dissatisfaction, unrest and social problems are low and stress falls (Wilkinson and Pickett 2009).

High levels of stress reduce our ability to be empathic. If there is low trust and high tension, dissatisfaction and envy in the social climate, then stress will rise and empathy fall. If a society is to maintain its well-being, it is critical that the empathy 'trainers' of tomorrow's citizens – parents – enjoy conditions of low stress if they are to connect, attune and emotionally communicate with their children. And yet it is young parents in general, and mothers in particular, who are often the least supported and the most stressed.

Hrdy's concept of cooperative parenting, in which mothers enjoy extensive support from family, friends and community, reminds us of the value of an empathically literate society (Hrdy

2009). Cooperation, trust and social harmony depend on the presence of empathy and fairness. Social capital is greatest in societies where the bonds of trust, friendship and shared endeavour are most strong.

Pinker (2011), although he acknowledges that we still live in violent times, nevertheless argues controversially that when we take the long view, there has actually been a steady decline in violence and mass killings. Compared to the historical past when murder, casual violence and torture were routine, the past century, in spite of wars and genocide, has actually grown increasingly more peaceful. This decrease in violence can be observed at the interpersonal level, in the actions of governments, in our treatment of animals.

There is no guarantee that this long-term trend will continue, but Pinker offers a number of explanations, many of which witness an expansion in people's empathy and an attitude that sees violence as a problem to be solved rather than a contest to be won. All of this is nicely summarized by Naughton:

> [Pinker] identifies a number of forces that were key factors in curbing mankind's capacity for inhumanity: the slow emergence of states capable of playing the role of Hobbes's 'Leviathan'; the pacifying impact of commerce and trade on behaviour; the impact of the Enlightenment on the way people thought about others; the evolution of notions of etiquette over the centuries; the way print and literacy expanded the 'circle of empathy' beyond people's immediate family; the importance of women in civilising men; and the 'long peace' that followed the second world war.
>
> (Naughton 2011: 8)

Empathy helps us raise our social game. It is all too easy for the self to be selfish. Selfish selves promote a win–lose world, where some gain at the expense of others, and tension and conflict are rife. However, in worlds where there is selflessness, the collective gains can be enormous. Give-and-take attitudes promote cooperation, and cooperation has a habit of producing win–win outcomes in which everyone gains. Baron-Cohen's career-long interest in empathy has helped him recognize its remarkable properties:

> Empathy is like a universal solvent. Any problem immersed in empathy become soluble. It is effective as a way of anticipating and resolving interpersonal problems, whether this is marital conflict, an international conflict, a problem at work, difficulties in a friendship, political deadlocks, a family dispute, or a problem with a neighbour.
>
> (Baron-Cohen 2011: 127)

Empathy and fairness, justice and forgiveness

Principles of justice and morality typically have a touch of empathy about them. Sensing how we would feel if we were the victim of some injustice, we tend to support social systems that uphold notions of fairness. We sympathize with those who are on the receiving end of some wrongdoing – a deception, a trick, a robbery, an act of discrimination. But quite what we judge to be 'fair' is less settled.

Those who have done well in life while believing that merit, hard work and productivity account for their success tend to favour payment by results and personal freedom. They might empathize with a person who feels angry when the boss's son is promoted before them, or when positive discrimination sees the appointment of a less well-qualified person instead of them. Others might measure fairness in terms of equality and the principle of 'each according to his or her need'. They might sympathize with those who suffer poverty and hardship because they have been exposed to sexual or racial discrimination in the job market.

The tension between principles of freedom and equality, liberty and security, productivity and need, and the strong feelings that these principles evoke, has led political philosophers to conceive what they believe would be a fair and just society. For example, Rawls's theory of justice (Rawls 1999) attempts to reconcile these conflicting principles by recognizing that merit and hard work should be rewarded, but that the needs of society's least advantaged (the old, sick and injured) should also be met to a level that everyone agrees is fair based on the idea that 'there but for the grace of God go I'. Although Rawls emphasizes the rational in his theory, there seems a good case to be made that empathy and the construction of moral principles, particularly around ideas of what is fair, are closely linked.

The concept of restorative justice also relies on the reformative powers of empathy. Criminals who have caused harm and emotional suffering to others by robbing them, hurting them or cheating them are brought face to face with their victims. The victims talk about how their lives have been blighted by the crime. They describe how their feelings of well-being and safety have been undermined, their mental health upset.

The belief is that by exposing the perpetrators to the personal consequences of their crimes, their empathy will be aroused. Offenders, who typically run low on the empathy stakes, might also be encouraged to get involved in intense role-taking exercises and group discussions, or be challenged to imagine how their offensive behaviour might have been experienced by their victims. The hope is that feelings of empathy make us less likely to harm others. In this way, restorative justice hopes to bring about change and healing in those who have unthinkingly and without feeling hurt others and destroyed their peace of mind. Restorative Justice Online (n.d.) has up-to-date reviews of current research on the effectiveness of victim-awareness and empathy-based interventions.

Similar thoughts lie behind the truth and reconciliation commissions that have brought racists, terrorists and torturers face to face with their victims, for example in South Africa, Argentina and Northern Ireland. Of course, people vary in their willingness to forgive. The most forgiving people tend to have trusting natures. They are typically emotionally stable. They are blessed with the empathic ability to see and understand others and why they did what they did. People who forgive also avoid ruminating about past hurts and injustices; they are good at living in and trying to make the most of the present.

It is extraordinary to discover that so many victims who have been willing to meet their perpetrators have also been able to forgive them. To forgive is an act of deep humanity, or even one of saintliness if common wisdom is to be believed, for 'To err is human; to forgive divine'. Being forgiven begins the healing process. Empathy is in fact a good predictor of forgiveness (Fincham 2010). True, it is often the case that the closer we are to someone, the more difficult we find it to forgive them, especially if they have hurt us. Nevertheless, a wife who has had an affair is more likely to be forgiven if her husband scores high on measures of empathy (Toussant and Webb 2007). It seems that forgiveness, and therefore empathy, is an important factor in whether relationships are destined to be successful.

Conclusion

Empathy makes social life possible, it makes it smooth. We are attracted to people possessed of high empathy. We feel understood; and feeling understood is both ontologically and existentially a life-affirming experience. Benefits, though not directly sought, also accrue to empathizers. They tend to be successful in their relationships, with lovers, friends, colleagues and strangers.

Only when societies stretch the difference between rich and poor, the strong and the weak, does empathy's capital fall. One of the rarest but most powerful examples of high empathy is to be found in those willing and able to forgive those who have harmed them. Holding no bitterness in their hearts, they can move on. And those who have been forgiven, though humbled, might also learn something of empathy's virtues and power to heal. So it seems fitting to end this brief book with a short chapter on the part that empathy plays in what makes us human and what lies at the heart of our humanity.

16
Human Being

Shared fate

Our social nature gives rise to our empathy and empathy allows us to be sociable. Our sociability is inextricably linked with our ability to love and show compassion. When we empathize, we see ourselves in the other and the other in ourselves. Empathy dissolves the boundaries between the self and others as my life expands into yours and yours into mine. In the words of the poet Friedrich Schiller (quoted in Scheler 1954: 250):

> If you would know yourself, take heed of the practice of others.
> If you would understand others, look to your own heart within you.

We recognize our own hopes and fears as we listen to others talk of their hopes and fears. To lose our empathy would be to lose our humanity. 'There is nowhere else for one to obtain humanness', claims Agosta (2010: xvi), 'than from another human being.' Human being, becoming and being human, is not an individual enterprise. Empathy and its dependence on our socially embedded nature are ontological, a matter of our very being.

The other as subject, the other as object

Modern life emphasizes the self as independent and isolated, not interconnected and interdependent. Although the self is experienced as subject, other people are viewed as object. Viewing others as objects – to be used commercially, exploited sexually, observed scientifically, assessed clinically, judged legally – frustrates the understanding of the other as subject. Others are too frequently seen and dealt with instrumentally, as objects that might impede or further one's own ends.

In this sense, we relate with others on an *I–It* basis, subject to object (Buber 1958). Treating other people as objects reveals a lack of empathy. Little or no thought is given to their experience. Other people are viewed simply as a means to an end: to provide sex, to supply labour, to make a profit, to help the organization meet its goals.

These kinds of relationship dehumanize other people. Many of us, maybe fleetingly as we single-mindedly (that is, not other-mindedly) pursue our own goals and interests, might treat others instrumentally, without empathy. But when self-interest and self-centredness become our *modus vivendi* and *modus operandi* – that is, our way of living and way of working – then we suffer an empathy deficit. Single-minded attention, by definition, rules out consideration of other people's states of mind. Treating people as objects and lacking empathy mean that people become indifferent to the feelings of others, and indifference can easily pave the way to cruelty.

In contrast, as we saw earlier, *I–Thou* relationships are those that take place between people as subjects, two centres of meaningful experience. For Buber (1958), I only become myself as I relate to the other. And I can only relate fully with others when I discover myself: 'I become through my relation to the *Thou*; as I become *I*, I say *Thou*' (Buber 1958: 11, emphasis in original). In an I–Thou relationship, the self and other meet as equals, with mutual needs and goals. The other is not a means to my end (van Deurzen and Arnold-Baker 2005: 165–6). In this philosophy, we can only meet others as they come out to meet us (Gardner 2011: 56). And in this meeting a 'subjective truth' is experienced by the two participating agents (Kierkegaard 2011[1843]). Only when we meet in the 'in between', when the relationship is *I–Thou*, do we grow.

Social being and human being

Our psychological selves emerge out of our relationships with others. This echoes Marx's famous aphorism: 'It is not the consciousness of men that determines their being, but, on the contrary, their social being that determines their consciousness' (Marx 1859: 363). To become human we have to relate with empathic others. As a clinical psychologist and passionate advocate of the power of empathy, Ciaramicoli proclaims:

> In my work and life I have discovered one absolute truth – empathy is the light that shines through the darkness of our pain and our fear to reveal what we have in common as human beings.
>
> (Ciaramicoli and Ketcham 2000: x)

Empathy is therefore both an extraordinary human skill and a fundamental requirement to the process of becoming, and being, human.

Throughout life, from infancy to old age, our humanity arises out of and is sustained by our relationships with empathic others. 'All real living', said Buber (1958: 11), 'is meeting.' Empathy can only be a participant activity. Empathy, claims Stewart, is 'an activity requiring a belief in persons as the ultimate term of reference, as the ultimate reality, not minds, not bodies, not concepts, but persons, actual or imagined' (Stewart 1956: 134, quoted in Clark 2007: 76). 'Human beings', believes Agosta (2010: 30), 'are designed to be affected by each other's feelings.' To be cut off from the emotional interest of others and to have no interest in the emotions of others is to suffer the fate of not being known or not knowing. Without empathy, we remain strangers and estranged. Those unfortunate enough to have suffered brain damage or dysfunction through accident, biology or disease, with the result that they can no longer recognize and show interest in their own or other people's emotions, remain cut off and socially isolated, no longer the 'person' whom their family and friends once knew.

It is in our empathic dealings with other people that we continue to learn, develop, mature and become more moral. As I recognize me in you, and you in me, not only do I begin to understand the nature of being human, I also become a little wiser, a mite more humble. 'Empathy ... enables me to develop myself more fully as a reflective and self-critical individual, since

it enables me to recognize the opinions of others about myself'
(Stueber 2006: 9).

Deep down, empathy is a reminder of our shared frailties and
our common strengths. Rifkin (2009: 161) talks of empathy as
'the soul of democracy'. When empathy wanes, democracy is
diminished. The erosion of empathy robs us of our humanity,
without which any sense of community, shared interests and
shared fates is lost.

> The great transformation from 'I think, therefore I am' to 'I
> participate, therefore I am' places empathy at the very center
> of the human story – a place it has always inhabited but
> which society has never fully acknowledged or recognized.
> Polish philosopher Henryk Skolimowski writes '*[t]o be a*
> *person in the participatory universe entails the recognition of the*
> *bond of participation* ... If we recognize this bond, then we ipso
> facto recognize empathy.'
> (Rifkin 2009: 153, emphasis in original; Skolimowski 1995:
> 373)

On this reckoning, life's meaning is to be found in our relationships with others. 'To sum up,' says Rifkin, 'if reality is experience and experience is always in relationship to the other, then
the more extensive the relationships, the deeper we penetrate
the various layers of reality and the closer we come to understand the meaning of existence ... Empathy is a celebration of
life, in all of its corporeality (Rifkin 2009: 155, 273–4).

The cycle of empathy

The story of empathy begins with evolution selecting for the skills
of empathy and minds that can read other minds: what they are
feeling, desiring, planning. Empathy and mind reading offer a
huge boost to behaviours that are cooperative, collaborative and
collective. Empathy and sociability allow communities and societies to grow ever more complex, sophisticated and adaptive,
conferring huge evolutionary advantages on the human species.

Nature's other great trick that she weaves into this story is her
ability to capitalize on the human infant's extremely immature

and vulnerable state at birth. The helplessness of babies means that they are dependent on primary carers for many, many years. This dependency sets up a relationship in which survival depends on parents and kin being caring, compassionate and protective. The sensitivity demanded by these tasks requires empathy and attunement, as well as the skills of mind reading and mind-mindedness. The infant's brain, relatively undeveloped at birth, is exquisitely set up to develop and neurologically organize itself to make sense of the environment in which it finds itself.

As we learned in Chapter 5, the young brain is programmed to make sense of experience, but it needs exposure to experience before it can make sense of it. One of the major environmental experiences to which the baby's brain is exposed is parents and other kin relating to it as an independent self and mental being, emotionally, socially, empathically, psychologically and as mind readers. Being programmed to make sense of these experiences means that the young brain gradually learns to make sense of and practise the very things of which it has been on the receiving end, namely the skills of empathy, emotional intelligence, social understanding, intentionality and psychological selfhood. So, lo and behold, children gradually develop empathy, attunement and mentalization, the very factors that allow them to become socially competent. These are also the qualities that make them human.

Empathy is vital if children are to join the community of others with all the skills and virtues that define our species at its best. With empathy, we can love, listen, understand and imagine. We can work together, share and create. We can tolerate, forgive, show mercy, apologize, repair and hope. We know what empathy is. We know how it can be nurtured. We just need the will to continue finding the way to do so.

We noted at the very beginning of this book that there has been an explosion of interest in empathy by many disciplines and practices, ranging from the brain sciences to restorative justice, evolutionary psychology to counselling, the arts to education. The shared belief is that empathic people are more successful social players and more cooperative colleagues. They become better counsellors and more skilful social workers. In the worlds of health and education, they are well regarded by patients and pupils.

All of this argues for raising empathy's presence at every opportunity. There is no set way to achieve this. Indeed, one of the hopes of this book is that simply recognizing and appreciating empathy's nature, origins and wide-ranging virtues itself heightens our empathic sensitivities. I argue that it is not so much training people in a formal manner that increases our empathy, but rather recharging our interest in other people, the wonders of the human mind and our extraordinary talent as a species for 'doing' social life. This takes more effort than might be apparent at first sight. To sustain our interest in what other people might be thinking and feeling, and to be forever curious about why we do and say the things we do, takes a great deal of mental effort. Few of us can keep up such concentration for long, but when we do, it connects us to others in ways that see the best of human being – care, concern, cooperation, compassion, love, interest, understanding, fascination, forgiveness.

As we have seen, it is never too late to develop and improve our empathic sensibilities. However, most advocates acknowledge that empathy comes most easily and naturally when it is introduced into relationships during the early years. To this end, the more parents are helped to recognize, understand and enjoy their infants as emotionally complex, psychologically fascinating, social skilled burgeoning beings, the more their children will grow up to be secure and empathic (Sroufe *et al.* 2005; Szalavitz and Perry 2011). Indeed, the subtitle of Sunderland's excellent book, *What Every Parent Needs to Know: The Remarkable Effects of Love, Nurture and Play on Your Child's Development*, captures all of this most beautifully (Sunderland 2006).

Many teachers and educationalists have become equally enthusiastic about helping older children develop their empathic capacities (Breakstone *et al.* 2008; Williams 2011). Although teaching emotional literacy and promoting empathic classroom behaviour were often triggered by worries about bullying, these skills are now seen as part and parcel of everyday classroom practice. Chapter 13 described the government-sponsored SEAL programmes run by schools in England and

Wales (DfES 2005; DCSF 2007). These are designed to improve emotional literacy in general and empathy in particular. Mary Gordon's *Roots of Empathy* (2009) programmes for schools have also proved very attractive to educators across the world. They have now been widely adopted by schools in the United States, Canada, Australia, Ireland, Scotland and England.

And beyond the school years, the value of promoting empathy in adults is being increasingly recognized as a way of sponsoring healthier and happier, safer and more creative societies. In his book *The Age of Empathy: Nature's Lessons for a Kinder Society* (2010), Frans de Waal argues that empathy creates a sense of social responsibility. It is the 'social glue' that helps to hold communities together. For Rifkin (2009), empathy lies at the heart of decency and democracy. Similarly, David Brooks, in his politically influential book *The Social Animal* (2011), believes that qualities such as emotional intelligence and empathy are key to growing successful societies in which cooperation, community mindedness and general well-being are the natural order of things.

However, perhaps the most established, committed and best thought-through users of empathy are counsellors, psychotherapists and those who work in the personal social services. Although the aim of this book has been to celebrate empathy's value and scope, my belief is that an appreciation of empathy's richness and relevance, not just in the clinical setting but beyond in the world of the arts, biology, psychology and philosophy, helps power and nurture our empathic natures.

The more we recognize and understand empathy in all its guises, the more likely it will be that our parenting will be sound, our communications alert, our friendships good, our behaviour decent, our schools stimulating, our therapies successful, our practices effective, and our societies civilized.

Bibliography

Agosta, L. (2010). *Empathy in the Context of Philosophy*. Houndmills: Palgrave Macmillan.

Allen, J. G. (2006). Mentalizing in practice. In J. G. Allen and P. Fonagy (eds) *Handbook of Mentalilzation-Based Treatment*. Chichester: Wiley, pp 3–30.

Alligood, M. (1992). Empathy: The importance of recognising two types. *Journal of Psychosocial Nursing*, 30: 14–17.

Allport, G. (1938). *Personality: A Psychological Interpretation*. London: Constable.

Alvarez, A. (2001). *Poker: Bets, Bluffs, and Bad Beats*. San Francisco: Chronicle Books.

Alvarez, J. R. (2007). The psychological impact of kidnap. In E. K. Carll (ed.) *Trauma Psychology*. Westport, CT: Praeger, pp 61–90.

Anckarsäter, H. and Cloninger, C. R. (2007). The genetics of empathy and its disorders. In T. Farrow and P. Woodruff (eds) *Empathy in Mental Illness*. Cambridge: Cambridge University Press, pp 261–88.

Archer, R., Foushee, H., Davis, M. and Aderman, D. (1979). Emotional empathy in a courtroom simulation: A person–situation interaction. *Journal of Personality and Social Psychology*, 60: 241–53.

Armstrong, K. (2005a). *The Spiral Staircase*. London: HarperCollins.

Armstrong, N. (2005b). *How Novels Think: The Limits of Individualism from 1719–1900*. New York: Columbia University Press.

Aronson, E. and Patnoe, S. (1997). *Cooperation in the Classroom: The Jigsaw Method*. New York: Longman.

Aronson, E., Wilson, T. D. and Akert, R. M. (2005). *Social Psychology* (5th edn). Upper Saddle River, NJ: Pearson.

Baron, R. A., Byrne, D. and Branscombe, N. R. (2006). *Social Psychology* (11th edn), Boston: Pearson.

Baron-Cohen, S. (1987). Autism and symbolic play. *British Journal of Developmental Psychology*, 5: 139–48.

Baron-Cohen, S. (1995). *Mindblindness: An Essay on Autism and Theory of Mind*. Cambridge, MA: MIT Press.

Baron-Cohen, S. (2004). *The Essential Difference*. London: Penguin.

Baron-Cohen, S. (2011). *Zero Degrees of Empathy: A New Theory of Human Cruelty*. London: Allen Lane.

Baron-Cohen, S. and Wheelwright, S. (2004). The Empathy Quotient

(EQ): An investigation of adults with Asperger Syndrome or High Functioning Autism, and normal sex differences. *Journal of Autism and Developmental Disorders*, 34: 163–75.

Baron-Cohen, S., Wheelwright, S. and Hill, J. (2001) The 'Reading of the mind in the eyes' test, revised version: A study with normal adults and adults with Asperger Syndrome or high functioning autism. *Journal of Child Psychology and Psychology*, 42: 241–52.

Baron-Cohen, S., Ring, H., Bullmore, E., Wheelwright, S., Ashwin, C. and Williams, S. (2000). The amygdala theory of autism. *Neuroscience and Behavioural Reviews*, 24: 355–64.

Barrett, L., Dunbar, R. and Lycett, J. (2002). *Human Evolutionary Psychology*. Basingstoke: Palgrave Macmillan.

Barrett-Lennard, G. T. (1981). The empathy cycle: Refinement of a nuclear concept. *Journal of Counseling Psychology*, 28: 91–100.

Batson, C. D. (1991). *The Altruism Question toward a Social Psychological Answer*. Hillsdale, NJ: Lawrence Erlbaum.

Batson, C. D. (2010). Empathy-induced altruistic motivation. In M. Mikulincer and P. R. Shaver (eds). *Prosocial Motives, Emotions, and Behavior*. Washington, DC: American Psychological Association, pp 15–34.

Batson, C. D., Fultz, J. and Schoenrade, P. (1987). 'Distress and empathy: Two qualitatively distinct vicarious emotions with different motivational consequences. *Journal of Personality*. 55: 19–39.

Baumeister, R. F. and Leary, M. R. (1995). The need to belong: Desire for interpersonal attachments as a fundamental human motivation. *Psychological Bulletin*, 117: 497–529.

Baumeister, R. F. and Tierney, J. (2011). *Willpower: Rediscovering Our Greatest Strength*. London: Allen Lane.

Beadle, J. N., Brown, V., Keady, B., Tranel, D. and Paradiso, S. (2012). Trait empathy as a predictor of individual differences in perceived loneliness. *Psychological Report*, 110(1): 3–15.

Beeghly, M. and Cicchetti, D. (1994) Child maltreatment, attachment and the self system: Emergence of an internal state lexicon in toddlers at high social risk. *Developmental Psychopathology* 6: 5–30.

Bentall, R. (2009). *Doctoring the Mind: Why Psychiatric Treatments Fail*. London: Allen Lane.

Bierman, K. L. and Erath, S. A. (2008). Promoting social competence in early childhood: Classroom curricula and social skills coaching programs. In K. McCartney and D. Phillips (eds) *Blackwell Handbook of Early Childhood Development*. Oxford: Blackwell, pp 595–615.

Björkqvist, K. (2007). Empathy, social intelligence and aggression in adolescent boys and girls. In T. Farrow and P. Woodruff (eds) *Empathy in Mental Illness*. Cambridge: Cambridge University Press, pp 76–88.

Blair, R. (2007). Empathic dysfunction in psychopathic individuals. In T. Farrow and P. Woodruff (eds) *Empathy in Mental Illness*. Cambridge: Cambridge University Press, pp 3–16.

Blair, R., Mitchell, D. and Blair, D. (2005). *The Psychopath*. Oxford: Blackwell.

Bloom, P. (2004). *Descartes' Baby: How Child Development Explains What Makes Us Human*. London: Heinemann.

Bohart, A. C. and Greenberg, L. S. (1997). *Empathy Reconsidered: New Directions in Psychotherapy*. Washington, DC: American Psychologist.

Bohart, A. C., Elliot, R., Greenberg, L. and Watson, J. (2002). Empathy. In J. C. Norcross (ed.) *Psychotherapy Relationships That Work: Therapist Contributions and Responsiveness to Patients*. Oxford: Oxford University Press, pp 89–108.

Bowlby, J. (1969) *Attachment and Loss. Vol. I: Attachment*. London: Hogarth Press.

Bowlby, J. (1988). *A Secure Base: Clinical Applications of Attachment Theory*. London: Hogarth Press.

Bradley. M. M., Codispoti, M., Sabatinelli, D. and Lang, P. (2001). Emotion and motivation II: Sex differences in picture processing. *Emotion* 1: 300–19.

Breakstone, S., Dreibblatt, M. and Dreiblatt, K. (2008). *How to Stop Bullying and Social Agrression: Elementary Grade Lessons and Activities That Teach Empathy, Friendship and Respect*. Thousand Oaks, CA: Corwin Press.

Brewer, M. B. and Caporael, L. R. (1990). Selfish genes versus selfish people: Socio-biology as origin myth. *Motivation and Emotion*, 14: 237–43.

Brooks, D. (2011). *The Social Animal*. London: Short Books.

Brufee, K. A. (1999). *Collaborative Learning: Higher Education, Interdependence, and the Authority of Knowledge* (2nd edn). Baltimore: Johns Hopkins University Press.

Brune, M. (2005). 'Theory of mind' in schizophrenia: A review of the literature. *Schizophrenia Bulletin*, 31: 21–42.

Bruner, J. (1990). *Acts of Meaning*. London: Harvard University Press.

Buber, M. (1958). *I and Thou* (2nd edn). Edinburgh: T. and T. Clark.

Bush, T. (2003). Communicating with patients who have dementia. *Nursing Times* 99(48): 42.

Carpendale, J. and Lewis, J. (2006). *How Children Develop Social Understanding*. Oxford: Blackwell.

Carter, C. S., Harris, J. and Porges, S.W. (2011). Neural and evolution-ary perspectives on empathy. In B.Weber, E. Marsal and T. Dobashi (eds) *The Politics of Empathy*. Munster: LIT Verlag, pp 169–82.

Cartwright, J. (2000). *Evolution and Human Behaviour*. Basingstoke: Macmillan.

Caspi, A., McClay, J., Moffit, T., Mill, J., Martin, J., Craig, I., Taylor, A. and Poulton, R. (2002) Role of genotype in the cycle of violence in maltreated children. *Science* 297: 851–4.

Cassels, T., Chan, S., Chung, W. and Birch, S. (2010). The role of culture in affective empathy: Cultural and bicultural differences. *Journal of Cognition and Culture*, 10: 309–26.

Castonguay, L. G. and Beutler, L. E. (2006). Common and unique principles of therapeutic change: What do we know and what do we need to know? In L. G. Castonguay and L. E. Beutler (eds) *Principles of Therapeutic Change That Work*. Oxford: Oxford University Press, pp 353–69.

Chakrabarti, B. and Baron-Cohen, S. (2006). Empathizing: Neurocognitive developmental mechanisms and individual differ-ences. *Progress in Brain Research*, 156: 403–17.

Chartrand, T. L. and Bargh, J. A. (1999). The chameleon effect: The perception–behavior link and social interaction. *Journal of Personality and Social Psychology*, 76: 893–910.

Chartrand, T. L., Maddux, W. W. and Lakin, J. L. (2005). Beyond the perception–behavior link: The ubiquitous utility and motivational moderators of nonconscious mimicry. In R. Hassin, J. Uleman and J. Bargh (eds) *Unintended Thought II: The New Unconscious*. New York: Oxford University Press, pp 334–61.

Cheng, C. M. and Chartrand, T. L. (2003). Self-monitoring without awareness: Using mimicry as a nonconscious affiliation strategy. *Journal of Personality and Social Psychology*, 85: 1170–79.

Churchill, S. and Bayne, R. (1998). Psychological type and concep-tions of empathy in experienced counsellors. *Counselling Psychology Quarterly* 11(4): 379–90.

Churchland, P. S. (2011). *Braintrust: What Neuroscience Tells Us about Morality*. Princeton: Princeton University Press.

Ciaramicoli, A. and Ketcham, K. (2000). *The Power of Empathy: A Practical Guide to Creating Intimacy, Self-Understanding, and Lasting Love*. London: Piatkus.

Clark, A. J. (2007). *Empathy in Counseling and Psychotherapy: Perspectives and Practices*. Mahweh, NJ: Lawrence Erlbaum Associates.

Coleridge, S. T. (1798[1983]). *Biographica Literaria. Vol. I: Collected*

Works of Samuel Taylor Coleridge, eds J. Engell and W. Bate. London: Routledge.

Coles, R. (1997). *The Moral Intelligence of Children*. New York: Random House.

Cooper, M. (2001). Embodied empathy. In S. Haugh and T. Merry (eds) *Empathy*. Ross-on-Wye: PCCS Books, pp 218–29.

Coplan, A. (2011). Understanding empathy: Its features and effects. In A. Coplan and P. Goldie (eds) *Empathy: Philosophical and Psychological Perspectives*. Oxford: Oxford University Press, pp 3–18.

Coplan, A. and Goldie, P. (2011). Introduction. In A. Coplan and P. Goldie (eds) *Empathy: Philosophical and Psychological Perspectives*. Oxford: Oxford University Press, pp ix–xlvii.

Covey, S. R. (1990). *The 7 Habits of Highly Effective People: Powerful Lessons in Personal Change*. New York: Free Press.

Cozolino, L. (2002). *The Neuroscience of Psychotherapy*. New York: Norton.

Cozolino, L. (2006). *The Neuroscience of Human Relationships*. New York: Norton.

Crittenden, P. (2008). *Raising Parents: Attachment, Parenting and Child Safety*. Cullompton: Willan Press.

Cupitt, D. (1990). *Creation out of Nothing*. London: SCM Press.

Darwin, C. (1871). *The Descent of Man and Selection in Relation to Sex*. London: John Murray.

Davies, S. (2011). Infectious music: Music-listener contagion. In A. Coplan and P. Goldie (eds) *Empathy: Philosophical and Psychological Perspectives*. Oxford: Oxford University Press, pp 134–48.

Davis, M. H. (1994). *Empathy: A Social Psychological Approach*. Madison, WI: Brown and Benchmark.

Davis, M. H. (2004). *Test Your EQ: Find Out How Emotionally Intelligent You Really Are*. London: Piatkus.

Dawes, R. M., van de Kragt, A. J. C. and Orbell, J. M. (1988). Not me or thee but we: The importance of group identity in eliciting cooperation in dilemma situations. *Acta Psychologica*, 68: 83–97.

Dawkins, R. (1976). *The Selfish Gene*. Oxford: Oxford University Press.

de Hennezel, M. (2011). *The Warmth of the Heart Prevents Your Body from Rusting*. London: Rodale/Pan Macmillan.

de Waal, F. B. M. (2009). Putting altruism back into altruism: The evolution of empathy. *Annual Review of Psychology*, 59: 279–300.

de Waal, F. (2010). *The Age of Empathy: Nature's Lessons for a Kinder Society*. London: Souvenir Press.

Decety, J. and Ickes, W. (eds) (2011). *The Social Neuroscience of Empathy*. Cambridge, MA: MIT Press.

Decety, J. and Jackson, P. L. (2004). The functional architecture of human empathy. *Behavioral and Cognitive Neuroscience Reviews*, 3: 71–100.

Decety, J. and Meltzoff, A. N. (2011). Empathy, imitation, and the social brain. In A. Coplan and P. Goldie (eds) *Empathy: Philosophical and Psychological Perspectives*. Oxford: Oxford University Press, pp 58–81.

Dekeyser, M., Elliott, R. and Leijssen, M. (2011). In J. Decety and W. Ickes (eds) *The Social Neuroscience of Empathy*. Cambridge, MA: MIT Press, pp 113–24.

Denham, S. A. (1998). *Emotional Development in Young Children*. New York: Guilford Press.

Department for Children, Schools and Families (2007). *Social and Emotional Aspects of Learning for Secondary Schools*. Nottingham: DCSF Publications.

Department for Education and Skills (2005). *Excellence and Enjoyment: Social and Emotional Aspects of Learning (Guidance)*. Nottingham: DfES Publications.

Dolan, M. and Fullam, R. (2007). Empathy, antisocial behaviour and personal pathology. In T. Farrow and P. Woodruff (eds) *Empathy in Mental Illness*. Cambridge: Cambridge University Press, pp 33–48.

Domes, G., Heinrichs, M., Michel, A., Berger, C. and Herpertz, C. (2007). Oxytocin improves 'mind-reading' in humans. *Biological Psychiatry* 61(6): 731–3.

Dovidio, J., Johnson, J., Gaertner, S., Pearson, A., Aguy, T. and Ashburn-Nardo, L. (2010). Empathy and intergroup relations. In M. Mikulincer and P. R. Shaver (eds) (2010) *Prosocial Motives, Emotions, and Behavior: The Better Angels of Our Nature*. Washington, DC: American Psychological Association, pp 393–408.

Dunbar, R. (1996). *Grooming, Gossip and the Evolution of Language*. London: Faber and Faber.

Dunbar, R. and Aiello, L. (1993). Neocortex size, group size, and the evolution of language. *Current Anthropology*, 34(2): 184–93.

Dunn, G. and Bentall, R. (2007). Modelling treatment effect heterogeneity in randomized controlled trials of complex interventions (psychological treatments). *Statistics in Medicine*, 26: 4719–45.

Dunn, J. and Cutting, A. L. (1999). Understanding others, and individual differences in friendship interactions in young children. *Social Development*, 8: 201–19.

Dunn, J., Brown, J. and Beardsall, L. (1991). Family talk about feeling states and children's later understanding of others' emotions. *Developmental Psychology*, 27: 448–55.

Dunn, J., Cutting, A. L. and Demetriou, H. (2000). Moral sensibility, understanding others, and children's friendship interactions in the preschool period. *British Journal of Developmental Psychology*, 18: 159–77.

Edmunds, M. (1992). Co-dependency and counselling. Unpublished MSW transcripts, University of East Anglia, Norwich.

Egan, G. (2010). *The Skilled Helper: A Problem-Management and Opportunity-Development Approach to Helping* (9th edn). Belmont, CA: Brooks/Cole Cengage Learning.

Ehrlich, P. R. and Ornstein, R. E. (2012). *Humanity on a Tightrope: Thoughts on Empathy, Family, and Big Changes for a Viable Future.* Lanham, MD: Rowman and Littlefield.

Einstein, D. and Lanning, K. (1998). Shame, guilt, ego-development, and the five-factor model of personality. *Journal of Personality*, 66: 555–82.

Eisenberg, N. (1986). *Altruistic Emotion, Cognition, and Behavior.* Hillsdale, NJ: Lawrence Erlbaum Associates.

Eisenberg, N. (2010). Empathy-related responding: Links with self-regulation, moral judgment, and moral behaviour. In M. Mikulincer and P. R. Shaver (eds) (2010) *Prosocial Motives, Emotions, and Behavior: The Better Angels of Our Nature.* Washington, DC: American Psychological Association, pp 129–48.

Eisenberg, N. and Eggum, N. (2011). Empathic responding: Sympathy and personal distress. In B. Weber, E. Marsal and T. Dobashi (eds) *The Politics of Empathy.* Munster: LIT Verlag, pp 71–83.

Eisenberg, N. and Miller, P. A. (1987). The relation of empathy to prosocial behaviour and related behaviors. *Psychological Bulletin*, 101: 91119.

Eisenberg, N., Valiente, C. and Champion, C. (2004). Empathy-related responding: Moral, social, and socialization correlates. In A. G. Miller (ed.) *The Social Psychology of Good and Evil.* New York: Guilford Press, pp 386–415.

Eisenberg, N., Zhou, Q. and Koller, S. (2001). Brazilian adolescents' prosocial moral judgment and behaviour. *Child Development*, 72: 518–34.

Eisenberg, N., Guthrie, I., Cumberland, A., Murphy, B., Shepard, S. and Zhou, Q. (2002). Prosocial development in early adulthood: A longitudinal study. *Journal of Personality and Social Psychology*, 67: 611–26.

Eliot, G. (1963[1856]). The natural history of German life. In T. Pinney (ed.) *Essays of George Eliot.* London: Routledge, pp 266–99.

Elliott, R., Watson, J., Goldman, R. and Greenberg, L. (2004).

Learning Emotion-Focused Therapy: The Process-Experiential Approach to Change. Washington, DC: American Psychological Association.

Fabes, R. A., Gaertner, B. M. and Popp, T. K. (2008). Getting along with others: Social competence in early childhood. In K. McCartney and D. Phillips (eds) *Blackwell Handbook of Early Childhood Development.* Oxford: Blackwell, pp 297–316.

Fairbairn, G. J. (2009). Empathy, sympathy, and the image of the other. *Peace Review,* 21(2): 188–97.

Fairbairn, R. (1952). *Psychoanalytic Studies of the Personality.* London: Tavistock.

Farmelo, G. (2009). *The Strangest Man: The Hidden Life of Paul Dirac, Quantum Genius.* London: Faber and Faber.

Farrow, T. (2007). Neuroimaging of empathy. In T. Farrow and P. Woodruff (eds) *Empathy in Mental Illness.* Cambridge: Cambridge University Press, pp 201–16.

Fernandez-Duque, D., Hodges, S., Baird, J. and Black, S. (2010). Empathy in frontotemporal dementia and Alzheimer's disease. *Journal of Clinical and Experimental Neuropsychology,* 32(3): 289–98.

Feshbach, N. D. (1987). Parental empathy and child adjustment/maladjustment. In N. Eisenberg and J. Strayer (eds) *Empathy and Its Development.* Cambridge: Cambridge University Press.

Feshbach, N. D. (1989). Empathy training and prosocial behaviour. In J. Groebel and R. A. Hinde (eds) *Aggression and War: Their Biological and Social Basis.* New York: Cambridge University Press, pp 101–11.

Feshbach, N. D. and Feshbach, S. (1987). Affective processes and academic achievement. *Child Development,* 58: 1335–47.

Feshbach, N. D. and Feshbach, S. (2011). Empathy and education. In B. Weber, E. Marsal and T. Dobashi (eds) *The Politics of Empathy.* Munster: LIT Verlag, pp 85–97.

Figley, C. R. (2002). Compassion fatigue: Psychotherapists' chronic lack of self-care. *Journal of Clinical Psychology,* 58: 1433–41.

Fincham, F. D. (2010). Forgiveness: Integral to a science of close relationships? In M. Mikulincer and P. R. Shaver (eds) *Prosocial Motives, Emotions, and Behavior: The Better Angels of Our Nature.* Washington, DC: American Psychological Association, pp 347–65.

Finlay, K. A. and Stephan, W. G. (2000). Improving intergroup relations: The effects of empathy on racial attitudes. *Journal of Applied Social Psychology,* 30: 1720–37.

Fitts, W. H. (1965). *The Experiences of Psychotherapy: What It's Like for Clients and Therapist.* Princeton, NJ: Van Nostrand Reinhold.

Fonagy, P. and Target, M. (1997) Attachment and reflective function: Their role in self-organization. *Development and Psychopathology*. 9: 679–700.

Fonagy, P., Gergely, G., Jurist, E. and Target, M. (2002). *Affect Regulation, Mentalization, and the Development of the Self*. New York: Other Press.

Frady, M. (2002). *Martin Luther King, Jr*. New York: Penguin.

Freedberg, D. and Gallese, V. (2007). Motion, emotion and empathy in esthetic experience. *Trends in Cognitive Sciences* 11(5): 197–203.

Frith, U. and Frith, C. D. (2001). The biological basis of social interaction. *Current Directions in Psychological Science*, 10: 151–5.

Gallese, V., Fadiga, L., Fogassi, L. and Rizzolatti, G. (1996). Action recognition in the premotor cortex. *Brain*, 119: 593–609.

Gardiner, J. K. (1989). *Rhys, Stead, Lessing, and the Politics of Empathy*. Bloomington: Indiana University Press.

Gardner, S. T. (2011). The evolution of connectivity. In B. Weber, E. Marsal and T. Dobashi (eds) *The Politics of Empathy*. Munster: LIT Verlag, pp 51–9.

Gelso, C. J. and Hayes, J. A. (2002). The management of countertransference. In J. Norcross (ed.) *Psychotherapy Relationships That Work: Therapist Contributions and Responsiveness to Patients*. Oxford: Oxford University Press, pp 267–83.

Gerdes, K. E. (2011). Empathy, sympathy, and pity: 21st-century definitions and implications for practice and research. *Journal of Social Service Research*, 37: 230–41.

Gerhardt, S. (2004). *Why Love Matters: How Affection Shapes a Baby's Brain*. Hove: Brunner-Routledge.

Gilbert, P. (2005). Compassion and cruelty: A biopsychosocial approach. In P. Gilbert (ed.) *Compassion: Conceptualisations, Research and the Use of Psychotherapy*. London: Routledge, pp 9–74.

Gillberg, C. (2007). Non-autism childhood empathy disorders. In T. Farrow and P. Woodruff (eds) *Empathy in Mental Illness*. Cambridge: Cambridge University Press, pp 111–25.

Gilson, A. and Moyer, D. (2000). Predictors of empathy in dementia staff. *American Journal of Alzheimers Disorders*, 15(July/August): 239–51.

Golan, O., Baron-Cohen, S., Wheelwright, S. and Hill, J, (2006). Systematising empathy: Teaching adults with Asperger Syndrome to recognise complex emotions using interactive multi-media. *Development and Psychopathology*, 18: 589–615.

Golan, O., Baron-Cohen, S., Ashwin, E., Granader, Y., McClintock, S., Day, K. and Leggett, V. (2010). Enhancing emotion recognition in children with autistic spectrum conditions: An intervention using animated vehicles with real emotional faces. *Journal of Autism and Developmental Disorders*, 40: 269–79.

Goleman, D. (1999). *Working with Emotional Intelligence*. London: Bloomsbury.

Gordon, M. (2009). *Roots of Empathy: Changing the World Child by Child*. New York: The Experiment.

Grandin, T. (2006). *Thinking in Pictures*. London: Bloomsbury.

Graziono, W. G., Habashi, M. M., Sheese, B. E. and Tobin, R. M. (2007). Agreeableness, empathy, and helping. *Journal of Personality and Social Psychology*, 93: 583–99.

Greenberg, L., Watson, J., Elliot, R. and Bohart, A. (2001). Empathy. *Psychotherapy: Research, Theory and Training*. 38: 380–84.

Greenspan, S. and Benderely, B. L. (1997). *The Growth of the Mind: And the Endangered Origins of Intelligence*. Reading, MA: Addison Wesley.

Gross, D. R. and Capuzzi, D. (2007) Helping relationships: From core dimensions to brief approaches. In D. Capuzzi and D. R. Gross (eds) *Counseling and Psychotherapy* (4th edn). Upper Saddle River, NJ: Pearson, pp 3–25.

Guardian Review (2011). 'I will have to make it up.' *Guardian Review*, 26 March, pp 2–5.

Gunter, T., Vaughn, M. and Philibert, R. (2010). Behavioral genetics in Antisocial Spectrum Disorders and Psychopathy: A review of the recent literature. *Behvioral Sciences and the Law*, 28(2): 148–73.

Halpern, J. (2001). *From Detached Concern to Empathy: Humanizing Medical Practice*. New York: Oxford University Press.

Hamann, S. and Canli, T. (2004). Individual differences in emotion processing. *Current Opinion in Neurobiology*, 14: 233–8.

Hamilton, W. D. (1964). The genetic evolution of social behaviour. *Journal of Theoretical Biology*, 7: 1–51.

Haney, C., Banks, W. and Zimbardo, P. (1973). Interpersonal dynamics in a simulated prison. *International Journal of Criminology*, 1: 69–97.

Hazler, R. J. (2006). Person-centred theory. In D. Gross and D. Capuzzi (eds) *Counseling and Psychotherapy: Theories and Interventions* (4th edn). New York: Merrill, pp 189–215.

Hazlitt, W. (1998[1805]). An essay on the principles of human action, being an argument in favour of natural disinterestedness of the human mind. In D. Wu (ed.) *The Selected Writings of William Hazlitt: Vol. I*. London: Pickering and Chatto, pp 1–82.

Heard, D. and Lake, B. (1997). *The Challenge of Attachment for Caregiving*. London: Routledge.

Heidegger, M. (1992[1927]). *Being and Time*, trans. J. Macquarrie and E. Robinson. Oxford: Blackwell.

Heim, C., Young, L., Newport, D., Mletzko, T., Miller, A. and Nemeroff, C. (2008). Lower CSF oxytocin concentrations in women with a history of child abuse. *Molecular Psychiatry*, 14(10): 954–8.

Hein, G. and Singer, T. (2010). Neuroscience meets social psychology: An integrative approach to human empathy and prosocial behavior. In M. Mikulincer and P. R. Shaver (eds) *Prosocial Motives, Emotions, and Behavior: The Better Angels of Our Nature*. Washington, DC: American Psychological Association, pp 109–25.

Held, V. (2006). *The Ethics of Care: Personal, Political, and Global*. New York: Oxford University Press.

Hennessey, R. (2011). *Relationship Skills in Social Work*. London: Sage.

Hietolahti-Ansen, M. L. and Kalliopuska, M. (1991). Self-esteem and empathy among children actively involved in music. *Perceptual and Motor Skills*, 72: 1364–6.

Hill, C. E. (2004). *Helping Skills: Facilitating Exploration, Insight, and Action* (2nd edn). Washington, DC: American Psychological Association.

Hobson, P. (2002). *The Cradle of Thought*. London: Macmillan.

Hobson, P. (2007). Empathy and autism. In T. Farrow and P. Woodruff (eds) *Empathy in Mental Illness*. Cambridge: Cambridge University Press, pp 126–41.

Hoffman, M. (2000). *Empathy and Moral Development*. Cambridge: Cambridge University Press.

Hogan, R. (1969). Development of an empathy scale. *Journal of Consulting and Clinical Psychology*, 33: 307–16.

Holmes, J. (2006). Mentalizing from a psychoanalytic perspective. In J. Allen and P. Fonagy (eds) *Handbook of Mentalization-Based Treatment*. Chichester: Wiley, pp 31–49.

Hosking, G. and Walsh, I. R. (2005). *The WAVE Report: Violence and What to Do about It*. Croydon: WAVE Trust.

Howe, D. (1989). Birth Mothers: The Post-Adoption Centre, The First Three Years. Research Report No. 4. Norwich: University of East Anglia.

Howe, D. (1993). *On Being a Client: Understanding the Processes of Counselling and Psychotherapy*. London: Sage.

Howe, D. (2005). *Child Abuse and Neglect: Attachment, Development and Intervention*. Houndmills: Palgrave Macmillan.

Hrdy, S. (2009). *Mothers and Others: The Evolutionary Origins of Mutual Understanding*. Cambridge, MA: Belknap Press.

Humphrey, N. (1986). *The Inner Eye*. London: Faber and Faber.

Hume, D. (1978[1739]). *A Treatise on Human Nature*. Oxford: Clarendon Press.

Husserl, E. (1964). *The Idea of Phenomenology*. The Hague: Martinus Nijhoff.

Iacobini, M. (2007). Existential empathy: The intimacy of self and other. In T. Farrow and P. Woodruff (eds) *Empathy in Mental Illness*. Cambridge: Cambridge University Press, pp 310–21.

Iacoboni, M. (2008). *Mirroring People: The Science of How We Connect with Others*. New York: Farrar, Straus and Giroux.

Iacoboni, M. (2009). Imitation, empathy, and mirror neurons. *Annual Review of Psychology*, 60: 653–70.

Ickes, W. (1997). Introduction. In W. Ickes (ed.) *Empathic Accuracy*, New York: Guilford Press, pp 1–16.

Ickes, W. (2011). Empathic accuracy: Its links to clinical, developmental, and physiological psychology. In B. Weber, E. Marsal and T. Dobashi (eds) *The Politics of Empathy*. Munster: LIT Verlag, pp 57–70.

Ickes, W., Gesn, P. R. and Graham, T. (2000). Gender differences in empathic accuracy: Differential ability or differential motivation? *Personal Relationships*, 7: 95–109.

Irvin, R. and Pederson, P. (1995). The assessment of multicultural competencies. In J. G. Ponterotto (ed.) *Handbook of Multicultural Counseling*. Thousand Oaks, CA: Sage, pp 287–311.

Jacob, S., Brune, C. W., Carter, C. S., Leventhal, B., Lord, C. and Cook, E. H. Jr (2007). Association of the oxytocin receptor gene (OXTR) in Caucasian children and adolescents with autism. *Neuroscience Letters*, 417: 6–9.

Johnson, D. R. (2012). Transportation into a story increases empathy, prosocial behaviour, and perceptual bias toward fearful expressions. *Personality and Individual Differences*, 52(2): 150–55.

Johnson, R. (1971). *Existential Man*. London: Pergamon Press.

Johnson, S. M. (2004). Attachment theory: A guide to healing couple relationships. In W. S. Rholes and J. A. Simpson (eds) *Adult Attachment: Theory, Research and Clinical Implications*. New York: Guilford Press, pp 367–87.

Kagan, J. (1994). *Galen's Prophecy: Temperament in Human Nature*. New York: Basic Books.

Kalliopuska, M. and Ruokonen, I. (1993). A study with follow-up of the effects of music education on holistic development of empathy. *Perceptual and Motor Skills*, 76: 131–7.

Karen, R. (1998). *Becoming Attached: First Relationships and How They Shape Our Capacity to Love*. New York: Oxford University Press.

Karlsson, R. (2005). Ethnic matching between therapist and patient in psychotherapy: An overview of findings, together with methodological and conceptual issues. *Cultural Diversity and Ethnic Minority Psychology*, 11: 113–29.

Kasl-Godley, J. and Gatz, M. (2000). Psychosocial interventions for individuals with dementia: An integration of theory, therapy, and a clinical understanding of dementia. *Clinical Psychological Review* 20(6): 755–82.

Katz, R. L. (1963). *Empathy: Its Nature and Uses*. London: Collier Macmillan.

Kaufman, J. and Charney, D. (2001). Effects of early stress on brain structure and function: Implications for understanding the relationship between child maltreatment and depression. *Development and Psychopathology*, 13: 451–71.

Keen, S. (2007). *Empathy and the Novel*. Oxford: Oxford University Press.

Kennedy, A. (2008). Impressing the need for empathy. *Counseling Today*, May: 30–31.

Kidd, S. M. (2005). A common heart: A best selling novelist argues for empathy through fiction. *Washington Post* Book World, Sunday 4 December, p. 9.

Kierkegaard, S. (2011[1843]). *Fear and Trembling*. London: Penguin Classics.

Knafo, A. and Israel, S. (2010). Genetic and environmental influences on prosocial behaviour. In M. Mikulincer and P. R. Shaver (eds) *Prosocial Motives, Emotions, and Behavior: The Better Angels of Our Nature*. Washington, DC: American Psychological Association, pp 149–67.

Kohut, H. (1959). Introspection, empathy, and psychoanalysis: An examination of the relationship between mode of observation and theory. *Journal of the American Psychoanalytic Association*, 7: 459–83.

Kohut, H. (1977). *The Restoration of Self*. Madison, CT: International Universities Press.

Kohut, H. (1985). *Self Psychology and the Humanities*. New York: W. W. Norton.

Kohut, H. (1990). Introspection and empathy: Further thoughts about their role in psychoanalysis. In P. H. Ornstein (ed.) *The Search for the Self: Selected Writings of Heinz Kohut: 1978–1981*. Madison, CT: International Universities Press, pp 83–101.

Kosfeld, M., Heinrichs, M., Zak, P., Frisbacher, U. and Fehr, E. (2005). Oxytocin increases trust in humans. *Nature Neuroscience*, 435(June): 673–6.

Kreisman, J. J. and Straus, H. (1989). *I Hate You, Don't Leave Me: Understanding the Borderline Personality*. New York: Avon.

Lakin, J. L., Jeffries, V. E., Cheng, C. M. and Chartrand, T. L. (2003). The chameleon effect as social glue: Evidence for the evolutionary significance of nonconscious mimicry. *Journal of Nonverbal Behavior* 27(3): 145–62.

Lawrence, D. and Luis, H. Z. (2001). Cross-cultural empathy and training the contemporary psychotherapist. *Clinical Social Work Journal*, 29: 3.

Leary, M. R. and Hoyle, R. H. (2009). Situations, dispositions, and the study of social behavior. In M. R. Leary and R. H. Hoyle (eds) *Handbook of Individual Differences in Social Behavior*. New York: Guilford Press, pp 3–11.

Leary, M. R. and Kelly, K. M. (2009). Belonging motivation. In M. R. Leary and R. H. Hoyle (eds) *Handbook of Individual Differences in Social Behavior*. New York: Guilford Press, pp 400–9.

Lessing, D. (1987). *Prisons We Choose to Live Inside*. New York: Harper and Row.

Lewin, K. (1936). *Principles of Topological Psychology*. New York: McGraw-Hill.

Lide, P. (1966). Dynamic mental representation: An analysis of the empathic process. *Social Casework*, March: 146–51.

Liew, J. Eisenberg, N., Losoya, S., Guthrie, I. and Murphy, B. (2003). Maternal expressivity as a moderator of the relations of children's vicarious emotional responses to their regulation, emotionality, and social functioning. *Journal of Family Psychology*, 17: 584–97.

Liotti, G. and Gilbert, P. (2011). Mentalizing, motivation, and social mentalities: Theoretical considerations and implications for psychotherapy. *Psychology and Psychotherapy: Theory, Research and Practice*, 84: 9–25.

Lipps, T. (1903). Einfühlung, Innere Nachahmung und Organempfindung. *Archiv für gesamte Psychologie*, 1, 465–519. Translated as Empathy, inner imitation and sense-feelings in M. Rader (ed.) (1979) *A Modern Book of Esthetics*. New York: Holt, Rinehart and Winston, pp 374–82.

Luborsky, L., Rosenthal, R., Diguer, L., Andrusyna, T., Berman, J., Levitt, J., Seligman, D. and Krause, E. (2002). The Dodo bird verdict is alive and well – mostly. *Clinical Psychology: Science and Practice*, 9: 2–12.

Main, M. and George, C. (1985). Responses of abused and disadvantaged toddlers to distress in agemates. *Developmental Psychology*, 21: 407–12.

Mar, R. A., Oatley, K. and Peterson, J. B. (2008). Exploring the link between reading fiction and empathy: Ruling out individual differences and examining outcomes. *Communications*, 34: 407–28.

Mar, R. A., Oatley, K., Hirsh, J., dela Paz, J. and Peterson, J. B. (2006). Bookworms versus nerds: Exposure to fiction versus non-fiction, divergent associations with social ability, and the simulation of social worlds. *Journal of Research in Personality*, 40: 694–712.

Marangoni, C., Garcia, S., Ickes, W. and Teng, G. (1995). Empathic accuracy in a clinically relevant setting. *Journal of Personality and Social Psychology*, 68(5): 854–69.

Markram, H., Rinaldi, T. and Markram, K. (2007). The Intense World Syndrome – an alternative hypothesis for autism. *Frontiers in Neuroscience* 1(1): 77–96.

Marx, K. (1859). Preface to *A Contribution to the Critique of Political Economy*. In K. Marx and F. Engels (1962) *Karl Marx and Frederick Engels: Selected Works, Vol. I*. London: Lawrence and Wishart, pp 361–5.

Mathur, V. A., Harada, T., Lipke, T. and Chiao, J. Y. (2010). Neural basis of extraordinary empathy and altruistic motivation. *NeuroImage*, 51: 1468–75.

Maurer, R. E. and Tindall, J. H. (1983). Effect of postural congruence on client's perception of counselor empathy. *Journal of Counseling Psychology*, 30: 158–63.

McCluskey, U. (2005). *To Be Met as a Person: The Dynamics of Attachment in Professional Encounters*. London: Karnac.

McCrae, R. R. and Costa, P. T. (1999). A Five-Factor theory of personality. In L. A. Pervin and O. P. John (eds) *Handbook of Personality Psychology*. New York: Guilford Press, pp 139–53.

McWilliam, C. (2011). *What to Look for in Winter: A Memoir in Blindness*. London: Vintage Books.

Mead, G. H. (1934). *Mind, Self and Society*. Chicago: University of Chicago Press.

Meaney, M. (2003). Maternal care, gene expression, and the transmission of individual differences in stress reactivity across generations. *Annual Review of Neuroscience*, 24(1): 1161–92.

Meaney, M. J. (2010). Epigenetics and the biological definition of gene ¥ environment interactions. *Child Development*, 81(1): 41–79

Mearns, D. and Cooper, M. (2005). *Working at Relational Depth in Counselling and Psychotherapy*. London: Sage.

Mearns, D. and Thorne, B. (1999). *Person-Centred Counselling in Action* (2nd edn). London: Sage.

Mehrabian, A., Young, A. and Sato, S. (1988). Emotional empathy and associated individual differences. *Current Psychology: Research and Reviews*, 7: 221–40.

Meins, E. (1997) *Security of Attachment and the Social Development of Cognition*. Hove: Psychology Press.

Meins, E., Fernyhough, C., Wainwright, R., Gupta, M., Fradley, E. and Tuckey, M. (2002) Maternal mind-mindedness and attachment security as predictors of Theory of Mind understanding. *Child Development* 73(6): 1715–26.

Mensch, J. R. (2011). Empathy and rationality. In B. Weber, E. Marsal and T. Dobashi (eds) *The Politics of Empathy*. Munster: LIT Verlag, pp 17–24.

Milgram, S. (1974). *Obedience to Authority*. New York: Harper.

Morse, J., Anderson, G., Bottorff, J., Yonge, O., O'Brien, B., Solber, S. and McIlveen, K. (1992). Exploring empathy: A conceptual fir for nursing practice. *Image*, 24: 273–80.

Moursund, J. P. and Erskine, R. G. (2004). *Integrative Psychotherapy: The Art and Science of Relationship*. Pacific Grove, CA: Brooks/Cole.

Naughton, J. (2011). Fighting talk: The prophet of peace. *The Observer*, London, 16 October, pp 8–11.

Norcross, J. C. (2002). *Psychotherapy Relationships That Work: Therapist Contributions and Responsiveness to Patients*. Oxford: Oxford University Press.

Nussbaum, M. C. (1997). *Cultivating Humanity: A Classical Defence of Reform in Liberal Education*. Cambridge, MA: Harvard University Press.

Oberman, L. M. and Ramachandran, V. S. (2007). The simulating social mind: The role of the mirror neuron system and simulation in the social and communicative deficits in autism spectrum disorders. *Psychological Bulletin*, 133(2): 310–27.

Oliner, S. P. and Oliner, P. M. (eds) (1988). *The Altruistic Personality: Rescuers of Jews in Nazi Europe*. New York: Free Press.

Penner, L. A. and Orom, H. (2010). Enduring goodness: A person-by-situation perspective on prosocial behaviour. In M. Mikulincer and P. R. Shaver (eds) *Prosocial Motives, Emotions, and Behavior: The Better Angels of Our Nature*. Washington, DC: American Psychological Association, pp 55–72.

Pfiefer, J. H. and Dapretto, M. (2011). In B. Weber, E. Marsal and T. Dobashi (eds) *The Politics of Empathy*. Munster: LIT Verlag, pp 183–97.

Pfiefer, J. H., Iacoboni, M., Mazziotta, J. C., and Dapretto, M. (2008). Mirroring others' emotions relates to empathy and interpersonal competence in children. *NeuroImage*, 39: 2076–85.

Phillimore, P. (1981) *Families Speaking: A Study of Fifty-One Families' Views of Social Work*. London: Family Service Unit.

Piaget, J. (1932). *The Moral Judgment of the Child.* London: Routledge and Kegan Paul.

Pinker, S. (2011). *The Better Angels of Our Nature: The Decline of Violence in History and Its Causes.* London: Allen Lane.

Plomin, R. (1994). *Genes and Experience: The Interplay between Nature and Nurture.* Thousand Oaks, CA: Sage.

Pollak, S. and Kistler, D. (2002). Early experience is associated with the development of categorical representations for facial expressions of emotion. *Proceedings of the National Academy of Sciences USA,* 99(13): 9072–6.

Preston, S. D. and de Waal, F. B. M. (2002). The communication of emotions and the possibility of empathy in animals. In S. G. Post and L. G. Underwood (eds) *Altruism and Altruistic Love.* Oxford: Oxford University Press, pp 284–308.

Prunetti, E., Framba, R., Barone, L., Fiore, D., Sera, F. and Liotti, G. (2008). Attachment disorganization and borderline patients' metacogntive responses to therapists' expressed understanding of their states of mind: A pilot study. *Psychotherapy Research,* 18: 28–36.

Ramachandran, V. (2003). *The Emerging Mind: The Reith Lectures 2003.* London: Profile.

Rankin, K. P., Gorno-Tempini, M. L., Allison, S. C., Stanley, M., Glenn, S., Weiner, M. and Miller, B. (2006). Structural anatomy of empathy in neurodegenerative disease. *Brain* 129(11): 2945–56.

Rasoal, C., Eklund, J. and Hansen, E. (2011). Toward a conceptualization of ethnocultural empathy. *Journal of Social, Evolutionary, and Cultural Psychology.* 5(1): 1–13.

Rawls, J. (1999). *A Theory of Justice: A Revised Edition.* Cambridge, MA: Harvard University Press.

Reik, T. (1964). *Listening with the Third Ear.* New York: Pyramid Books.

Reis, H. T. and Shaver, P. (1988). Intimacy as a personal process. In S. Duck and D. Hay (eds) *Handbook of Personal Relationships: Theory, Research and Interventions.* Chichester: Wiley, pp 367–89.

Rennie, D. L. (1998). *Person-Centred Counselling: An Experiential Approach.* London: Sage.

Restorative Justice Online (n.d.) http://restorativejustice.org/prison 02victim-awareness-and-empathy-programmes, accessed 8 July 2012.

Ridley, C. R. and Lingle, D. W. (1996). Cultural empathy in multicultural counselling: A multidimensional process model. In P. B. Pedersen and J. G. Draguns (eds) *Counseling across Culture* (4th edn). Thousand Oaks, CA: Sage, pp 21–46.

Ridley, C. R. and Udipi, S. (2002). Putting cultural empathy into practice.

In P. Pedersen, J. Draguns, W. Lonner and J. Trimble (eds) *Counseling across Cultures* (5th edn). Thousand Oaks, CA: Sage, pp 317–33.

Rifkin, J. (2009). *The Empathic Civilization: The Race to Global Consciousness in a World in Crisis*. Cambridge: Polity Press.

Rizzolatti, G., Craighero, L. and Fadiga, L. (2002). The mirror system in humans. In A. Stamenov and V. Gallese (eds) *Mirror Neurons and the Evolution of Brain and Language*. Philadelphia: John Benjamins, pp 37–59.

Rizzolatti, G., Fadiga, L., Gallese, V. and Fogassi, L. (1996). Premotor cortex and the recognition of motor actions. *Cognitive Brain Research*, 3: 131–41.

Robinson, R., Roberts, W., Strayer, J. and Koopman, R. (2007). Empathy and emotional responsiveness in delinquents and non-delinquent adolescents. *Social Development*, 16: 555–79.

Rodrigues, S. M., Saslow, L., Garcia, N., John, O. and Keltner, D. (2009). Oxytocin receptor genetic variation relates to empathy and stress reactivity in humans. *Proceedings of the National Academy of Sciences*, 106(50): 21437–41.

Roessing, L. (2005). Creating empathetic connections to literature. *The Quarterly*, 27(2): 1–6.

Rogers, C. (1949). The attitude and orientation of the counsellor in client-centred therapy. *Journal of Consulting Psychology*, 13: 82–94.

Rogers, C. (1951). *Client-Centered Therapy: Its Current Practice, Implications, and Theory*. Boston: Houghton Mifflin.

Rogers, C. (1957). The necessary and sufficient conditions of therapeutic personality change. *Journal of Consulting Psychology*, 21: 95–103.

Rogers, C. (1958). Reinhold Niebuhr's *The Self and the Dramas of History*: A criticism. *Pastoral Psychology*, 9: 15–17.

Rogers, C. (1964). Toward a science of the person. In T. W. Wann (ed.) *Behaviorism and Phenomenology*. Chicago: Chicago University Press, pp 109–40.

Rogers, C. (1980). *A Way of Being*. Boston: Houghton Mifflin.

Rogers, C. (1986). Rogers, Kohut, and Erickson: A personal perspective on some similarities and differences. *Person-Centered Review*, 1: 125–40.

Romero-Canyas, R., Anderson, V., Reddy, K. and Downey, G. (2009). Rejection sensitivity. In M. R. Leary and R. H. Hoyle (eds) *Handbook of Individual Differences in Social Behavior*. New York: Guilford Press, pp 466–79.

Rorty, R. (1979). *Philosophy and the Mirror of Nature*. Princeton: Princeton University Press.

Rorty, R. (1989). *Contingency, Irony, and Solidarity*. Cambridge: Cambridge University Press.

Rowe, D. (2011). The missing pot of gold. *Guardian Review*, 16 April, p 9.

Sapolsky, R. M. (1998) *Why Zebras Don't Get Ulcers*. New York: W. H. Freeman.

Schaffer, H. R. (1996). *Social Development*. Oxford: Blackwell.

Scheler, M. (1954). *The Nature of Sympathy*. London: Routledge and Kegan Paul.

Schmid, P. (2003). The characteristics of a person-centred approach to therapy and counseling: Criteria for identity and coherence. *Person-Centered and Experiential Psychotherapies*, 2(2): 104–20.

Schmid Mast, M. and Ickes, W. (2007). Empathic accuracy: Measurement and potential clinical implications. In T. Farrow and P. Woodruff (eds) *Empathy in Mental Illness*. Cambridge: Cambridge University Press, pp 408–27.

Schmidt, M. and Sommerville, J. (2011). Fairness expectations and altruistic sharing in 15-month-old infants. *PLoS ONE* 6(10): e23223.

Schulte-Rüther, M, Markowitsch, H., Shah, N. J., Fink, G. and Piefke, M. (2008). Gender differences in brain networks supporting empathy. *NeuroImage*, 42: 393–403.

Schutz, A. (1973). *Collected Papers I*. The Hague: Martinus Nijhoff.

Scott, N. E. and Borodovsky, L. G. (1990). Effective use of cross-cultural role taking. *Professional Psychology: Research and Practice*, 21(3): 167–70.

Seabright, P. (2012). *The War of the Sexes: How Conflict and Cooperation Have Shaped Men and Women from Prehistory to the Present*. Princeton: Princeton University Press.

Shamay-Tsoory, S. G. (2011). Empathic processing: Its cognitive and affective dimensions and neuroanatomical basis. In J. Decety and W. Ickes (eds) *The Social Neuroscience of Empathy*. Cambridge, MA: MIT Press, pp 215–31.

Shamay-Tsoory, S. G., Tomer, R., Berger, B. D. and Aharon-Peretz, J. (2003). Characterization of empathy deficits following pre-frontal brain damage: The role of the right ventromedial prefrontal cortex. *Journal of Cognitive Neuroscience*, 15: 324–37.

Shapiro, J. (2007). Using literature and the arts to develop empathy in medical students. In T. Farrow and P. Woodruff (eds) *Empathy in Mental Illness*. Cambridge: Cambridge University Press, pp 472–94.

Shapiro, J., Morrison, E. and Boker, J. (2004). Teaching empathy to first year medical students: Evaluation of an elective literature and medicine course. *Education for Health*, 17: 73–84.

Sharma, R. (1993). *Understanding the Concept of Empathy and Its Foundations in Psychoanalysis*. Lewiston, NY: Edwin Mellen Press.

Shaver, P., Mikulincer, M. and Shemish-Iron, M. (2010). In M. Mikulincer and P. R. Shaver (eds) *Prosocial Motives, Emotions, and Behavior: The Better Angels of Our Nature*. Washington, DC: American Psychological Association, pp 73–92.

Shelley, P. B. (1973). A defence of poetry. In H. Bloom and L. Trilling (eds) *Romantic Poetry and Prose*. New York: Oxford University Press.

Siegel, D. (1999). *The Developing Mind: Towards a Neurobiology of Interpersonal Experience*. New York: Guilford.

Siegel, D. (2007). *The Mindful Brain: Reflection and Attunement in the Cultivation of Wellbeing*. New York: Norton.

Siegel, D. J. (2009) Foreword. In M. Gordon (ed.) *Roots of Empathy: Changing the World Child by Child*. New York: The Experiment, pp xiii–xvi.

Siegel, D. (2010). *The Mindful Therapist*. New York: W. W. Norton.

Silko, L. M. (n.d.) Workshop 7 – Who am I in this story? *In Search of the Novel*. http://www.learner.org/workshops/isonovel/Pages/subpage7.html, accessed 17 June 2011.

Simpson, J. A. and Beckes, L. (2010). Evolutionary perspectives on prosocial behaviour. In M. Mikulincer and P. R. Shaver (eds) *Prosocial Motives, Emotions, and Behavior: The Better Angels of Our Nature*. Washington, DC: American Psychological Association, pp 35–53.

Singer, T. (2006). The neuronal basis and ontogeny of empathy and mind reading: Review of literature and implications for future research. *Neuroscience and Biobehavioral Reviews*, 30: 855–63.

Singer, T., Seymour, B., O'Doherty, J., Stephan, K., Dolan, R. and Frith, C. D. (2004). Empathy for pain involves the affective but not sensory components of pain. *Science* 303(20 Feb.): 1157–62.

Skolimowski, H. (1995). *The Participatory Mind*. London: Penguin.

Slade, A. (2005). Parental reflective functioning: An introduction. *Attachment and Human Development*, 7(3): 269–81.

Slote, M. A. (2007). *The Ethics of Care and Empathy*. London: Routledge.

Smith, A. (1759), *The Theory of Moral Sentiments*. In D. Raphael and A. Macfie (eds) *Glasgow Edition of the Works and Correspondence of Adam Smith, Vol. I*. Oxford: Oxford University Press.

Smith, M. L. and Glass, G. V. (1977). Meta-analysis of psychotherapy outcome studies. *American Psychologist*, 32: 752–60.

Spiegel, M. and Charon, R. (2004). Editor's preface: Narrative, empathy, and proximity. *Literature and Medicine*, 23(2): vii–x.

Spinelli, I. (1989). *The Interpreted World: Introduction to Phenomenological Psychology*. London: Sage.

Sroufe, A. (1989). Talk at City University, New York, Graduate Center, 10 February. Cited in Robert Karen (1998) *Becoming Attached*. New York: Oxford University Press, p 195.

Sroufe, L. A., Egeland, B., Carlson, E. and Collins, W. A. (2005). *The Development of the Person: The Minnesota Study of Risk and Adaptation from Birth to Adulthood*. New York: Guilford Press.

Stanford Encyclopedia of Philosophy (2008). Empathy. http://plato.stanford.edu/entries/empathy/, accessed 10 June 2011.

Stark, W. (1954). Editor's introduction. In M. Scheler (1913) *The Nature of Sympathy*. London: Routledge and Kegan Paul.

Stein, E. (1989). *On the Problems of Empathy (The Collected Works of Edith Stein, Vol. 3)* (3rd rev. edn), trans. W. Stein. Washington, DC: ICS Publications.

Stern, D. (1985). *The Interpersonal World of the Infant*. New York: Basic Books.

Steward, R. J., Jo, H. and Roberts, A. (1998). Empathy and cross-cultural sensitivity. Paper presented at the Great Lakes Regional Conference, Division 17, American Psychological Association, Bloomington, IN, 3–4 April.

Stewart, D. A. (1956). *Preface to Empathy*. New York: Philosophical Library.

Stompe, T., Ritter, K. and Northoff, G. (2010). Empathy, culture and brain – proposal for a large-scaled cross cultural study. *World Cultural Psychiatry Research Review* Summer: 43–8.

Stotland, E. (1969). Exploratory investigations of empathy. In L. Berkowitz (ed.) *Advances in Experimental Social Psychology*. New York: Academic Press, pp 271–314.

Strupp, H. H. (1996). Some salient lessons from research and practice. *Psychotherapy*, 33: 135–8.

Stueber, K. R. (2006). *Rediscovering Empathy: Agency, Folk Psychology, and the Human Sciences*. Cambridge, MA: MIT Press.

Sunderland, M. (2006). *What Every Parent Needs to Know: The Remarkable Effects of Love, Nurture and Play on Your Child's Development*. London: Dorling Kindersley.

Szalavitz, M. and Perry, B. (2011). *Born to Love: Why Empathy Is Essential and Endangered*. New York: Harper.

Taylor, M. (2002–03). The illusion of independent agency: Do adult fiction writers experience their characters as having minds of their own? *Imagination, Cognition and Personality*, 22: 361–80.

Thompson, S. and Thompson, N. (2008). *The Critically Reflective Practitioner*. Houndmills: Palgrave Macmillan.

Titchener, E. B. (1909). *Lectures on the Experimental Psychology of Thought-Processes*. New York: Macmillan.

Torrance, F. (2011). Experience: I feel other people's pain. *Guardian Weekend*, 19 March, p. 14.

Toussant, L. and Webb, J. R. (2007). Gender differences in the relationship between empathy and forgiveness. *Journal of Social Psychology*, 145(6): 673–85.

Trivers, R. L. (1985). *Social Evolution*. Menlow Park, CA: Benjamin/Cummings.

Trobst, K., Collins, R. and Embree, J. (1994). The role of emotion in social support provision: Gender, empathy, and expressions of distress. *Journal of Social and Personal Relationships*, 11: 45–62.

Trommsdorff, G., Friedlmeier, W. and Mayer, B. (2007). Sympathy, distress and prosocial behavior of preschool children in four cultures. *International Journal of Behavioral Development*, 31: 284–93.

Truax, C. B. and Carkhuff, R. R. (1967). *Toward Effective Counseling and Psychotherapy: Training and Practice*, Chicago: Aldine.

van Baaren, R., Decety, J., Dijksterhuis, A., van der Leij, A. and van Leeuwen, M. L. (2011). Being imitated: Consequences of nonconsciously showing empathy. In J. Decety and W. Ickes (eds) *The Social Neuroscience of Empathy*. Cambridge, MA: MIT Press. pp 31–42.

van Baaren, R., Maddux, R., Chartrand, T., de Bouter, C. and van Knippenberg, A. (2003). It takes two to mimic: Behavioral consequences of self-construals. *Journal of Personality and Social Psychology*, 84: 1093–102.

van Deurzen, E. and Arnold-Baker, C. (2005). The self. In E. van Deurzen and C. Arnold-Baker (eds) *Existential Perspectives on Human Issues: A Handbook for Therapeutic Practice*. Houndmills: Palgrave Macmillan.

van Kaam, A. L. (1959). Phenomenal analysis: Exemplified by a study of the experience of 'really feeling understood'. *Journal of Individual Psychology*, 15: 66–71.

Vernon, M. (2010). *The Meaning of Friendship*. Houndmills: Palgrave Macmillan.

Vischer, R. (1994[1873]). On the optical sense of form: A contribution to aesthetics. In H. F. Mallgrave (ed.) *Empathy, Form and Space*. Los Angeles: Getty Center for the History of Art and the Humanities, pp 89–123.

Wampold, B. E. (2001). *The Great Psychotherapy Debate: Models, Methods, and Findings*. Mahweh, NJ: Laurence Erlbaum Associates.

Wang, Y.-W., Bleier, J., Davidson, M., Savoy, H., Tan, J. and Yakushko,

O. (2003). The scale of ethnocultural empathy: Development, validation, and reliability. *Journal of Counseling Psychology.* 2: 221–34.

Watson, J. C. and Greenberg, L. S. (2011). Empathic resonance: A neuroscience perspective. In B. Weber, E. Marsal and T. Dobashi (eds) *The Politics of Empathy.* Munster: LIT Verlag, pp 125–37.

Weber, B. (2011). Sympathy instead of rationality? Richard Rorty and the reconstruction of public space. In B. Weber, E. Marsal and T. Dobashi (eds) *The Politics of Empathy.* Munster: LIT Verlag, pp 25–38.

White, S. J. (1997). Empathy: A literature review and concept analysis. *Journal of Clinical Nursing,* 6: 253–7.

Wilkinson, R. (2000). *Mind the Gap: Hierarchies, Health and Human Evolution.* London: Weidenfeld and Nicolson.

Wilkinson, R. and Pickett, K. (2009). *The Spirit Level: Why Greater Equality Makes Societies Stronger.* London: Bloomsbury Press.

Williams, D. M. (2011). *Teacher Empathy and Middle School Students' Perception of Care.* Saarbrucken: Lambert Academic Publishing.

Williams, R. (1965). *The Long Revolution.* London: Penguin.

Wilson, E. O. (1975). *Sociobiology: The New Synthesis.* Cambridge, MA: Harvard University Press.

Wimmer, H. and Perner, J. (1983). Beliefs about beliefs: Representation and contraining function of wrong beliefs in young children's understanding of deception. *Cognition,* 13: 103–28.

Wingler, H. (1969). *Bauhaus.* Cambridge, MA: MIT Press.

Winnicott, D. (1967). Mirror-role of mother and family in child development. In P. Lomas (ed.) *The Predicament of the Family.* London: Hogarth Books, pp 26–33.

Winnicott, D. (1984). *Through Paediatrics to Psychoanalysis.* London: Karnac.

Wispé, L. (1986). The distinction between sympathy and empathy. *Journal of Personality and Social Psychology,* 50: 314–21.

Wix, L. (2009). Aesthetic empathy in teaching art to children: The work of Friedl Dicker-Brandeis in Terezin. *Art Therapy,* 26(4): 152–8.

Woodruff, P. (2007), Foreword. In T. Farrow and P. Woodruff (eds) *Empathy in Mental Illness.* Cambridge: Cambridge University Press, pp ix–xxii.

Woodward, J. (1988). *Understanding Ourselves: The Uses of Therapy.* London: Macmillan Press.

Woolf, V. (1925[1919]) *Modern Fiction/The Common Reader.* New York: Harcourt.

Worsley, R. (2009). *Process Work in Person-Centred Therapy*. Basingstoke: Palgrave Macmillan.

Zahn-Waxler, C., Radke-Yarrow, M. and King, R. (1979). Child rearing and children's prosocial initiations towards victims of distress. *Child Development*, 50: 319–30.

Zanger, A. (1968). A study of factors related to clinical empathy. *Smith College Studies in Social Work*, February: 116–32.

Subject Index

Author Index